D0065019

TASTE MATTERS

TASTE MATTERS

Why We Like the Foods We Do

John Prescott

REAKTION BOOKS

Published by Reaktion Books Ltd
33 Great Sutton Street
London ECIV ODX, UK
www.reaktionbooks.co.uk

First published 2012

Copyright © John Prescott 2012

Foreword copyright © Heston Blumenthal 2012

Printed and bound in Great Britain
by MPG Books Group

British Library Cataloguing in Publication Data
Prescott, John, 1954–
Taste matters: why we like the foods we do.
1. Food preferences.
2. Taste.
3. Nutrition – Psychological aspects.
I. Title
394.1'2-dc23
ISBN 978 1 86189 914 9

Contents

Foreword

HESTON BLUMENTHAL

In the preface to this book, John mentions the Icelandic dish hakarl, in which a shark is buried in gravel until it rots, then dug up and eaten. Apparently, these fish don't pee the way other animals do; instead, they expel uric acid through their skin. So if you inter one and leave it a while, the acid turns to ammonia, tenderizing and preserving the flesh.

I've had my own run-in with hakarl, when I was in Iceland looking for ideas for a fish feast that I wanted to create. It's hard to describe what a horrible experience it is. The smell alone made me want to gag. (Think of the most eye-wateringly pungent blue cheese you've ever smelled, then up it by a factor of ten.) I chewed my morsel of putrefied shark for about fifteen seconds before spitting most of it out and rinsing my mouth with the local spirit, brennivín. This is the traditional accompaniment to the dish, although ordinarily it's drunk from a glass as a chaser, rather than straight from the bottle and swilled like mouthwash!

The fact that someone could think up a dish like hakarl, and that some people actually enjoy it, shows just how complex our food likes and dislikes are. We tend to think of our food preferences as personal – unique expressions of our personality – but, as John demonstrates in this fascinating book, our likes and dislikes are actually the result of a labyrinth of different influences, many of which we are oblivious to. Evolution and our genetic inheritance prompt us to respond positively to particular tastes, especially saltiness and sweetness, and to be wary of others, such as bitterness. Not surprisingly, we also pick up a lot from our parents, both psychologically (by copying their food choices) and physically (research has shown that if a newborn regularly ingests a particular flavour via breast milk, they are likely to grow up with a liking for foods containing that flavour). Society plays a part: whether we realize it or not, we are all influenced by the culinary values of the society in which we live, which can lead to radically different ideas about what's acceptable to eat. The Japanese will happily eat live soft-shelled crab, which many of us would refuse to do, yet they find rice pudding repulsive. And, on top of this, we subconsciously make all kinds of associations between food and particular experiences that govern how we respond to that food in the future.

John is the perfect guide through this labyrinth. He has all the latest scientific developments and thinking at his fingertips and explains it all in simple, accessible, jargon-free language, backed up by lots of vivid, instructive examples and case histories. Among these pages, for example, we learn that newborns appear to prefer soup to which MSG has been added, which suggests we are genetically predisposed to like and seek out the savoury umami taste. We learn that the fear of food novelty (neophobia) can be inherited: identical twins are more likely to show similar levels of neophobia than non-identical twins. We learn that food aversion is sense-dependent: animals such as humans and rats, which use smell and taste to track down food, tend to become averse to a taste or aroma associated with a food that has made them ill, whereas quails, which hunt by means of sight, are more likely to register the colour of a food that has made them ill, and be wary of that instead. We even learn that vampire bats are the only mammal that doesn't have food aversions! (John's book is full of intriguing little facts like this that you'll find yourself lobbing into conversations.)

In one of the scientific studies John quotes, participants were all fed an identical dish, but were given different descriptions of what it was. Some were told that it was cold smoked salmon mousse; others that it was smoked salmon ice cream. There was a markedly more positive response among those who thought they were eating a mousse, which shows how important expectations are in our enjoyment of food. The notion of a seafood mousse is familiar and therefore offers no impediment to enjoyment; fish-flavoured ice cream, on the other hand, is unexpected and therefore more difficult to make sense of. The catalyst for this research was a crab ice cream that I developed as a garnish for crab risotto at my restaurant, The Fat Duck. I noticed that people not only found it easier to accept the ice cream if I called it frozen crab bisque, they also thought it tasted much less sweet. It was probably at this point that I realized just how complicated and subjective are our food likes and dislikes, and began talking about the subject with scientists like John. What I discovered undoubtedly had a powerful influence on the direction my cooking has taken.

Taste Matters is of huge interest to the cook because it offers valuable insights into what is actually going on as we eat, and is likely to inspire all kinds of ideas about how to produce food that is pleasurable and memorable. But it's not just for cooks and scientists. Food is such a central part of our lives that what's in these pages will be of interest to everyone, whether you're a parent looking for ways to get your children to eat more widely or a reader just trying to work out what makes us humans tick.

Brussels Sprouts and Ice Cream

If you live in Europe, the USA, Australia or a host of other countries, strongly flavoured, fermented beans – *natto* – are not a natural breakfast choice, as they are in Japan. But no Japanese consumer was born liking *natto*, any more than I was born liking fried slices of fatty pig meat. How did I end up liking bacon for breakfast and my notional Japanese counterpart, *natto*?

It is not difficult to find food preferences in other cultures that fall into the category of 'How can anyone possibly eat . . .?' Thus, to prepare the traditional Icelandic food *hakarl*, you start with a poisonous Greenland shark, its meat rich in uric acid, then bury it in gravel for two or more months so that it rots, and then serve, ideally accompanied by a shot or two of *brennivín*, a high-potency vodka equivalent (translation: 'burning wine'). The flavour, apparently much appreciated by Icelandic gourmands, is reminiscent of concentrated ammonia. There is no doubt that this dish, like many culturally specific delicacies – and no list is complete without crisp grasshoppers, sheep's eyes, tea with yak butter and Vegemite – tends to be considered with a shudder if you happen not to be from that culture. In other words, some food preferences are puzzling.

To say that such food preferences are a matter of culture only partly addresses the question. While culture is clearly an important influence on food likes, I could ask the same question *within* my own, or indeed any other, culture. Not everyone I know likes bacon for breakfast – in fact, the idea has no appeal at all for some, otherwise reasonable, omnivores. How did our food preferences develop differently in a culture in which bacon has a history of being a prototypical breakfast food?

Just as important a question as why we do not all like the same foods is why we have so many likes and dislikes in common. Again, the impact of culture is of course evident. If your main food staple is rice or corn, disliking either is not a viable option within that culture. However, in industrialized and affluent countries, variety is a characteristic of our diet as never before, and nowadays the range of foods available transcends cultures and seasons. So why do you and I love ice cream so much and with the same passion dislike Brussels sprouts? What is it about chocolate that makes it popular wherever it is introduced? And why has *hakarl* not taken off as an exotic delicacy wherever sharks are found?

As I will show through the course of this book, the answer to these questions – the origins of both differences and commonalities in food preferences – lies in the different ways that the sensory properties of foods – their tastes, odours, textures, appearance – come to be liked. This book is called *Taste Matters* because it focuses on the sensory basis of food preferences.

A main focus of this book is the role of pleasure in shaping likes and dislikes for the sensory properties of foods. The pursuit of pleasure for its own sake – hedonism – has traditionally been frowned upon because it seems to be at odds with more serious or worthwhile pursuits. But food pleasures, like those of sex, have been absolutely crucial to our survival. It is not, I am sure, a great revelation that eating is associated with pleasure. I expect that most of us are happy about this, and we tend to feel sorry for those unfortunate few who view foods merely as fuel. Is the fact that foods provide pleasure just a lucky coincidence? *Taste Matters* aims to show just how the hedonic aspects of foods – that is, their ability to evoke pleasure – has been central in helping us to survive as a species. Enjoying food is an evolution-grounded pleasure that is crucial to maintain adequate nutrition.

For many of us, most of the time, an emotional response of like or dislike to the taste of a food determines whether or not a food is consumed. Underlying this seemingly simple decision is a remarkable range of emotions – from blissful appreciation of haute cuisine to a profound rejection elicited by an emotion that is clearly linked to food consumption, namely *disgust*. Unlike its nutritional worth, though, a food's hedonic value is based in the person, not the food itself. And while the hedonic value can therefore differ significantly between individuals and across cultures, it is nevertheless, in developed countries at least, probably the strongest determinant of diet.

Do you feel perhaps that your food likes and dislikes are accidental or even random? Or that they reflect a conscious decision on your part to steer yourself towards an ideal diet? For the most part, neither is true. We have evolved a variety of ways in which we are guided through pleasure towards food likes and dislikes that maximize our survival. The development of food likes and dislikes, like many other complex human behaviours, reflects the operation of multiple influences – our genetic inheritance, maternal diet, child-raising practices, learning, cognition and culture – each of which is expressed through hedonic responses to sensory qualities. In fact, the development of food preferences may be an ideal illustration of the interplay of these influences during our lifespan.

As the story of this book unfolds, it will become clear that in some cases, such as our liking for basic tastes such as sweetness, preferences are innate. In contrast, many food likes and dislikes are the result of mechanisms that allow us to learn that food flavours are likely to be accompanied by energy or other nutrients that will keep us alive. Other automatic processes encourage dietary variety, once again aiding us in ensuring that we receive an adequate supply of the different nutrients we require.

When food sources are scarce, there is motivation to explore potential new sources of food, and we can take advantage of this because we are omnivores. But this advantage carries with it the worry of consuming something that might poison us. Hence the other great driver of food selection in maximizing our survival has been harm minimization. Again, innate taste preferences mean that many bitter-tasting toxins are avoided, while learning allows us to automatically respond hedonically to those foods that might, or alternatively probably will not, make us ill. We even inherit a predisposition to be wary about foods generally early in our development, just at that time of our lives when increasing mobility and freedom mean that ingesting something unfortunate becomes a real possibility. Perhaps most impressive of all, we have a harm minimization emotion – disgust – that works to ensure that potentially serious sources of disease or other contamination are not eaten.

These are mechanisms that we all possess. In other words, regardless of our culture, our bodies, through the intermediary role of taste preferences, drive us towards the nutrients that we need. But this is not the same as driving us towards particular foods. Our differing cultures and our individual physiological and genetic make-ups mean that food selection is not fixed either within or between cultures.

Why write this book? I presume that I will be telling you quite a few things of which you were unaware. This is worthwhile if you are interested in food as a topic and I am hoping that you are. But in addition, we are at a stage in our history – and by 'our' I mean affluent societies – when our relationship with food has changed. Food is increasingly not about intake of needed nutrients; it is about sensory, and even sometimes intellectual, pleasure. This is certainly in contrast to much of humanity's history. Once you take for granted that you have enough to eat, what happens? If our food preferences are a survival mechanism, what are the consequences when these mechanisms become redundant? Well, it is impossible to know unless you know that food likes and dislikes are shaped by the innate and learned influences mentioned above.

Given that foods are palatable for a reason, namely to encourage our consumption of particular nutrients, perhaps we can sit back and relax and let our food preferences inform us how to keep alive and healthy. But we all know this is not the case. No discussion of food palatability can these days avoid the rather bulky elephant in the room, namely obesity, and the risks that it carries: high blood pressure, heart disease, diabetes and cancer.

There is thus an intriguing paradox. While our food preferences have historically been the route to survival, in affluent societies today, where foods high in fats and carbohydrates are freely available and inexpensive, one consequence may be obesity and increased risk of cardiovascular and other diseases. Of course, part of this conundrum reflects the fact that obtaining food sources once required significant energy expenditure. In contrast, a characteristic of modern diets is the ease of access to energy. We literally do not work for our food, and energy in the form of sugars and fats has become the most freely available of all nutrients. This situation is part of what has been referred to as the *obesogenic environment* – that is, a food environment that actively promotes weight gain.

If our eating were governed mainly by fluctuating energy needs, none of this would be a problem. But the currency of our food preferences is sensory pleasure, and seeking such pleasure in food has become in many cases far more important than any consideration of a need for energy or other nutrients. Even food cravings are only very rarely about something we need; most often they are about what we want. So not only are our diets increasingly unrelated to survival, but they have also been hijacked by the desire for food as sensory pleasure.

Our response to the problems associated with eating for pleasure, particularly in Western societies, has been widespread, chronic attempts to restrict intake of just those foods that provide most sensory pleasure. As a way of addressing the decoupling of energy needs and eating, dieting too often fails because it ignores the fact that eating itself is motivated by the desire to obtain such pleasure.

The focus in *Taste Matters* is on likes and dislikes for the food and its flavour, rather than on other influences affecting what food is chosen. It is instructive, though, to consider what happens when our responses to the sensory properties of foods are potentially in conflict with other reasons for food choice.

Over the past few decades, there has been a dramatic increase in consumer concerns for risks associated with the health consequences – primarily obesity, and its attendant health risks – of consumption of high-fat, high-sugar foods. In response to such concerns, we have seen a remarkable upsurge in the marketing of low-fat versions of foods, as well as foods sweetened by non-calorific sweeteners such as aspartame, saccharin and various sweetener blends. In parallel, at least with some segments of the consumer population, there has been an emphasis on 'healthy eating', including concerns regarding food additives. Such a noticeable groundswell of consumer sentiment could suggest that the motives for food consumption have perhaps shifted from immediate gratification by highly palatable, but 'potentially harmful', foods to a more considered response in which the nutritional value of the food has become more important. The dramatic increase in the emphasis on organic foods in many Western countries seems to point to this. Originally, organic foods were seen as a worthwhile choice because of fears that pesticide residues may be harmful over a long period of consumption. Now, however, claims for organic foods include that they are somehow more 'healthy' in general. But the whole idea of 'healthy foods' creates an unfortunate dichotomy: foods are either healthy or palatable, and in turn this attitude underlies the fact that diets typically fail.

In fact, there is no evidence that, overall, such a shift in motives has occurred, despite an increasing focus on food and health. Palatability remains the primary motivating force in what foods we want to consume. If a food is highly palatable, we are likely to consume it in preference to other foods, both in frequency and quantity. In other words, the sensory properties of foods still determine to a great extent what we want to eat and indeed how much we eat of a particular food. As a result, the total number of calories we consume remains under the control of taste. Avoiding palatable foods, while achievable (indeed it is the basis for most diets), reflects a denial of inherent and learned internal motivations and of the way that our bodies have evolved.

Yet another consequence of the fact that sensory pleasure has been decoupled from nutrition is rather less of a concern. Sensory pleasure is the underlying principle motivating food consumption once basic nutritional needs have been met, and for the majority in affluent societies this means that taste is the only factor to consider. Food appeal is mass appeal. The recent major sales successes of cookbooks rely at least as much on the sensory pleasure contained in the book's food illustrations as in the practical skills they impart. The emergence of molecular gastronomy in the past decade, and the elevation of the major exponents of these techniques to stellar chef status, recognizes that food consumption for at least some segments of populations can be an issue only of sensory or intellectual pleasure. Restaurants that excel in the 'science' of creating unexpected combinations of flavours and textures are focused primarily on creating sensory pleasure without consideration of either nutrition or satiety. This may or may not be the future of food, but this approach is popular precisely because it does address honestly one of the main reasons for eating.

But what of the multitude of other reasons behind why certain foods are consumed? Food choices can of course reflect a huge variety of influences, including anticipated health consequences or the belief that some foods are more appropriate, ethically or environmentally, as well as such practical considerations as price, availability and convenience. Cross-cultural similarities and differences have also been identified in those factors that people say are important reasons for choosing one food over another, such as price, convenience and natural content. In particular, commonalities appear to derive from ethnic origins. Consumers in New Zealand, Finland, the USA and the UK all rate taste as the number one motivation to consume particular foods. Although Chinese populations – whether in China, Taiwan or Malaysia – tend to place a greater emphasis on the potential of foods to have health-giving properties and for weight control, they still nominate sensory appeal as crucial.[1] Even in cultures that do not rate taste as the *most* important factor, it is still highly likely that it is a necessary minimum requirement for food acceptance. Once the requirement for foods to taste good has been met, then factors such as cost, nutrition, convenience and weight control have various amounts of influence on food choices.

Purchasing a food for the first time obviously relies on something other than first-hand experience of its taste. This might be curiosity, interesting packaging or an appeal by the manufacturer to your newly diet-conscious self in their advertising. However, it is our responses to a food's odour, taste, flavour and texture that provide the basis for repeated consumption and, ultimately, for food acceptance.[2] So, while this is only one aspect of food choice, it is the most crucial one. That is why the book's focus is on the influences that shape hedonic responses to the foods themselves, their flavours and other sensory qualities.

The primacy of taste vis-à-vis other influences on food choice is also evident in much research.[3] One of my own studies examined the impact of adding monosodium glutamate (MSG) to a vegetable soup. Based on previous research, added MSG was expected to make the soup richer and more savoury, and better liked, than the version without added MSG. However, that was only part of what we did. In many countries in recent years, the use of MSG as a food additive has received adverse publicity because of claims that it produced allergic reactions in some people – a phenomenon sometimes known as *Chinese Restaurant Syndrome*. This has led to food manufacturers, and even Chinese restaurants, labelling their foods as having 'No Added MSG'. This is disingenuous at best. 'No Added Sulphuric Acid' labels would be just as useful and accurate. One consequence of such labelling is a widespread belief that MSG is somehow a harmful food additive, despite a lack of evidence for this.

These beliefs provided an ideal context in which to examine whether information about the MSG content of a food might influence the extent to which the food's flavour was judged positively. To do this, we recruited groups of consumers, the majority of whom agreed that it was 'better to choose foods without added MSG'. They were asked to evaluate the two soups using rating scales for overall liking, richness, saltiness, natural taste and purchase intent. For a psychologist, no study is truly satisfying unless we deceive participants. So, with the soup samples, the participants received an ingredients list that specified either 'No Added MSG' or 'Contains Added MSG'. However, for all participants both labels were paired with both soups so that the labels were sometimes accurate and sometimes not. The results were straightforward: the labels had no impact whatsoever. Samples of soup containing MSG were liked more; they were judged as having a more natural taste and being richer and saltier, and the participants were more likely to purchase this version of the soup. So, despite their beliefs about MSG, participants responded only to the enhanced flavour.[4]

Food manufacturers implicitly recognize these basic motivations by making sure that so-called 'healthy' foods are also designed and marketed with a focus on their sensory appeal. They know that being labelled as 'healthy' is, for a food, much like you or I being labelled as having a 'good personality' – in both cases, the appeal is for something more enduring, something we *should* like. In the end, however, some rather more basic drive tells us that we might not get exactly what we want. Fortunately for our waistlines, it is possible to select foods that have both taste and nutritional appeal, and increasingly the food and beverage industry is focusing on developing fat, salt and sugar substitutes that taste like the 'real thing'. Even with organic foods, there has been increasing emphasis on promoting such produce as better tasting, despite no evidence that this is actually true.

The aim of this book is to tell the story of how our likes and dislikes for the sensory properties of foods arise. The material on which this story is based is the science of food preference* and food choice. Although this is a relatively young field of investigation, the science is proving crucial to our understanding of how our food preferences develop and the implication of those preferences for both our health and our enjoyment of life. This makes it an exciting field in which to work and I hope that you can share some of this excitement in *Taste Matters*.

Enjoy the book. If you are just having a nibble at it, perhaps in a book shop, deciding whether or not to buy, my advice is: go on, make a meal of it.

---

* Throughout the book, I use the term 'preference' interchangeably with 'liking'. Of course, this is strictly inaccurate. I can like two foods – pizza and scrambled eggs – equally, but if you ask me which one I prefer, it will depend on what I feel like at that time of day. One way to think about this is that relative liking varies with context.

ONE

Taste Sensations

When is the last time you paused while munching on an apple and wondered at the complexity of the sensory experience? Even a humble piece of fruit provides an enormously varied set of sensations that begins prior to the first bite. The sight and smell of a food that you are about to eat sets up expectations of the flavour to follow, and the extent to which it is likely to make you feel full. But it is only after you have taken a bite that the characteristic flavour of a food – odours, tastes and tactile or *mouthfeel* sensations such as astringency, spiciness and texture – emerges. Yet unless we are particularly enthusiastic about our beverage or food experiences, we seldom analyse those experiences, other than to decide whether or not we like what we are eating. So, before focusing on the hedonic properties of foods, it is worth considering briefly the nature of what we experience – our food perceptions.

Smell

Flavours are more than just tastes and, as we will see in this and later chapters, our likes for the various aspects of flavours come about in different ways. We start, therefore, with a very common misunderstanding about food flavours, namely the role of taste. Whatever you think taste is (and my apologies if you are the exception), it probably is not. Much of what is commonly referred to as the taste of a food is actually its aroma or odour. Odours consist of volatile (gaseous) chemical compounds. The mixture of compounds that we perceive as apple odour reach the olfactory receptors that lie at the top and back of the complex maze of passages within the nose, and it is these receptors that ultimately signal that it is an apple that we are eating. Chocolate is not a taste, and neither are orange, coffee and peach. Consider that if you close your eyes and hold your nose, this (unsurprisingly) has no effect on the sense of taste. However, with sight and smell now temporarily disabled, you will be unable to tell the difference between an apple and an onion, red and white wine, or beef and lamb, and you will have no possibility of identifying whether the juice you drink is orange, mango or peach, or a combination of all three!

After a food enters the mouth, the same aromas that you may have detected when the food was cooking, or when you sniffed it, are released and concentrated within the mouth by the combined actions of heating (the internal temperature of the mouth is 37°C / 98.6°F) and chewing. These aromas now reach the olfactory receptors via the nasopharyngeal passage at the back of the mouth. The main reason why we commonly refer to characteristic food qualities as tastes – apple taste, coffee taste, and so on – is because we are not conscious of this alternate route for the sense of smell. Odour and taste perceptions are so well integrated in flavours that there are seldom any obvious signs as to where one sense ends and the other begins. It is this uncertainty about which sensations are odours and which are tastes that gives rise to the illusion that, during eating, odour qualities are perceived in the mouth – and we naturally assume that it is our sense of taste that is responsible for these sensations.[1] Our language both reflects and encourages this confusion, in that we use the terms 'taste' and 'flavour' interchangeably. Simply holding the nose while a food or drink is in the mouth is sufficient, however, to demonstrate just how large a contribution the sense of smell makes to flavour. The complaint of loss of taste during a head cold is also a consequence of this misunderstanding. In fact, taste is largely unaffected, and it is the sense of smell that suffers.

The rich diversity of food flavours throughout the world's cuisines testifies to the fact that we can perceive thousands, if not tens of thousands, of distinct odours. Attempts have been made to classify odours into a set of basic prototype qualities, but this has been entirely without success. In the 1950s, for example, prominent olfactory scientist John Amoore proposed that all smell could be categorized into a distinct set of qualities: *camphoraceous, peppermint, floral, musky, ethereal, putrid* and *pungent*, or some mixture of these, but this classification system has never been widely accepted. In fact, our sense of smell appears to be almost *infinitely* receptive to new qualities. Thus combining different odours can produce a new quality entirely distinct from the components. Many of the foods we eat – chocolate and coffee are good examples – have many hundreds of different chemical compounds that combine to produce a distinctive odour/flavour that is unlike the odours of the individual compounds in the mixture.[2]

But the majority of food and drink odours and flavours are even more complex than that. A mixture of odours that smells like a food can also have *odour notes*. The best example of this is wine. We are all familiar with wine experts who can apparently describe the odour of a white wine in terms of tropical fruits, capsicum, cut grass, asparagus and – for a few lucky drinkers – cat's pee. Are they making this up? Is there something special about their olfactory abilities? In fact, anyone with a reasonable sense of smell could be trained to perceive the same qualities. Sometimes a note can be identified with a particular chemical compound in wine. Thus the buttery smell often found in wood-aged Chardonnay wines (and some beers) can be linked to the presence of the compound diacetyl. However, the links between particular chemicals and specific odour qualities are not always evident. One of the things that makes the sense of smell still relatively mysterious is that these notes *emerge* from the combination of different chemical compounds that make up wine odour, as does the overall wine odour. A wine can smell like wine and, simultaneously, a collection of odour notes. Some red wines, for example, are described in terms of the odours of cherries, chocolate and tobacco, to name only a few common terms.

Taste

At the same time as the odours in our apple are released during chewing, its acids and sugars stimulate taste receptors, giving rise to perceptions of sourness and sweetness, respectively. To be perceived as a taste, a chemical compound or food ingredient has to be soluble (for example, in water or saliva) in order to reach the taste receptors, which are grouped together in 3,000 or so taste buds, located mostly on the upper and side surfaces of the tongue. The taste buds are themselves located within structures on the tongue called *papillae*, which are most obviously seen as tiny bumps on the tongue's upper front surface. These are known as *fungiform papillae* for their resemblance to tiny mushrooms. Contrary to popular belief, taste buds are not specialized according to tongue location – we are capable of perceiving all tastes at any tongue location where taste buds are present (although our sensitivity to different tastes does vary somewhat across different locations). The so-called *tongue map* – sweetness and saltiness at the tip, sour at the sides, and bitter at the rear of the tongue – actually stems from the perpetuation of a misleading interpretation of a study originally published in German in the early part of the twentieth century. Even today this misinterpretation of the original study is found in university textbooks whose authors clearly have not gone to the original source of the information.

Compared to the rich, perhaps limitless, inventory of odours that do so much to define the distinctive properties of foods, the sense of taste initially seems remarkably unimpressive. Perhaps this is because, after subtracting odour qualities (and other sensations such as pungency and various aspects of mouthfeel) from the overall flavour of a food or beverage, we are left with a rather small group of sensory qualities – traditionally, sweetness, saltiness, sourness and bitterness. These four qualities have long been identified – from Aristotle onwards – as the basic tastes. From time to time, various other qualities have been proposed to increase this list. A metallic taste and the drying, puckering quality of astringency have been suggested as basic tastes, but are now generally accepted as arising from odours and tactile sensations, respectively. However, there is now a reasonable consensus that the rich, meaty quality of savoury foods reflects another basic taste quality, known most commonly by the Japanese term, umami, which translates approximately as 'savoury deliciousness'. There is also growing evidence that fat – or at least the fatty acids of which they are composed – may also be a basic taste quality.

This limited set of four or five, or perhaps six, taste qualities is clearly inadequate to describe much of the sensory complexity of any specific food, let alone a whole cuisine, no matter how they are combined. Unlike odours, tastes do not combine to form new qualities. Combining salt, sugar and lemon juice may result in changes in the intensity of the tastes involved (different tastes typically suppress one another in mixtures), but it will only produce a mixture with the qualities of saltiness, sweetness and sourness. Nor can any of these qualities be made from a combination of the other tastes, one of the key reasons we talk about a set of basic tastes.[3]

Saying that there are only a few different taste qualities is, of course, not the same as saying that only a few substances produce those qualities. Sour tastes are mostly produced by acids, such as the citric acid found in fruits and the acetic acid of vinegar. Similarly, saltiness is most commonly due to the presence of sodium in a compound. Sweetness and bitterness, however, can be produced by substances belonging to a wide variety of chemical classes: not only sugars, but also some proteins and amino acids are sweet. Other amino acids are bitter, as are alkaloids and some salts. Many chemical compounds also produce multiple tastes. For example, the artificial sweetener saccharin is both sweet and somewhat bitter.

Touch

Clear liquid flows freely from each nostril, your scalp, forehead and cheeks are hot and damp from perspiration, and there is a sensation much like being stabbed in the tongue with a sharp knife. What could be nicer? The answer, for about a quarter of the world's population – those who consume chilli daily – is nothing. Many of the most impressive food sensations relate neither to tastes nor odours. The sensations produced by chilli, as well as some of the other important ingredients that make up the flavours of foods and drinks, are more closely related to our sense of touch than they are to odours or tastes. If the acidity in a piece of fruit is high enough, we might also perceive a degree of 'bite' or 'sharpness'. This is due to the activation of receptors in nerves within the mouth and tongue responsive to a variety of sensations, including warmth, cooling and even, in the case of chilli, pain. These same nerves send branches into the eyes and nose, and the sensations they carry, often called *pungency* in the context of foods, are important to our appreciation of flavour in many foods and beverages. Pungent qualities are important sensory components of foods throughout the world, including Western diets. A cola drink without fizz, a glass of wine without its sharpness, and onions, mustard and horseradish without their bite or ability to induce tears, have all lost much of their defining quality.[4]

We often associate pungency with cultures such as Korea, Vietnam, Thailand and Mexico, whose cuisines use a lot of chilli. These cuisines provide much greater flavour impact than typical Western diets, and their recent popularity in Western countries may reflect not just increased availability, but a striving for new, intense culinary sensations. It was such a demand that led Christopher Columbus in the fifteenth century to attempt to reach the East Indies in search of spices such as pepper, valued in the European cuisines of his time. It is one of the ironies of food history that, in failing to find these spices, he returned with chilli. This much more potent spice established itself throughout the world, if not in all cuisines, then certainly as a food ingredient eaten by a substantial proportion of the world's population.

Even in cultures in which chilli failed to take hold initially, it is becoming increasingly popular, but within limits. A common complaint – apparently across cultures and particularly by infrequent chilli consumers – is that too much burn overwhelms other aspects of the flavour. Even regular chilli eaters feel that if the food is *too* hot, then appreciation of other aspects of flavour are spoiled. On the face of it, it seems self-evident that such a strong sensation should overwhelm a weaker one. We are used to the suppression of flavour and taste qualities by other flavours and tastes. For example, the sourness of lemon juice is decreased by adding sweetness. Yet the evidence for this occurring with chilli heat is weak, even with fairly subtle flavours, and the only reliable finding to date is that chilli heat reduces the sweetness of foods.[5]

That we cannot show an impact of chilli on food flavours is certainly contrary to popular belief and, perhaps, popular experience. Wine commentators commonly invoke the idea that hot foods reduce the intensity of 'subtle' wine flavours. It is not uncommon for wine columns in newspapers to grapple with the question of what to drink with spicy food, and a frequent conclusion is to recommend that spicy dishes be accompanied by beer instead (or sometimes a 'bold' red or a 'spicy' white). For some reason, beer flavour is thought immune to pungency, or perhaps the assumption is that beer drinkers do not worry about flavour as much as wine drinkers.

Moreover, attempts to convince reluctant and relatively naive hot-food eaters to consume a Thai meal or an Indian curry usually founder on this issue of the impact of pungency on other food qualities. If high levels of pungency do not reduce most tastes and flavours, why do individuals complain that food with too much chilli overwhelms the flavour? It seems unlikely that a simple sweetness reduction is being noticed, particularly in savoury foods. The most plausible explanation is that, particularly for the novice chilli consumer, attention may be dominated by the initial, strongest or most strongly positive or negative sensory experiences. Following consumption of highly spiced food, we may be left with a strong impression that flavours were reduced, whereas what really occurred was that the burn was simply more prominent. This impression may be reinforced by the persistence of the burning sensations long after the tastes and flavours have disappeared. Hence it may be the memory of the experience which lies behind the belief that the flavour was reduced. This may be particularly the case if the level of pungency is higher than the individual finds pleasant. However, repeated experience with the hot food not only leads to preferences for that overall food flavour but also to the burning sensations being less dominant.

Other, less obvious tactile sensations are also important in food acceptability. In particular, problems with texture are a common reason for rejecting foods. It is frequently noted that eating an oyster for the first time involved a certain amount of bravery. This has little or nothing to do with oyster flavour, which is subtle and hard to define. Far more pertinent is the oyster's appearance,* and particularly its texture. The oyster is certainly slippery, if not, as its critics claim, slimy. Its consumption requires little assistance from the consumer, with the oyster preferring instead to slide down the throat unchewed. Presumably, this would be fine for a bit of carrot or even a small piece of cooked meat. The oyster, however, is not only a whole, uncooked creature, but it is one that resists our most expert efforts to finely manipulate its passage around the mouth, or divide it into smaller, chewable pieces. Of course, for oyster-lovers, none of this is a problem, since part of the attraction is the oyster's *creamy* texture. For the rest of the world, though, the oyster is a pre-eminent example of the role that texture often plays as a reason for rejection of a food.

Less dramatic examples of the importance of texture are seen with everyday foods. It is unlikely that we will finish an apple if it is either mushy or rock-hard, or in any other way requires too much effort in chewing. Many textural sensations – for example, the crispness of a crisp / potato chip or the crunchiness of our apple – are derived not just from the food activating tactile fibres in the tongue, but also from pressure sensors in the jaw, and even the sounds that the foods make when we bite down or chew. Research that has artificially altered the sounds that we hear when crunching a potato chip, for example, has shown that perceptions of freshness or staleness could be increased or decreased, depending on which sound frequencies were manipulated.[6]

Sometimes in the past considered a taste, the property of *astringency* is now known to be a set of mouthfeel sensations.[7] Characteristic of foods and beverages containing tannins, including some fruits, nuts, tea and cranberry juice, astringency consists of sensations of drying, puckering and roughness felt on the mucous lining of the mouth. These sensations result when the tannins act on the proteins in saliva to reduce saliva's ability to lubricate the mouth. Although it

---

* Memorably described by food critic A. A. Gill as 'sea-snot on a half-shell' (*Sunday Times*, 8 November 2009).

sounds largely unpleasant, astringency is a good example of how responses to sensory qualities are often highly dependent on the context in which we experience them. One of the reasons that we might not eat a green banana is that it tends to leave the mouth feeling like a sandpit. Red wine drinkers, on the other hand, value these sensations, at least to some extent, and when a wine is described as 'dry', it is due to a significant extent to astringency.

Sensory Integration

Taste, smell, touch and even the appearance and sounds of foods are integrated during eating. It is the combination of these different senses that leads to a characteristic food flavour. Disturbing this integration can have a serious impact on our ability to recognize or enjoy foods. Thus textural properties are crucial in our ability to identify even very common, everyday foods. In one study, groups of tasters were asked to identify a variety of fruits and vegetables that had been puréed. Because many of the textural differences among these foods had been removed, identification relied heavily on odours and tastes. Among a group of students, only 41 per cent could identify banana, 30 per cent broccoli, 63 per cent carrot and 7 per cent cabbage. While these figures might be surprising, the sad news for all of us sooner or later is that the corresponding percentages for an group of elderly people were 24 per cent, 0 per cent, 7 per cent and 4 per cent. As well as indicating the decline in olfactory abilities that is common as we age, these findings highlight our difficulty in accurately identifying odours or flavour.[8]

Even expertise and knowledge can be discounted by the influence of the overall sensory context. Wine enthusiasts were asked to sniff white wines with all visual cues hidden, and to describe the aroma characteristics of the wine. When led to believe that they were sniffing a red wine, the words used matched those of red wines – blackcurrant, cherry, chocolate and so on. The same effect emerged when they were told to sniff 'white' wines and describe their properties.[9]

Our likes and dislikes naturally spring from the synthesis of sensations that we have learned to recognize as foods and which are therefore important to survival. Initial reactions to foods are almost always hedonic – that is, they are concerned with the overall pleasure provided by the food – and this naturally precedes accepting or rejecting the food. While we may analyse whether the taste, or texture or smell is responsible if a food is somehow not right, our 'gut' response is to the food overall – the steak or the glass of red wine – rather than a collection of separate odours, tastes and tactile sensations.

TWO

We Eat What We Like

Think for a moment about your favourite foods. Not the ones you eat every day, as these are often selected on criteria – healthiness, wholesomeness, convenience – that have little to do with likes and dislikes. But the ones you *would* eat every day if you had no concerns about weight gain, or heart attacks, or the need for balance in your diet; or perhaps the ones you reserve as a special treat. Now think about a few words to describe the general qualities of these foods. Do any of the following words fit: sweet, salty, creamy, rich, savoury, smooth, tangy? Notice that I am not including here qualities that might describe specific foods – no chocolatey, no crispy bacon, no pizza with pepperoni and mushrooms, but rather qualities that *many* of your favourites might possess.

These qualities are, to a large extent, anchored in basic tastes – sweet, sour, salty, bitter and umami. Because of recent discoveries about its taste properties, fat can also be included in this category. The distinction was made earlier between the vast array of odours that provide the defining characteristics of a majority of individual foods, and the relatively small number of basic tastes. The starting point for considering the origins of food likes and dislikes is to ask why there are so few basic tastes. The answer is that each of these taste qualities has a unique significance signalled by the distinctive hedonic responses that it elicits. This forms the first step in understanding food preferences. As already noted in chapter One, our imprecise use of the word 'taste' reflects our confusion about the different qualities that make up flavours. In compensation, our language does provide clues as to the nutritional implications of different taste qualities, and ultimately the role that taste plays in determining food preferences. So, in addition to describing food qualities, we also talk about tastes as a way of indicating good or bad characteristics, properties or judgements. These descriptions reflect the underlying structure of the taste experience itself.

Most obviously, there is sweetness. Of all the qualities that our senses perceive, is there anything more unequivocally positive? It makes unpalatable food acceptable and the medicine go down (at least when administered by the spoonful). Sweetness is embedded in our language as a metaphor for positive experiences in general: success (the sweet smell of . . .; victory is sweet), pleasure (sweet soul music), desire (sweetheart; my sweet), or that sensation of just getting it right (the sweet spot; 'sweeeet'). Substitute any other taste, even any other sensory quality, for any of these expressions and they not only sound odd, but we seem to lose all meaning. Red is a nice colour, but does not universally signal pleasure, success or victory. We like salty snacks, but 'saltyheart' as a term of endearment is relatively rare. We even use the word 'sweet' to add something positive to potentially objectionable foods. Calling certain kinds of offal 'sweetbreads' is done for good reasons, even if it is not very convincing. On the other hand, 'bitter' and 'sour' clearly reflect unpleasant emotions. One can become embittered by failure or loss, and bitter(ness) is a good substitute for disappointment, distaste, hatefulness or resentment. Similarly, someone who is 'sour' can be discontented or ill-tempered. Of course, the expression that someone has a sour face is more than just a metaphor, as watching someone sucking a lemon will demonstrate.

The origin of this use of tastes to describe such everyday emotions lies in the universal role that tastes play as in-built arbiters of what is good and bad in those things that we consume. This is mediated by the emotions that each taste quality produces. As long ago as 1825, the French gastronome Jean-Anthelme Brillat-Savarin noted in his meditations on food and eating, The Physiology of Taste, that taste can be reduced 'in the last analysis, in the two expressions, agreeable or disagreeable'.[1] More recent scientific explorations of taste hedonics have not contradicted Brillat-Savarin's conclusion. In contrast to our preferences for other food qualities – including odours – which are moulded by individual patterns of exposure and reinforcement from an early age (see chapters Three and Four), our emotional responses to basic taste qualities have been shown to be remarkably uniform.

While, of course, food preferences vary quite substantially in different cultures, hedonic responses to pure tastes in isolation appear to remain relatively independent of culture or diet in adults. Comparisons across cultures whose diets are very different find highly similar patterns of likes and dislikes for pure tastes, outside of the context of foods. The sweet taste of sucrose in water, for example, is optimally pleasant at around 10–12 per cent by weight (approximately the same as is found in many ripe fruits), regardless of whether you are from Japan, Taiwan or Australia. By contrast, at anything other than very low concentrations, for these same populations, bitter quinine and the sour taste of citric acid become increasingly disliked as concentration rises.[2]

The characteristic hedonic responses to sweetness, sourness, bitterness and umami are present at birth, while there seems to be a developmental lag of a few months for saltiness. Again, as far as we know, this holds across all cultures. The picture on p. 32 shows the distinctive hedonic responses to the sweetness of sucrose and the bitterness of quinine in two newborns, each only a few hours old. For each, their first post-natal experience of taste has come as part of a study in which pure tastants were placed on their tongues. Of course, at this age, the experience of pleasure has to be inferred from overt behaviours. In this famous study, conducted by Israeli taste researcher Jacob Steiner, the presence of sweet tastes on the tongue was reliably followed by sucking, lip smacking and smiling – each suggestive of a quality that the baby might want to ingest.[3] Perhaps unsurprisingly, breast milk is very sweet, meaning that its taste will be inherently acceptable.

Putting bitter quinine on the tongue produces a rather different outcome, in a display of nose-wrinkling, gaping and tongue protrusion, the meaning of which is fairly unambiguous. Humans are not alone in such responses – placing sweet or bitter compounds on the tongue of a rat, a monkey or a gorilla will produce essentially identical facial expressions. This provides further evidence for both

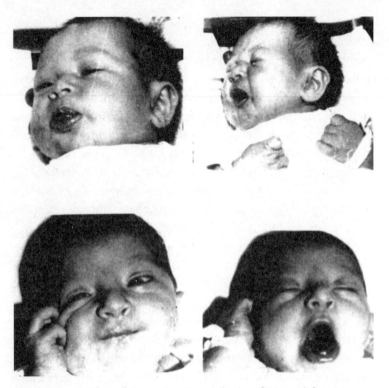

Facial expressions of two newborns to application of a sweet (left panels) and a bitter (right panels) taste prior to any experience of foods (including bottle- or breast-feeding).

the universality of preferences for basic tastes and the importance of such innate responses in the evolution of mammals generally.

Given their age, the responses of the newborns shown here are clearly not learned, raising the strong possibility that such fixed responses to tastes at birth are genetically determined. Certainly, at least in the case of preference for sweetness and for common sweet foods, there is strong family heritability, although it is difficult to completely rule out the influence of the maternal diet while we are in *utero* (see, for example, the role that maternal diet has in shaping preferences for flavours in infants, covered in chapter Three).[4] In either case, the significance of uniform hedonic responses to pure tastes appears to lie in the nutritional implications of these qualities, and this provides the key to understanding why we have evolved to be sensitive to these qualities specifically.

As discussed below, taste palatability, and ultimately the palatability of foods, seems to reflect either provision of energy or other vital nutrients, or, conversely, a warning of the presence of a potential toxin. We can think of our instinctive reactions to tastes therefore as a survival strategy, a way of motivating us to consume what will keep us alive and avoid what will poison us before we have an opportunity to learn about foods and their consequences.

Eat!

It is unfortunate that the list of most of those things that our body innately registers as good to ingest – sugar, fat, salt – reads like a set of disease risk factors. This seems at once to put our biological drives at odds with the nutritional advice we hear about every day. To whom do we listen: our bodies or our nutritional advisors? In fact, this question confuses preference for specific foods and food qualities with nutritional balance and dietary behaviour (see chapter Twelve for further discussion of this apparent contradiction). As we will see, each of these substances generates pleasure in the foods we eat, and this is a signal for a nutrient that is physiologically useful. Moreover, the pleasure serves a purpose, namely as a motivation to ingest. Removing any of these nutrients from our diet will result in illness and eventually death, generally considered a poor nutritional outcome.

Sweet

The search for sources of sweetness has been a major influence on the development of the modern world. Providing European consumers with sugars for their foods and drinks through cultivation and trade in sugar cane was a major impetus for trade and exploration from the 1600s onwards. Such trade has caused wars, driven the development of the slave trade and spurred European nations to build empires.[5]

What is so special about sweetness? Where is the race to find high-potency acids that will make drinks more sour? Why weren't slaves shipped in large numbers to cultivate and harvest the cinchona tree, whose bark is used to make bitter-tasting quinine? In other words, why are only sweet tastes so pervasively positive? While a wide range of chemical compounds possess a sweet taste, at least for humans, the sweetness of those compounds found in plants have a vital nutritional function in that they very commonly signal the presence of carbohydrates. Our survival depends on our ability to take in energy from our diet, and one of the major sources of such energy is carbohydrates, which include sugars. Sweetness, therefore, is an excellent signal for the presence of energy.

Humans, while omnivores, have relied on plants to provide a substantial proportion of required energy and other nutrients. To our distant ancestors wandering through the forest in search of food, the sweetness of a piece of fruit within reach was a signal that needed calories were available, and hence that the fruit should be consumed. Our hairy predecessors did not require a *What Fruit Is That?* guidebook to make a decision about what to eat – the mere presence of a sweet taste produced a sensation of pleasure that motivated consumption. Hence the fact that we respond innately to sweetness positively is an important part of our ability to survive.

In order to maximize energy intake, preferences generally rise with sweetness intensity.[6] Human newborns not only respond positively to sugars, they also discriminate between different sugars, consuming more if given free access to those that are more sweet (sucrose and fructose), as compared to less sweet glucose and lactose. In other words, the sweeter the better, as far as newborns are concerned. Once again, plant-eating humans are not alone in responding to sweetness to maximize energy intake. In photosynthesizing plants, sugars increase during the day, then decrease at night. Herbivores like cattle, sheep, horses and rabbits will selectively prefer and eat more of forage cut later in the day, when sugars are highest. Carnivorous cats, on the other hand, are indifferent to sweet tastes (at least at low concentrations) – a reflection of the importance of sweet tastes primarily as an indicator of ripeness or sugar content in plants.

Given that concerns are often raised about 'sugar addictions', especially in children, it is not difficult to think about the universal pleasure derived from sweetness in terms of drug-like properties. This analogy has some substance. It is now known that sweetness palatability is mediated by the same opioid (morphine-like) biochemical systems in the brain that are thought to be the basis for all highly rewarding activities, including recreational drug-taking. A drug such as naloxone, which blocks the activity in brain opioid systems and will eliminate the effects of heroin and other opioid drugs, will also reduce food palatability and intake, especially that of sweet foods.[7] The activation of opioid systems also explains why sweetness has been shown to act like an analgesic. For example, a sweet taste applied to the tongue – whether a carbohydrate like sucrose or an artificial sweetener such as aspartame – will reduce crying in infants and is consequently sometimes used as a pacifier during painful procedures in hospitals.[8] In adults, a sweet taste, and even a sweet smell, can increase the willingness to tolerate more pain.[9]

Such parallels do not of course demonstrate 'sugar addictions'; they simply illustrate that sweet tastes are rewarding (which we know), as are the effects of some other substances. Whether or not other properties of addictions such as craving occur with respect to tastes, or foods in general, will be examined in chapter Six. That the majority of foods self-selected by children in Western societies are nevertheless primarily sweet reflects the innate pleasure that sweetness provides, but of course may also indicate just how available and promoted sweet foods are. This undoubtedly underlies the fears expressed by anxious parents that their children are addicted to sweet things. But such fears are almost certainly unjustified with regard to long-term consequences. There is very little evidence that strong preferences for sweet foods in childhood necessarily lead to hyperactivity or adult obesity, or even to continued high consumption of sweet foods beyond puberty. In terms of the body's needs, a high preference for sugars makes sense when energy needs are high, as they often are (or at least traditionally have been) in childhood. In any case, despite parental concerns about intake of sweet foods, the reward inherent in sweetness is recognized as crucial in many circumstances. Sweet foods continue to be used as pacifiers and rewards, and predominate within pleasant social contexts such as parties and outings.

Sweetness continues to influence food palatability in adults, even if preferences for, and consumption of, sweet foods declines relative to childhood. Especially in combination with fats (see below), we find the presence of sweetness in foods highly palatable, and for some foods, such as desserts, palatability remains entirely dependent on their sugar content.[10] There is also truth in the idea that some of us retain the 'sweet tooth' of our childhood. Adults can be classified into sweet-likers or dislikers, although the 'dislike' shown by this latter group – around 30 per cent of us in Western societies – is a relative, rather than an absolute, dislike.[11] Since this distinction between sweet-likers and dislikers is usually made in research studies on the basis of responses to sugar solutions, it is reasonable to ask whether or not likers eat more sweet foods than dislikers. Unfortunately, we do not know this for sure, but it would be a reasonable assumption since the sweetness of a food is a strong influence on the amount consumed by adults (see chapter Eight).

When asked to eat until they are comfortably full, most people will consume much greater quantities of sweet than savoury or salty foods (see also chapter Six). This appears to be the result not of some effect in the digestive system, or a need for the energy that a sweetener might provide. Rather, it has to do with the taste, since it occurs even if we use sweeteners that do not provide calories. Such effects show that our innate responses are to sweetness itself, and not in anticipation of the calories that are very often associated with sweetness. In fact, in modern Western diets, sweet taste and energy consumption have been increasingly decoupled. Because it is so innately rewarding, sweetness does not always need to be accompanied by calories for it to be pleasurable or influence food consumption. We have evolved to recognize and like sweetness for the energy value it signals. Even though non-nutritional (artificial) sweeteners have had no role in our evolution, they still evoke pleasure. It is the quality of sweetness itself that our bodies respond to, since its meaning has previously been unambiguous. Hence sweet tastes can exert effects on palatability and consumption in the absence of any effect it has on our metabolism. This has an upside in terms of its effects on calories consumed. Dieters who eat foods that are sweet – but without calories (for example, sweetened with aspartame) – are better able to comply with their diets and lose weight.

Given our awareness of the role of sweet carbohydrates such as sucrose and fructose in obesity, our attitudes to these sweet substances (and the foods that contain them) has changed in recent times; however, our attitudes to sweetness per se have not. Today, the food industry spends considerable sums attempting to develop artificial, and often high-potency, sweeteners such as saccharin, aspartame and sucralose to act as substitutes for sucrose and other plant-based sweeteners. This is driven by a perceived consumer demand for diet drinks and other low-calorie products, as well as the potential for lower manufacturing costs associated with the use of high-potency sweeteners. But the important thing to note is that our concerns about obesity have not suddenly opened up promising markets for unsweetened soda drinks. If you are a Diet Coke drinker, but it is unavailable, you are unlikely to choose sparkling mineral water; instead you will probably choose plain old, un-Diet Coke, sweetened with sucrose or fructose.

Fat

The other major source of energy in Western diets is fat, which is more energy-dense than sugars. One of fat's major contributions to food acceptability is through providing pleasant textures: sensations of creaminess, crunchiness, smoothness, crispness and richness are all a consequence of a food's fat content. Fat is also the major carrier for flavours in many foods. Hence low-fat versions of foods seldom suffer from the 'too much flavour' problem. Recent research has pointed to the strong possibility that, as with a basic taste such as sweetness, there may be taste mechanisms involved in the detection and recognition of fats, or the fatty acids of which they are made.[12] Although the mechanisms are not yet fully understood, foods that contain genuine fats produce increases in levels of the fatty acids in the blood, a process that prepares the body to utilize the fat's energy. Foods using thickeners that mimic fat's textural properties (for example, as used in low-fat cream cheese) can be essentially indistinguishable in terms of texture and odour, but are far less effective in eliciting this response from the body.[13]

Fat palatability, like that of sweetness, may be the body's way of ensuring sufficient energy intake. It is not surprising, therefore, that our first experience of fat in foods is via breast milk, which typically has more fat than full-cream milk. Preferences for fat also tend to be high in childhood, but in contrast to those for sweetness, persist at much the same level throughout adulthood. The drive to consume high-fat foods is evident whenever such foods are freely available, in particular when in combination with sugar.[14] Although much dietary fat comes from meat products, attempts to reduce fat intake tend to focus particularly on foods that are both sweet and high-fat – cakes, dairy drinks, ice cream and other desserts. What characterizes such foods is their extreme palatability, which makes them the most difficult to resist in a diet. Moreover, as with that of sweetness, the palatability of fat appears to be a consequence of its sensory properties (either texture or taste), rather than fat's actual energy content. Like sweetness, for the vast duration of our evolutionary history the sensory properties of fat have been very reliable signals to our body for the associated energy value.

Salt

While we tend to be indifferent to salt taste at birth, by the time we are six months old, slightly salty water is preferred to plain.[15] The significance of this apparently universal preference is even more apparent for saltiness than it is for sweetness. Saltiness is an excellent signal for the presence of sodium, necessary for maintaining the body's fluid balance. A diet with dramatically reduced sodium is likely to result in illness and, if maintained, death. Unsurprisingly, a liking for salt, while present at all times, grows substantially if we are deprived of it below what is physiologically necessary.[16] There is strong evidence for the existence of salt craving in such circumstances (see also chapter Six).

From a health point of view, low-salt diets are not a major concern. Salt intakes throughout much of the world are well in excess of what is physiologically required and what is recommended by bodies such as the World Health Organization.[17] The INTERSALT study, involving 32 countries, found that the most common daily intake of sodium (assessed via urinary excretion) was typically more than twice the recommended intake for men and somewhat less for women (a difference probably accounted for by greater food intake in men).[18] In Western societies, three-quarters of our salt intake arises from consumption of processed foods, including those from restaurants, plus an additional 10 per cent or so that is added at the table. Especially important sources of salt are processed cereals, including breakfast cereal and bread, and meat products. By contrast, in China and Japan, condiments such as soy sauce, plus salt added during cooking, are the major sources.

It is possible to survive on far less dietary salt than we typically consume. The Yanomamo Indians of Brazil, for example, consume only around 1 per cent of the sodium found in most Western diets. What could explain our high salt intakes relative to what is needed physiologically or recommended to avoid risk of diseases such as stroke? The most obvious reason, now that it is seldom used for food preservation as it once was, is that salt increases food palatability.[19] Of course, overt saltiness is an important part of the appeal of many snack foods. But salt is important to food likes in two other ways. The first of these is that it enhances food flavours through chemical interactions within foods – a process known as 'salting-out'. Second, it adds flavour impact, even in foods that do not seem overly salty. The best example of this is bread. Some salt in bread – no more than 50 per cent of what is commonly added – is necessary for functional reasons – that is, for the baking process. However, eliminating the additional salt in bread produces a product not especially different in flavour from cardboard, at least for those with typical salt intakes.

Hence salt can strongly influence palatability, even in products that are not within a 'salty food' category. This suggests that the high salt intakes throughout the world are driven by its palatability effects on food.[20] Further indications of this comes from studies in which volunteers, placed on diets that are extremely low in salt for a week or so, report increased desire for salty foods – anchovies, pizza, bacon.[21] They also complain that all the foods that they do eat are 'tasteless' and unpalatable, even when attempts have been made to compensate for the low salt by making the food more spicy. Salt's main impact on food palatability is therefore not necessarily to add overt saltiness, but rather to increase flavour and flavour liking more generally.

The great mystery surrounding tomatoes is why, since they are fruit, we do not put them into fruit salad. Strangely, unlike most fruits, tomatoes seem more suited to savoury foods – they themselves can have a 'meaty', rich quality, which can be incorporated into sauces, stews and casseroles. Like the chilli, the tomato is a sixteenth-century import from South America that has infiltrated cuisines throughout the world. What sets the tomato apart from most other fruits, and the main reason for its common inclusion in savoury rather than sweet dishes, is that it is a good source of glutamate, a form of glutamic acid (an amino acid present in all proteins). The effects of glutamate are to produce the quality that we previously referred to as savoury, but that is now increasingly known by the Japanese word *umami*.

In the early twentieth century, a Japanese scientist, Kikunae Ikeda, first synthesized glutamate from the seaweed *konbu*, commonly used as a soup base in Japanese cuisine. He used the term umami to describe the quality that glutamate produced when added to savoury foods. Ikeda described umami as the 'peculiar taste which we feel as "Umai (meaning brothy, meaty, or savory)", arising from fish, meat and so forth'.[22] Over the past two decades, the scientific evidence has increasingly pointed to umami as a distinct basic taste.

Glutamate as a taste outside food, for example dissolved in water, is not particularly palatable, and it is hard to define in its quality. However, when added to suitable foods, its effects include increases in savouriness, richness and an almost tactile mouth-filling quality. The word umami may be relatively unfamiliar to Western consumers, but it is an everyday practice in most cuisines to make foods more palatable by adding glutamate to savoury foods.[23] Mostly, this is achieved by the addition of common ingredients in soups, sauces and stews. The preparation of a pasta sauce from basic ingredients such as onions, carrots, celery, tomatoes, mushrooms, chicken stock and Parmesan cheese is fundamentally an exercise in getting glutamate to our taste buds.[24] We can also add glutamate, in the absence of the other qualities offered by glutamate-rich vegetables and meats, by using a powder in which it is bound to sodium, namely mono-sodium glutamate (MSG). Glutamate-rich ingredients are encountered in all cuisines. Many Asian cultures increase the umami quality of their cuisines through sauces based on fermented vegetables or fish – soy sauce and the fish sauces of Vietnam and Thailand are examples. A Roman equivalent of fish sauce, 'liquamen', was being used 2,000 years ago as a way of enhancing food flavours.

As with sweetness, there is evidence that hedonic reactions to umami taste is innate. Newborns show facial responses to clear vegetable soup indicative of dislike – pursed lips, gaping mouth and wrinkled nose. However, when MSG is added to the same soup, the infants respond with facial expressions similar to those seen with liked sweet tastes, including licking, mouthing and sucking.

Why does glutamate elicit these signs of acceptance? As noted above, it has been argued that sweetness and fat are highly liked because of the body's response to the energy that they signal. If umami is a basic taste quality, a question arises about the evolutionary significance of the hedonic impact of glutamate in foods. Unlike salt or the energy that is signalled by sweet or fat tastes, we do not need to take in glutamate in the diet to survive. The palatability of glutamate may mean, therefore, that it is a marker for some other nutrient with which it is reliably associated. Because glutamic acid is an amino acid present in animal and vegetable protein, umami taste may act as a signal for the presence of protein, with its effects on palatability therefore promoting consumption.[25]

This hypothesis has been difficult to prove. Because the body manufactures most of its own glutamate, we cannot show the effects of glutamate deficiency, in the way that this can be shown for salt. Nevertheless, there have been studies showing that people with very low protein intakes prefer higher concentrations of glutamate than those whose protein intake is adequate.[26] In other studies, glutamate has been shown to increase food palatability irrespective of the taster's nutritional state.[27] An alternative idea to explain the palatability effect of glutamate comes from evidence that dietary glutamate is involved in crucial metabolic processes within the body, possibly even acting as an energy source for such processes in the gut.[28] In any of these cases, our preference for umami tastes reflects the value that the body places on the glutamate that we ingest in foods.

Don't Eat!

Bitter

Earlier, we considered the taste qualities that foods we like might have in common. Doing the same for foods we dislike is more difficult, if only for the reason that we do not eat them. In practice, foods are rejected for all sorts of reasons – many for their texture, their unfamiliarity or for being too sweet or salty, or not sweet or salty enough. However, when it comes to tastes, bitterness is the most common source of rejection. It is the reason, for example, that Brussels sprouts and spinach are not high on most children's lists of special treats. It is also the reason why we need time to develop a liking for black coffee and beer, as distinct from the ready acceptability that coffee-flavoured milk and lemonade enjoy. But since coffee and beer are the world's most popular beverages, we can conclude that disliking bitterness cannot be absolute. However, while preference for foods that are bitter can develop, it is unlikely that we ever experience a liking for bitter tastes per se. That is, outside of a particular food or drink, bitterness never becomes liked. Though we expect tonic water to be bitter, and drink it because it is, it did not escape the attention of tonic water manufacturers that they also needed to add a sweetener to ensure repeat purchase.

The strong dislike that we naturally have for bitterness also has nutritional implications, since it is thought to protect us against consuming potentially poisonous substances. Many plants manufacture toxins as a defence against predators, and very many of these toxins are bitter. Not surprisingly, then, we not only dislike bitterness, but tend to be extremely sensitive to it. For our foraging ancestors, bitterness was a signal much like sweetness was, but in this case it induced reluctance to consume the bitter food. One consequence of treating bitterness as a sign of potential poisons is that we often reject levels of bitterness that are not in fact toxic to humans. The average child may treat the poor Brussels sprout as though it were toxic, but this is really just evidence that bitterness as a signal for poison is imperfect, at least in the context of modern diets. Nevertheless, in order to offer adequate protection against the range of compounds that are both bitter and toxic, we have evolved multiple genes that encode for the different chemical structures that are perceived as bitter.

Sour

The significance of our dislike for high levels of sourness or acidity is not as clear-cut as it is for bitterness, even though newborns respond to citric acid on their tongues with the same unambiguous facial puckering as adults. It may be a signal for unripeness/spoilage in foods, or the fact that concentrated, and thus extremely sour, acids can be physiologically harmful. Sourness within foods, and especially drinks, can of course be highly liked, but typically only if it is in some sort of balance with sweetness. Again, this recalls the taste combinations found in ripe fruit – sour, but not too sour. Relative to this, both unripe fruits and fruits that have begun to spoil both show increased acidity. Those ripe fruits whose acid levels are very high relative to sugar – lemons are the best example – tend to be eaten, if at all, only in combination with other sweeter foods or ingredients. High levels of acidity also activate pain nerves in the mouth. A lemon drink may be sour, but concentrated lemon juice is both sour and irritating, producing sensations of 'bite' that are similar to those produced by strong alcohol.

Guarding the Gut

There remains some uncertainty about the adaptive significance of taste, especially with respect to sourness and umami. Nevertheless, the existence of a small number of discrete taste qualities with characteristic hedonic properties seems to reflect distinct adaptive processes related to ensuring nutrient intake and avoiding toxicity. One approach to providing evidence for this idea has been to examine the relationship between just how palatable or unpalatable a substance is and how likely these substances are to poison us. In general, this relationship is very strong. Many highly toxic compounds are rejected as unpalatable by both humans and many animals, and this is most commonly due to their bitter taste. In fact, the more poisonous something is, the more likely it is to be bitter. Conversely, substances that are palatable tend to be both low in toxicity and sweet. This relationship has led to the hypothesis that the innate pleasure or displeasure that tastes elicit is the means by which our bodies maintain their physiological well-being.[29] This makes considerable sense if we see our sense of taste inhabiting the interface between the external environment – the world of potential foods – and the internal environment of our body, which is vulnerable to substances that can be indigestible or even poisonous. Taste can therefore be seen as being a 'gatekeeper' whose function is to ensure that ingested substances maximize our survival. Consistent with this idea, regions of the brain responsible for processing information about tastes also receive signals from the gut, and as a result there are important mutual interactions between taste perceptions and internal metabolic processes that provide feedback about the usefulness of the ingested nutrients (see also chapter Four).

Taste in Context

While sweetness, fattiness and saltiness may be highly liked as qualities, and sourness and bitterness disliked, we seldom if ever experience these qualities on their own. Within the context of foods or drinks, it is evident that any quality may be liked or disliked, depending on the context and our expectations based on prior experience. This is true of our overall diet, too. While foods that are dominated by sweetness are highly liked, overall, for the majority of us, our diets do not consist of foods that are overtly and predominantly sweet. Nor do we like unlimited amounts of sweetness – for each food, there is a 'just right' level. From infancy onwards, our experience of sweetness is usually within foods or drinks that have a characteristic sweetness level. Hence our response to sweetness in foods becomes highly context-dependent. We are less likely to hear the complaint from children that a food is too sweet, but as we become more familiar with a particular level of sweetness within a food or drink, that level becomes the preferred one. Most tea or coffee drinkers will have an opinion about how much sweetener to add. If you take no sweetener, then any is too much. If you take two spoonfuls, then any variation up or down will leave you dissatisfied. In other words, 'appropriate' sweetness levels are learned. We can be very sensitive to these appropriate taste levels in the foods that we eat regularly, with any deviation seen as a defect.

This dependence on context is not restricted to sweetness, of course, but applies equally to all tastes – indeed, it applies to most if not all sensory properties in foods. Dietary salt is not only dependent on context because of our experience with specific salt levels in foods, but our liking for salt in food also relies on the fact that the amount of sodium in the diet is reflected in the sodium content in our saliva.[30] Thus if the diet is high in salt, we have a high saliva sodium content. The consequence of this is that our taste buds are adapted to a particular sodium level, meaning that only a sodium level above that contained in our saliva will be tasted as salty. This accounts, at least partly, for the changes that occur following efforts to reduce salt in the diet. The salt reduction is reflected in our saliva, with the result that lower salt levels can now be detected. Foods that had previously not seemed at all salty are now unpleasantly so.

Palatability also arises from tastes occurring in a context with other tastes, odours and textures. Liking for sourness in the context of sweetness has already been mentioned as an instance of this. But perhaps the strongest example of this synergy is the combination of sweetness and fattiness. In any list of most-preferred foods, those with cream and sugar typically rank very highly. As an evolutionary strategy, this makes a lot of sense, as such a preference clearly seeks to maximize energy intake. When cocoa arrived in Europe from the New World in the 1500s, there was no obvious reason why it should have been combined with fat and sugar except perhaps to reduce cocoa's bitter taste.[31] Like coffee, chocolate was originally served as a drink. It later found an enduring partner in sugar – itself becoming more widely available and used at that time – as chocolate drinks were increasingly consumed sweetened, in contrast to coffee. It is quite plausible that, without this, or the incorporation of cocoa into fat-dense blocks, chocolate might have remained at the fringe, rather than the universally loved product that it became.

Of course, the quality that we recognize as chocolate is not a taste, even though sweetness and the textural and taste properties of fat are integral to its identity and appeal. The fact that we learn to like tastes in contexts and at particular levels is only one aspect of how our experiences with foods shape our preferences for them. It is possible, though, to develop a liking for flavours like chocolate in a wide variety of contexts and, as noted earlier with the examples of beer and coffee, even to come to like flavours that are not overtly sweet, salty or rich.

Our ability to learn to like foods that we have previously never encountered is one of the important strengths of being an omnivore. It means not only that we can expand our repertoire of foods as required, but, perhaps more importantly, that we can adapt our diets when environmental circumstances dictate. If the food that makes up our normal diet becomes scarce for whatever reason, then new food sources need to be discovered and consumed. Such flexibility means that we can move beyond the useful, but limited, reliance on innate taste preferences. How, for example, when faced with a novel food can we make decisions about the likelihood that it will contain the nutrients we need to keep us alive? How this happens is explained in chapters Three and Four, where the crucial role that exposure, experience and learning in the development of food likes is explored.

THREE

We Like What We Eat

Broccoli . . . Be Very Afraid!

Simon has two smart, sociable and food-savvy daughters, aged six and ten. As siblings often do, the girls differ in their personalities. But they do have one characteristic in common – they are both extraordinarily fussy eaters. This hardly makes them unique, but it is perhaps surprising given Simon's devotion to food. The girls have been exposed to the preparation of quality home cooking all their lives and, since they were old enough to reach the kitchen bench, they have assisted in the ritual of the Sunday roast chicken. If this sounds like the perfect preparation to develop a rich, varied diet and an openness to new foods, it probably is.

Both girls like sweet foods, as we might expect, but of course most foods are defined more by their distinctive flavours and textures than they are by the predominant taste. So where does the fussiness come from? The girls differ in their response to food. The elder girl has a well-developed palate, derived from regular experience with a variety of different flavours, knows what she wants, and will happily order from any restaurant menu. In contrast, the six-year-old is more concerned with what she does not want. Despite a quite extraordinary focus on food at home, meal selection for her is an exercise in eliminating all those things she has never tried, but will not eat. Many parents will recognize this scenario. In fact, food *neophobia* – literally, fear of new foods – is common enough to have been a topic of considerable research interest for the past three decades. From about two years of age, up to six or seven, or sometimes older, food neophobia is common enough to be seen as a stage of childhood development.

During this stage, statements of 'I don't like it' to foods that have never passed the child's lips are a feature of mealtimes.[1]

On the face of it, an impulse to restrict food variety, thus potentially limiting intake of important nutrients at a time of rapid growth, does not sound like a sensible stage of development. But consider the food world that the two-year-old is leaving and the one they are about to enter. In the first year or two, we exist in a highly protected environment in which parents act as gatekeepers between us and the food supply. To a large extent, the source of the food – that is, trusted parents – during this period is a guarantee of safety. One two-year-old I know, Luce, is a good example of this. She seems highly sophisticated in her food choices, eating olives, prosciutto, and even having sips of wine when dad turns his back. But the reality is that she eats what her parents eat. Her acceptance of these and other 'adult' foods is based on her recognition that the adult diet she observes is both safe to eat and enjoyable.

Child development is, however, all about increasing independence, and this carries with it contact with new stuff – some potentially edible and some not – outside direct parental influence. Imagine you are the independent-minded child of one of your distant ancestors, wandering the forest, knuckles lightly brushing the undergrowth, searching for a nice morsel. What strategy could you employ that would guard against poisoning by eating something that may or may not be a food?

In these circumstances, reluctance to consume something unfamiliar, and therefore potentially unsafe, may well be crucial to survival. This strategy builds on the inherent knowledge that makes us dislike bitter and very sour substances, and provides additional protection against the inedible. Neophobia thus becomes very sensible when faced with a world of potential foods whose safety is uncertain, and is therefore worth inheriting. And, in fact, wariness in the face of food novelty does seem to be strongly heritable, since identical twins are much more likely to show similar levels of neophobia than non-identical twins.[2] This points strongly to genes being a more important influence in determining the degree of neophobia than shared influences such as parental attitudes or other factors found in the first few years of life.

WE LIKE WHAT WE EAT

The notion of neophobia as an inherited survival strategy is consistent with what has become known as the *Omnivore's Paradox*.[3] On
the one hand, as omnivores, we have access to a large range of
potential foods – meats and seafood of various kinds, dairy products,
and fruits and vegetables. However, as a result, in nature at least,
we are much more likely to be exposed to substances that might
just be part of the last meal we ever eat! In terms of the human
diet, many plants contain toxins that are an important part of their
survival strategy, but which might be a serious problem for ours.
Mushroom or toadstool? Tasty berry or little ball of poison? Bitterness, as noted in chapter Two, is one sign of potential toxicity, but
its absence is not a guarantee that a plant is not toxic. Neophobia
is useful precisely because our innate responses to tastes are an
imperfect guide to what we should eat. Some bitter vegetables are
perfectly safe, and sweetness is not an absolute guarantee that a
poison is not also present in a food. Thus we need to learn, first
and foremost, about what can safely be considered foods and what
cannot and, second, which potentially edible substances are low
risk. Such learning clearly requires caution, at least until our repertoire of safe foods is sufficient to provide a varied diet that contains
all the necessary nutrients for us to survive. Of course, to a large
extent, our culture now provides guidelines for food suitability, but
the legacy of this survival strategy endures in neophobia. We do not
endure this paradox alone, since other omnivores such as rats are
also food neophobic.

How do we learn which foods are safe? 'Trial and error' might
be effective in the long run, but we cannot risk too much of the
'error'. Observing the consequences of what others eat should
provide the necessary information, with little risk. Such social transmission of food preferences is commonly observed among rats and
mice. But, as a normally neophobic child, how would we know for
certain if a friend at school, after munching on their weird sandwich,
became ill? Because illness might be an unobserved consequence,
learning about safety in this way might be unreliable. In fact, the 'fear'
component of neophobia is not primarily about the potential consequences of ingested foods. While, in general, we do tend to regard
novel foods as somewhat more dangerous than familiar foods, at

least consciously, food neophobia is not directly underpinned by concerns about food safety.

With her colleagues, Patricia Pliner, from the University of Toronto, showed that the characteristic that distinguishes between low and high neophobic individuals is not whether or not they *like* novel foods once they are tasted – they do not differ in this regard – but rather the *fear* that they will not like the flavour of unfamiliar foods.[4] Hence neophobic avoidance arises from a belief – which in practice must often be mistaken – that food novelty is a sign of tasting bad. Of course, as a consequence of novel food avoidance, this belief is seldom tested. Our hedonic responses to the flavour of foods are therefore co-opted in the cause of survival, because the threat of a bad taste is a great motivator. How strongly would you resist eating a bad-smelling prawn, even if you knew that it did not carry a threat of illness? It is not that bad taste is itself taken as a sign of toxicity. Rather it is fear of a bad taste that drives the necessary degree of caution required if we are not to be exposed to too many potentially toxic substances.

The good news, from the point of view of dietary variety, is that most of us grow out of our extreme childhood neophobia, and increased willingness to try novel foods is often already apparent approaching the teenage years. Nevertheless, we all know adults whose dietary horizons still seem remarkably limited, and it is likely that at least some of those whose meal philosophy is strictly 'meat and three veg' are expressing adult food neophobia. The fact that a proportion of the population remains neophobic as adults tells us that food neophobia is more than a stage that we pass through as children.

As adults, we vary from one another in our degree of residual food neophobia, but one's own level is reasonably stable. Neophobia is therefore sometimes described as a food-related personality trait. The use of standard questionnaires that ask people to rate their degree of agreement with statements such as 'If I don't know what is in a food, I won't try it' or 'Ethnic foods are too weird to eat', show that this trait in adults is normally distributed – that is, the bulk of people are neither especially neophobic or *neophilic* (that is, predisposed to like novel foods – presumably a modern phenomenon).

There are smaller proportions of those who either love to sample new or exotic foods or, at the other, neophobic end of the spectrum, maintain the same sort of reluctance to try new foods that is seen in childhood.[5] Some estimates suggest that around 25 per cent of adults may be moderately to severely neophobic, although this percentage will vary depending on age (older adults are more neophobic), education (neophobia is lower in those who are more highly educated), whether the person is urban or rural (the latter are more neophobic), and almost certainly depending on the culture in which the person was raised.[6]

Neophobia in adults does differ somewhat from that in children, as might be expected given the inevitable exposure to new foods in the intervening years. It is more focused than it is in childhood, and it is especially strong for foods of animal origin such as unfamiliar meats, fish, dairy products or eggs. We can recognize a degree of caution regarding these protein-based foods even in those who are not otherwise especially neophobic. Because of the recent internationalization of many 'exotic' foods, raw seafood – such as oysters and sashimi – is now commonplace in many countries. But these are still polarizing foods, not just because some do not like their flavour, but rather because of a significant proportion that will not even try them. One reason for this may be the stricter food taboos that exist with regard to which animal products are culturally appropriate to consume. Hence the idea of eating beef, pork, snake or dog may be either disgusting or appealing, depending entirely on your culture. By contrast, you may not be familiar with such leafy greens as bok choy or cavolo nero, but neither are likely to evoke strong disgust.

For many parents, the food neophobia shown by their children is a major source of anxiety, although perhaps not for those whose children refuse to eat anything other than leafy green vegetables. But this scenario is unlikely, since childhood neophobia is particularly associated with reluctance to consume vegetables and fruits, in addition to animal proteins.[7] Highly neophobic children also tend have more food dislikes and a more limited range of foods that they like. Sweet carbohydrates – desserts, confectionery and so on – are, unsurprisingly, relatively immune.[8] Although childhood food neophobia is extremely common, many parents are nevertheless

A variety of infant facial expressions on their first exposures to the flavour of an unfamiliar food, green beans.

reluctant to simply accept that little Ruby or Henry can survive on a diet of chocolate and chips. This accounts for the culinary mime show of 'Mmmm, good!', played out at mealtimes in many families with young children. But what can be done when the approach fails, as it often does, to produce much progress?

Vegetables Exposed

At least in principle, reducing childhood neophobia ought to be straightforward, given what we know about how preferences develop when we encounter something new. We are all familiar with the way in which we come to like a new song or television show more once we have heard or seen it a few times. This change is sometimes referred to as the *mere exposure effect* (*mere* because it is thought that no other additional processes are involved). Novel experiences and sensations of all kinds, including music, pictures, smells and even abstract shapes, become more liked when they are repeated (at least for a while – the topic of *boredom* is discussed in chapter Five).[9]

While it is not exactly clear how mere exposure works, it has been suggested that the brain finds it a lot of effort to process novel stimuli and store them in memory. Repeated exposure is thought to produce faster and more efficient processing, the reduced effort of which translates to enhanced liking (although an alternative, but not necessarily contradictory, explanation is presented in chapter Four).[10] Perhaps surprisingly, changes in liking following repeated exposure are not always accompanied by either increased familiarity or even awareness that the repetition has occurred. Mere exposure effects have been shown, for example, by presenting novel shapes on computer screens for a few thousandths of a second, far too fast for us to be conscious of what is being presented. That rapid presentation of images without awareness can influence liking underpins subliminal television advertising, which uses brief repetitions of a brand or other product image to increase positive feelings about the brand.

The mere exposure effect appears to work just as effectively on liking for novel foods, if for no other reason than exposure to a food without adverse consequences is a signal of its safety. Perhaps because neophobia is so prevalent in childhood, much of the research involving food repetitions has focused on the development of preferences in our early years. One study of four- and five-year-old preschool children asked them to taste a small amount of tofu twice a week for nine weeks. The tofu came in three different versions – with added sugar, added salt or plain – but each child received only one type. During the exposure, they were asked several times to eat all three kinds and to rank the different types of tofu from most to least liked. Repeatedly eating one of these versions increased liking for the version they were given, with increasing amounts of exposure producing greater increases in liking. But this effect was quite specific, since liking for the versions of tofu that the children did not receive decreased. Nor did the exposure have an effect on the children's liking for other, similar novel foods such as ricotta, even if they were flavoured the same way as the tofu version they had received.[11]

Importantly, given concerns about children's vegetable intakes, such exposure strategies have worked with novel vegetables, increasing both liking and consumption, when children are encouraged on a daily basis to 'have a taste'.[12] Studies like these clearly have relevance for the ways in which parents can actively influence their children's diets, even from an early age.

How much exposure is enough to increase liking for a novel food or flavour? This clearly depends on the food itself, but a few exposures can be enough, and liking usually increases with more experience of the flavour. In one study of adults, a familiar soup with a much lower salt level than was preferred became liked after only four tasting occasions.[13] The unhappy infants shown on p. 52 consumed increased amounts of green beans after eight exposures to their taste, even though they continued to show grimaces and other signs of dislike.[14]

Most crucially, the effects of exposure on a child's food preferences operate even prior to their birth. A programme of research at the USA's Monell Chemical Senses Research Center, led by Julie Mennella, has established that the chemical compounds responsible for the flavour of foods in the maternal diet are found in amniotic fluid, which is ingested by the foetus. To a great extent, therefore, during the latter part of pregnancy, the mother's food experiences become those of the foetus as well. Following birth, these same maternal diet flavours are similarly expressed in breast milk.[15]

The implications of exposures to flavours prior to, and following, birth are profound and long lasting. Mennella has shown that a vegetable juice consumed by the mother either during the last trimester of pregnancy or while breastfeeding influenced the infant's later preferences once they were introduced to solid food. These infants unmistakeably preferred a version of their cereal to which this juice had been added, as shown by both the infants' facial expressions and reports by the mothers of how much their child enjoyed the food.[16] The transfer of flavours from mother to baby increases the baby's acceptance of foods that the mother eats and is an important way in which information about acceptable foods with that family, and indeed the whole culture, is transmitted across generations. Conversely, the mother's dislikes, as reflected in her avoidance of certain foods, means that these foods are more likely to be rejected as unfamiliar on first tasting.

The effects of flavour transmission can become evident for the first time later in development. Clancy is a bright two-year-old who has already been exposed to a varied diet, and consequently is receptive to very many foods. But even by twelve months old, she showed a distinct interest in black marinated Kalamata olives, so much so that she would reach for them if they were nearby. As soon as she started on solid foods, these olives became a regular part of her diet. Consistent with Mennella's findings, Clancy's mother Amy had developed a strong liking for the olives during pregnancy, and consumed them regularly. That this preference is not coincidental is strongly suggested by the complete lack of interest shown by Clancy in green olives, which Amy did not consume during her pregnancy.

Clancy's preference for black olives reveals two other interesting aspects of foetal exposure to flavours. The first of these is that it is likely that Clancy was first drawn to the Kalamata's distinctive odour because of the foetal exposure, and this accounts for her early interest prior to first consuming the olive. More important, though, it shows that her preference for the olive's flavour/odour overruled the instinctive response that she might have had to the olive's bitterness. This example thus provides an important insight into how exposure can modify our innate taste preferences and allow for liking to develop in the presence of otherwise unpalatable qualities such as bitterness.

The same exposure effects have also been observed following feeding infants with formulas that have distinctive flavours. There are strong differences in the flavour of formulas based on milk, soy or amino acids. In particular, the latter two are more bitter and sour, respectively, than those based on milk. The specific flavour of the formula experienced by the infant – even if it is initially unpleasant (as some based on amino acids are) – will become the most preferred, and in turn experiences with different formulas will shape food preferences once the infant goes on to solid foods. Tests of food likes in children even years after cessation of bottle feeding has found a strong relationship between the flavour of the formula and liking for bitter and sour foods and drinks, these being more preferred by those fed soy and amino-acid-based formulas as infants. These children also later show a greater preference for bitter vegetables such as broccoli.[17]

Early exposure to the maternal diet, and to different flavours in breast milk and formula, almost certainly has a snowball effect throughout our childhood and into our adult food preferences. One particularly striking example of such long-term effects of exposure to a specific flavour was evident in an ingenious experiment that took advantage of the fact that, for many years, vanilla flavour was added to infant formula marketed in Germany. At a Frankfurt fair, a group of German and Dutch researchers asked adults to taste two samples of tomato ketchup, one of which contained a very low level of vanilla, and to indicate which one they preferred. If anything, we might predict that adding vanilla would decrease liking for the sauce, since it is such an unusual combination. However, those tasters who, as infants, had been bottle-fed the formula containing vanilla showed a clear liking for the sauce containing vanilla, whereas those who had been breastfed did not – a strong demonstration that their early exposure to vanilla could still exert an influence decades later.[18]

Thus our adult food preferences, from their common origins in innate taste likes and dislikes, begin to diversify and become more complex, starting with the influence of the maternal diet during pregnancy and breastfeeding. However, one important consequence of early exposure is its effect not just on liking for specific foods, but on dietary variety in general. Food neophobia in children (or adults) is only a concern because of its potential to limit the intake of important nutrients that come from a varied diet. Of course, it can be argued that ignoring neophobia in children might also reduce the potential enjoyment that they might derive from eating different foods. Either way, the fact that neophobia may limit dietary variety is the issue that parents want to address. It turns out that exposure addresses this issue in two distinct ways. First, those children whose mothers themselves have a varied diet are obviously exposed to more flavours in utero and in breast milk, and are more likely to develop likes for those particular food flavours. But, in addition, exposure to variety seems to engender a preference for variety itself. Hence mothers who have a varied diet during pregnancy produce children who like variety in their own diet, beyond the particular flavours that were in the maternal diet. Following weaning, the introduction of variety in an infant's diet once again produces a greater likelihood that they will later be more receptive to other novel foods.[19] Therefore the culinarily adventurous among us can justifiably attribute their palates to mother's home cooking.

Exposure is the most fundamental strategy to reduce neophobia and promote liking for new foods and, in effect, all other processes that promote food likes are built on this. In the context of neophobia, mere exposure not only increases liking for the new food but also reduces the fear that the food will taste bad. These experiences appear to generalize so that repeated experience with novel foods without experiencing unpleasant tastes leads to less neophobia in general. That is, we can learn not to be neophobic if our experience of novel foods is generally taste-positive. Of course, some foods or drinks that are unpleasant for many when they are first tasted – bitter coffee and beer are good examples – do become liked following exposure. However, to some extent, this will be due to additional processes that occur during exposure, and these will be discussed in chapter Four.

The Taste Test

For exposure to increase liking for a food, that food has first to be tasted. But given that neophobia is all about a reluctance to try new foods, what can be done to encourage tasting? What would induce you to try something especially weird – perhaps the Icelandic shark dish hakarl, which, as noted in the Introduction, requires a few months buried in gravel to reach 'maturity'? Would you be more inclined to try it if I provided you with nutritional information: a detailed list of the important vitamins that it contained, or perhaps the message that it was low in fat, or just that it is good for you? Unsurprisingly, this is ineffective in encouraging children to eat novel foods, but does have a greater impact on teenagers and adults, in particular if nutrition is important to them.[20] In contrast, the impact of such information on the nutritionally uninterested is counter-productive, leading to a greater reluctance to try. This might best be seen as an example of the 'good personality effect', mentioned in the Introduction. That is, telling us only that a food is healthy could well be interpreted as a message that it actually tastes poor. Many food manufacturers have learned this the hard way with their low-fat products, which now often carry a 'good taste' label in addition to the smaller-print details of the nutritional benefits.

Unfortunately, the most commonly used strategies to encourage the consumption of foods such as spinach and broccoli are singularly counter-productive. Applying pressure through encouragements to 'eat it all up' not only fails to increase consumption of novel foods, but may also make mealtime an unpleasant experience for both child and parent as a battle of wills ensues.[21]

Using one food as a reward to increase consumption of another – a food that the *adult* wants the child to eat – also fails because the relative value of the foods soon becomes apparent. Understanding the message in an offer of ice cream once the spinach is eaten does not require advanced logic: ice cream is a good (taste) food – otherwise why use it as a reward? Spinach will clearly be pretty horrible, else why do I need to be rewarded for eating it? And, frankly, who is going to disagree? The unfortunate, if predictable, consequence is an increase in liking for ice cream and a further reduction in the stocks of spinach.[22] Incidentally, this is an excellent example of what is known to psychologists as the *overjustification effect*. This is the surprising finding that an activity undertaken because of the promise of a reward is actually valued less than if it were undertaken for its own sake – that is, where the reward comes from enjoyment of the activity itself. In this case, the *overjustification effect* means that preference for the spinach is actually undermined by using the ice cream as a reward.

The news is not all bad. Giving children *non-food* rewards to consume vegetables can work, at least in some circumstances. Both praise from an adult and tangible rewards (for example, a sticker) have been used in school settings to encourage young children to try initially non-preferred vegetables. When either or both of these rewards were used repeatedly, it increased both the children's ratings of liking and their intake of that vegetable.[23] One important aspect of this effect is that, in addition to the rewards motivating the child to try new foods, and hence allowing simple exposure to increase liking, they also seem to improve the effectiveness of exposure strategies alone.

Because a major part of the fear in neophobia is that the food may taste bad, we might expect that information about taste would be effective in overcoming reluctance to try new foods, and it is. Both the message that a novel food tastes like an already familiar food ('this broccoli tastes just like . . . er . . .') and indicating that others find the novel food pleasant-tasting ('everybody loves it!') can be effective encouragements to try the food, especially in children.[24] Clearly, though, the plausibility and sincerity of the messenger will be crucial – and this may account for the sometimes limited effectiveness when this is employed by parents, whose motives are likely to be transparent.

A more formal way of providing food flavour information has been used in Finnish studies as a strategy to induce children to be more open to new food experiences. This strategy involved educating eight- to eleven-year-old primary school children about the different categories of foods and their flavour and texture properties, using both lectures and restaurant visits. Relative to a similar group of children who did not receive this education, the programme improved the children's ability to describe foods in sensory terms and also produced an increased willingness, particularly in the younger children, to try novel foods.[25]

Another way of getting the good taste message across is by providing a model, someone shown 'surviving' the experience of consuming the novel food. This ought to work well with children, since they will often naturally imitate the food selections and preferences of their peers, even if this means changing their own original food likes and dislikes. A variety of ways of providing an eating model for both children and adults have been studied. One approach was to have five- to seven-year-olds watch videos that showed older children labelled as heroes called 'Food Dudes' eating a number of different new foods that the children had previously refused to eat. The programme, which also included rewards for reaching target consumption levels, generally induced the children to eat all of the target foods, which were presented to the children at mealtimes. Importantly, the effect appeared to be permanent. Months later, the children were still willing to eat most of the target foods.[26] Even infants younger than two years old are responsive to adult models shown eating a food, a far more effective strategy in inducing the infant to actually taste than simply offering the food to eat. Although this approach is particularly successful when the model is their mother, even adult strangers shown eating a food can encourage an infant to try something new.[27]

Similarly, highly neophobic adults can be induced to try novel foods if shown a model eating those foods, regardless of whether the model is on a video or physically present. While the model does not necessarily need to be shown *enjoying* the novel food for this process to be effective, there is probably an implicit assumption that if you observe someone selecting a food to consume, then its taste is probably liked. These effects do not seem to generalize to other novel foods – they are specific to the foods the model eats – which makes sense if the effectiveness of the model relies on reducing the fear associated with a particular food's taste. Continued observation of family and friends trying different foods, and in the process learning about which substances can be happily consumed, is probably the major reason for the decrease in neophobia in most of us as we leave childhood.

If the problem with novel foods is fear of the unfamiliar, then one solution is obvious, if a little unpalatable for the concerned home chef. In addition to the strategies for overcoming neophobia already mentioned, there is another that is regularly employed not only by parents, but also by neophobic children (and adults) themselves. What would Simon's six-year-old do if she was faced with the inevitability of eating a suspicious new food – we will call it 'broccoli' – and the tomato sauce was within reach? A slurp of ketchup not only adds a nice, sweet taste, but magically transforms this otherwise inedible vegetable into something familiar. This sounds a remarkably unsophisticated solution to the evolutionary conundrum of the Omnivore's Paradox, as reflected in childhood neophobia. Yet it is actually a successful way of introducing new foods into a diet. Both children and adults are much more willing to try novel foods when served with a familiar and liked food or ingredient such as a condiment or sauce.[28] Of course, there are likely to be limits to how much a familiar ingredient will help. Most obviously, the novel food must be recognizable as a food. This will be strongly influenced by culture, which plays the greatest role in defining those substances that individuals recognize as appropriate foods. For most cultures, no amount of tomato ketchup or chilli salsa is likely to be an effective inducement to sample a nice plate of fried spiders.

FOUR

Learning to Like

For all his brilliance as a scientist, the Nobel Laureate in physiology and medicine for 1904, Ivan Petrovich Pavlov, appears to have been remarkably inattentive to the world around him. Clearly, he never gave a second thought to the commonplace experience of entering a kitchen while hungry, and automatically reacting to the delicious cooking aromas with a rumbling stomach or a sudden increase in saliva. This is particularly odd since Pavlov's Nobel Prize was awarded for his important work on the physiology of gastric secretions, but he is generally better known for his work on 'psychic secretions', the flow of gastric juices and saliva in anticipation of receiving food. His experimental work with dogs showed that an otherwise meaningless signal, for instance, a sound, reliably occurring prior to the imminent arrival of food would – just like the food aroma – eventually cause the hungry canine's juices to flow as if the food were actually present. These studies, crucial in the foundation of behavioural psychology, provided the basis for understanding how we learn to associate environmental cues – sounds, smells or visual signals, for example – with something that is important biologically. This process of association, now typically referred to as classical or Pavlovian conditioning, means that, through learning, the signal or cue provides information that aids survival, whether it is by helping us find food, or water, or perhaps avoid impending danger.

By and large, classical conditioning occurs because we make a conscious link between, say, a red traffic light and the likely appearance of cars travelling across the intersection. Our response in the form of hitting the brake becomes automatic as we learn to drive.

Automatic responses are also seen when our bodies – Ivan Pavlov's included – have begun to associate cooking aromas with the food that follows. In anticipation of that food, secretions from our salivary glands and our stomachs increase to aid digestion, which we interpret as one of the signals of hunger. If we did not make a conscious link between the aroma and food, these learned secretions would not occur.

Powerful Associates

A very similar type of associative learning seems to occur without such awareness. Simply pairing a novel item, neither especially liked or disliked, with something that you already like increases your preference for that item. Put your favourite painting, for example, next to one that you have just been given, and you will develop a liking for the new work over and above seeing the new work repeatedly by itself. How this occurs is not certain, but it may be that the new and already-liked items become linked together as a pair in our memory. Thus viewing the newly liked painting may automatically, but unconsciously, evoke the original work, and its associated positive emotion. Whatever the mechanism, this form of learning, known as *evaluative conditioning*, appears not to require a conscious awareness of the original pairing – in other words, you have developed a preference, but you do not necessarily know why.[1] Of course, this runs somewhat counter to our belief that we make decisions or adopt attitudes or preferences after having rationally considered the reasons for those attitudes or preferences.

Evaluative conditioning may explain how many of our food preferences develop without any apparent effort or conscious awareness. As discussed in chapter Three, simple (mere) exposure to a flavour can produce increase in liking for that flavour. This appears to be the case, for example, when a foetus is exposed to flavours in the maternal diet. Increases in liking for a novel odour also occur when we repeatedly experience it. Moreover, there are good reasons to believe that simply experiencing a flavour is crucial in overcoming neophobic anxieties that it may taste awful. As such, mere exposure is the first step to developing a liking for that flavour. But this process, while important, has limitations because not all foods are of equivalent nutritional value. Thus we need a means of recognizing that a food odour, or the flavour in which the odour is embedded, is associated with the nutrients that our bodies require. This is something that we need to learn.

With the vast majority of our experiences with food flavours, the flavours do not occur in isolation. A food or drink always contains the odour component of flavours embedded in a chemical and physical environment that produces the tastes, textures, mouthfeel qualities, colours and temperatures that we encounter during consumption. Foods varying in preference are also eaten together. In what appears to be an example of evaluative conditioning occurring at an early age, the facial signs of distaste shown for green beans by the infants in the picture on p. 52 were reduced in those infants who were fed peaches after the green beans. Hence the liking for the sweet peaches was transferred to the flavour of green beans. Eating and drinking are also experienced in contexts, which may be social (dining alone or with family or friends) or physiological (eating while hungry or full). In each case, the context can provide important positive associations for food and drink flavours that encourage the development of preferences.

In order to appreciate how evaluative conditioning might typically operate in the development of food preferences, consider a typical sequence of events in trying a new product, for example a new brand of an iced tea drink. The most likely reason why you are aware of the tea is that you have seen an advertisement, probably on television, in which the advertiser will embed the consumption of the tea in a variety of what they judge are positive contexts. In addition to pairing with presumably appealing information, perhaps that the tea comes in an exciting range of exotic flavours, the tea might be shown being consumed by a famous TV personality or sportsperson, ideally in a glamorous location. Even in the absence of someone famous apparently being an early adopter of the tea, the selected tea consumers shown will often be young, attractive and fashionable (but not too fashionable, since we still need to be able to identify with the model). Signs of satisfaction, if not delight, will typically follow the tea's consumption. And, incredibly, the mere act of tea consumption seems to attract friends and admiring glances from strangers. Companies that use humour in their advertising also know that the positive mood that laughter produces can become 'attached' to their product or brand.

You no doubt feel immune to such obvious manipulation, but might feel nevertheless that the product deserves a try. It will probably be easy to spot in the supermarket, too, since the manufacturer will ensure that the pack colour and design will be new and attention-grabbing. But which flavour to try? Since they are all so exotic-sounding, you opt for one that seems to you to have a pleasant, pale green colour – 'Oolong tea'. The flavour is unusual, if not especially distinctive, but the drink is sweet enough to be pleasant. What is the context in which you sample this new drink? Is it with your friends, who may also be drinkers of the tea, at a social gathering, or while playing a favourite computer game? Are you relaxing? Indeed, we may be predisposed to consume novel flavours more often while in a positive state of mind, thus providing a ready association for the flavour.

Even such a brief account demonstrates the potential to associate the Oolong tea drink with positive experiences, concepts and qualities, including physical attractiveness, popularity, convivial environments, and even liked colours, designs and brand names. All of these factors influence the willingness to try a product as well as becoming part of the evaluative conditioning process. But from the point of view of effective development of a flavour preference, the key pairing is the Oolong tea flavour with sweetness. Chapter Three pointed out that one way of overcoming neophobia – often the result of unfamiliar odours – is to pair it with a quality that is liked and that signals familiarity. Of course, this is most easily done with the universally positive quality of sweetness – positive because it is an innate signal of the calories in carbohydrates. One consequence of such pairing is that the odour not only becomes more familiar but it also becomes liked – in essence, the positive aspects of the sweet taste are transferred to the odour. In other words, evaluative conditioning has taken place.

Since the drink is always consumed sweetened, how do we know that a preference for the Oolong tea *flavour* has developed? It could be simply that we are showing a liking for a sweet drink, irrespective of the flavour. In one of the earliest scientifically controlled demonstrations of this effect in foods, novel tea flavours were repeatedly tasted with or without added sugar. It could of course be predicted that the sweetened flavours would be preferred, but the important aspect of this study was that, following the pairing with sugar, these tea flavours were preferred even when no sugar was added.[2] In keeping with studies on this type of preference-development conducted with other stimuli (pictures, music, even random shapes), the effect seemed to involve the transfer of the positive emotion (that is, liking) from the sugar to the flavour. In controlled studies of this kind, the effect of pairing a flavour with a sweet taste is compared with the flavour repeatedly tasted in unsweetened water. The increase in liking for the sweet-paired flavour is therefore over and above any effect of exposure, since the unsweetened flavours were exposed equally often.

Potentially, dislikes can be formed using exactly the same mechanism. Repeated pairing of a novel flavour such as Oolong tea with just a bitter taste will lead to the flavour becoming disliked, even when later experienced without the bitterness.[3] In practice, it might seem unlikely that we would persist in consuming a drink or food that was unpleasantly bitter, but laboratory studies have demonstrated the formation of dislikes in this way. By contrast, consider that the two most popular drinks in the world (at least, after water) are beer and coffee, both distinctively bitter, while tea without milk is particularly astringent. Undoubtedly, in the case of preferences for these drinks, and for other bitter foods and drinks besides, the effects of pairing the flavour with a bitter taste are outweighed by other positive associations, including those mentioned above.

Beer, in particular, is advertised using attractive role models and the promise of being 'one of the boys/lads/men' (since such advertising is seldom targeted towards women). Sufficient mere exposure might then contribute to the development of a preference for beer flavour. Many beer consumers also appear to naturally adopt strategies to allow exposure to be more effective. Thus sweeter beers such as lager are often drunk prior to developing a taste for ales and more bitter beers. Moreover, marketers of some beers do not shy away from the challenge they present due to their relative bitterness, with advertising implying that a taste for this bitter brew is a mark of distinction and sophistication as a drinker.

Similar observations can be made about wine and other alcoholic drinks. Novice wine drinkers tend to favour sweeter wines, probably because initially unpleasant qualities like sourness and astringency are less prominent. The subsequent development of a preference for wine flavours is supported by this pairing with sweetness. Paradoxically, this leads to the development of a liking for the flavour of wines that are dryer, less sweet and less fruity as the wine flavour itself, and not just its sweetness, becomes preferred. In countries where wine is introduced to children at the family dinner table, the flavour is often made more initially acceptable by diluting with water. Similarly, for those whose early alcohol experiences include spirits such as Scotch, vodka or rum, the unpleasant irritation and bitterness are relieved by the addition of a variety of mixers, most of which both dilute the spirit and add sweetness.

Coffee is less targeted than beer in its advertising, but an enormous number of people act as role models for its consumption, and by the promise of a sophisticated lifestyle. Such so-called observational conditioning – that is, watching liked peers and role-models consume a food or drink – is known to be effective.[4] Children who repeatedly watch their peers at school consume a food that they do not particularly like become more likely to select that food if given an opportunity.[5] Why? Is the child learning that a food is safe to consume or is the liking that they have for their friends being transferred to the food? Both explanations may have some truth in them. Certainly, in some studies of observational learning, others' facial expressions – acting as cues to the acceptability of the flavour – have been shown to influence liking for a novel drink. Unsurprisingly, a model showing dislike appears to be particularly effective, probably because such negative facial expressions are unambiguous. Two-year-old Luce, who, as we saw in chapter Two, is highly accepting of any adult food, does so at least partly because she is modelling her parents' behaviour. She will not, for example, eat anything she perceives as being a special child's meal, or even anything that is presented in a way that is different from an adult meal.

In addition to forming associations between coffee and role models, this bitter beverage differs from beer in that it is commonly adulterated. Adding cream or milk, plus sugar, a common combination for novice drinkers, not only reduces the bitterness, but also provides the necessary positive tastes to produce liking for coffee flavour itself. This is why, even if you drink your coffee white and sweetened, the smell of black coffee brewing is so appealing. This also explains why the transition in coffee drinking is overwhelmingly from sweetened coffee to unsweetened coffee, rather than vice versa.

One of the most important aspects of evaluative learning, apart from lack of awareness that it is occurring, is its permanence. In the type of learning studied by Pavlov, the sound is a predictor that dog food will shortly arrive. It is, of course, highly profitable to survival to be able to predict when food will be available. But if, as Pavlov did in his later studies, the sound is subsequently made but the food does not arrive, Rex soon learns to ignore the sound. In effect, the sound loses its meaning. Although learned likes and dislikes seem to develop in much the same way – that is, through an association of a liked/disliked quality with something that is neutral – they do not diminish when the pairing stops. With coffee, for example, the initial pairing of the flavour with a sweet taste has the effect of producing a permanent liking for the flavour, with or without added sweetness. The distinction between the two forms of learning has its origins in what is learned. In Pavlovian learning, we learn cause and effect, to predict one event from another that occurs first. In evaluative conditioning, at least with foods, we learn whether a substance is likely to be safe to consume or not. We also learn whether it is likely to provide us with energy or other nutrients. So, while foods may fall out of favour for various reasons, foods that we have learned to like tend to stay that way, as do those we have learned to dislike, unless there is some strong additional association operating in the other direction (see the section on taste aversions below).

To add to this 'natural history' of how learned likes and dislikes develop, there are indications that these processes are also sometimes understood and consciously applied. Surveys in the USA have found that parents often intuitively understand the operation of associative learning of this type. Favoured methods for promoting food likes in children included demonstrating that target foods are liked by the parents, as well as involving the child in the (presumably) enjoyable activity of food preparation. Some part of this may reflect the fact that adult attention is generally positive for children, and has been shown, in itself, to promote liking for unfamiliar foods with which it is paired. Parents in these surveys also indicated that they recognized that pairing a food with something already liked or disliked would alter the child's attitude to that food, even if they did not always use this as a method of preference development themselves. It is probably much trickier than we imagine for parents to know with certainty what will be positive for a child and hence condition liking for a flavour or food. As we saw in chapter Three, praising a child for trying vegetables can be shown to be effective, as can providing something quite tangible such as a sticker. In addition, though, while both of these rewards also produced an increase in liking for the target vegetables, it was the sticker that was most effective in doing this. It is difficult to know, though, whether this type of reward would be as effective in different groups of children, across different cultures, or in five years time.

One explanation of how mere exposure produces liking is also via evaluative conditioning. The question is how the positive emotion – the equivalent of the liked sweet taste – is generated. The answer is not obvious, but it is possible that we automatically form associations between the context or environment in which the exposure occurs and the exposed item. For example, we know that those who enjoy participating in mere exposure experiments show the largest increase in liking for whatever is being exposed.[6] This suggests that the pleasure of participating transfers to the exposed item. Similarly, the context in which a food is consumed is obviously a crucial part of the eating experience and thus the degree to which a food or a meal is pleasurable. It has been shown that a familiar food or meal will be enjoyed more if it is eaten in an environment that is highly regarded, such as a restaurant, than if the same meal is consumed in a student cafeteria.[7] This is probably the reason why restaurant evaluations often emphasize the 'atmosphere', although which components of atmosphere – location, noise level, lighting, other diners, image and so on – might be important as promoters of food preferences are hard to specify exactly. Most likely it is the extent to which what is experienced fits with prior expectations, rather than any particular aspect, that will be an important determinant of enjoyment.

In some cases, while a pleasurable context might produce liking for a food, the food becomes strongly linked only to that context. Foods become part of the overall enjoyment of special occasions as in popcorn at the cinema, pies/hotdogs at sporting events, and any number of otherwise inedible items at funfairs or amusement parks. Who seeks out candyfloss (cotton candy/fairy floss) at any other time? In an exotic location, a local wine or *aperitivo* can seem like a taste of heaven while sitting at a taverna or trattoria on a warm summer evening, even if the same drink often sits unloved on the shelf at home once the holiday ends. The key to forming such strong links between the event or context and the food or drink is the positive emotion that is experienced at the time.

Flavours and odours are in general uniquely susceptible to becoming strongly linked to one's emotional experiences. A flavour, even out of the context in which it was experienced, can reactivate an emotion experienced at the time. In a famous passage from the first volume (*Swann's Way*, 1913) of French writer Marcel Proust's terminally dense work A *la recherche du temps perdu* (*In Search of Lost Time*), the narrator describes in detail how the flavour of a madeleine cake dipped in tea unexpectedly transports him back to happy times in his aunt's house where he had eaten these as a child.

It is not difficult to imagine that such pleasant emotions continue to reinforce the preference for the food's flavour. We can understand the almost universal liking – particularly at times of stress – for comfort food, food that is not only familiar but part of our childhood and culture and that reminds us of 'home'. If we are unhappy or fearful, it is unlikely that we would seek out innovative cuisine, no matter how delicious or interesting. Of course, mother's home cooking is liked for all those reasons already discussed. But her dishes, or food generally associated with happy times, also supplies the necessary emotional comfort because of the links between those food flavours and happiness or security, even if these associations are not recalled consciously. A recent study suggests that comfort food may even counteract feelings of loneliness by acting as a 'social surrogate' – a role that has been suggested for characters in favourite television programmes.[8] Because we can identify with television characters, we can feel part of their lives, and hence socially connected. Comfort foods may act in a similar way since they are foods that have most often been eaten in the company of those with whom we have important relationships, including parents, siblings and partners.

Another, more immediate, type of context that has a crucial impact on liking for food flavours is the food's physical properties, including its colour, temperature and texture, in which the flavour is embedded. Once again, the influence of these and other contexts is learned. For instance, we learn that a particular texture belongs with a particular food. There is nothing intrinsically likeable about crunchy, mushy or flaky as food qualities. When such qualities belong, respectively, to potato crisps/chips, peas and pastry, for very many of us, they are highly appealing. Conversely, crunchy pastry, mushy crisps and flaky peas are likely to be rejected. Food textures are highly dependent on preparation techniques and meal context. In turn, these vary by food, a fact that is specified within each culture's cuisine.

The same is true of serving temperature. While it may seem 'right' that tea is a hot beverage in the UK, this is only so because of how it has been most commonly consumed there.[9] In the USA, iced tea is a more common beverage. We can also learn to tolerate multiple versions or contexts – for example, tomatoes are a solid food, except when in soups or juice. In Japan, sake is sometimes served warm (winter) and sometimes cool (summer), as are some types of noodles. Violating the expectations generated by contexts can be a potent source of food rejections. A study of a savoury, smoked-salmon-flavoured 'ice cream/mousse' showed that its acceptance or rejection largely depended on the researchers' manipulation of the context. Telling participants in the study that they were consuming smoked salmon 'ice cream' provoked considerable dislike for the dish, whereas it was much more acceptable when labelled as cold smoked salmon mousse.[10] The crucial difference here is that the information provides a way of interpreting what is being eaten as either consistent with what we expect (a mousse can be savoury) or not (ice cream does not come in fish flavours*).

* This is a tentative statement. I have not, for example, surveyed the ice cream choices in Iceland.

Body Knows Best

A respected senior colleague of mine from the Netherlands, E. P. Koster, has spent more than 50 years researching the psychology of food choices. In addition to studying how preferences are formed generally, he has a poignant experience of his own that illustrates the power of a positive experience to shape a lifelong preference:

> In November 1944 there was extensive starvation in the Netherlands. I was 13 years old and extremely hungry. One day as I rattled along on my bicycle without tyres – if you had a bicycle with tyres the German soldiers would take it – I was passed by a convoy of German trucks. Then when they were a few hundred metres in front of me, the trucks suddenly stopped because their lookout had spotted two RAF fighter planes in the air. The drivers and other soldiers jumped off the trucks and went for cover in the grass by the roadside. I jumped off my bicycle and did the same. The planes dived, firing their guns and hitting the trucks, one of which caught fire. When they came a second time, flying low over the road to inspect the damage they had done, I got up and waved at them. They then circled low once more and while I was waving at them I saw one of the pilots reach into his jacket to pull something out, which he then threw from the cockpit. With the soldiers still distracted, I ran to pick it up. It was a pack containing three bars of Cadbury's Bourneville chocolate. Chocolate!!! I had not had that for years and I had almost forgotten the taste of it. I hid it in the bag on my bike and in fear that the Germans might take it from me, I made a large detour to my home. On the way back, I slowly sucked morsels of one bar. It was heaven. The other two bars I shared with my brother and we ate them for days, a little each day. For the rest of my life I have longed for the taste of that chocolate and whenever I came to Britain the first thing I did was to buy a bar of it. I admit that there may be finer chocolates than Cadbury's, but for me there is no chocolate more delicious.

The emotional power of this event and its association with Cadbury's chocolate is of course obvious. In addition, though, there is another powerful shaper of preferences at work here. The chocolate is delicious mainly due to the combination of sugar and fat, but the pairing of the chocolate flavour with these nutrients becomes especially potent in the context of extreme hunger – that is, when the body needs them most.

The ability of a sweet taste to produce liking for an odour with which it is paired in a flavour relies on the fact that sweetness is very commonly a signal for the energy value of a carbohydrate. This learning is considerably enhanced when our experience of the flavour is followed immediately by the *actual* energy – that is, *once the food is consumed*. Such flavour-nutrient learning appears to be a universal mechanism of food preference development since few, if any, foods contain no nutrients of potential value to the body (although there are suspicions about tofu). Even when nutritionists talk about foods having 'empty calories' they are explicitly referring to the fact that some foods supply only short-term energy to the body. But, from a survival perspective, the body values nutrients that supply such energy.

Carbohydrates like sucrose both taste sweet *and* provide energy. But we are able to show the effects of energy consumption as an additional influence on flavour preference beyond pairing with the liked sweet taste. This is achieved by comparing changes in liking for a novel food/flavour that contains an energy-containing sweetener such as sucrose, with the food/flavour when it is tasted but not consumed, or when it is consumed but contains a sweetener such as aspartame, which is sweet but provides no calories. Such studies do indicate that consuming a valued nutrient provides a stronger or quicker increase in liking than pairing with a liked taste alone.[11] The difference is essentially between a taste that is *usually* a reliable signal for calories to come versus the presence of the calories themselves. In animal studies, where more direct demonstrations are possible, nutrients including carbohydrates, fats and proteins introduced directly into the stomach increase liking for flavours that the animal had just experienced.[12] In studies with humans, these same nutrients all promote flavour liking.[13]

Other sources of nutrients that are of value to us similarly condition strong likes when consumed. The most important of these is fat, which, weight for weight, is an even more dense form of energy than sugar. It is therefore unsurprising that, at least in Western countries, some of our strongest preferences are for foods – chocolate, desserts, cakes – that are high in both fat and sugar. These foods are extremely palatable precisely for the reason that the body places such a high value on concentrated energy sources. Any flavour paired with this energy becomes an important signal for calories to come, and hence (potentially) a signal for survival. The apparently universal affection for chocolate flavour is due, therefore, to the form in which it is eaten – that is, embedded in blocks with sugar and fat, rather than anything intrinsic to the flavour itself.

In the same way, we can explain why pairing with a number of other sources of energy (the alcohol in beer and wine) and other positive benefits (alertness due to caffeine in coffee) can result in liked flavours.[14] The worldwide affection for these beverages reflects not only the processes of evaluative conditioning through pairing with liked sweet tastes, but learning about their physiological consequences following consumption as well.

Novel flavours repeatedly combined with glutamate (the prototypical umami taste) also become similarly liked, although the benefits are less obvious.[15] Unlike the taste of sweet carbohydrates, glutamate by itself is not an inherently pleasant taste. But adding glutamate to suitable meat- or vegetable-based savoury foods – soups, stews, pasta and other sauces – makes them richer and *fuller* tasting, and much more liked than those without added glutamate. But the question remains why? As noted in chapter Two, more than one explanation has been proposed, including that the increased liking for glutamate-rich foods reflects the fact that the umami taste is a signal for protein or that glutamate derived from the diet is used by the body for a variety of important metabolic processes.

Another situation in which nutrients become highly valued, and thus ought to be able to promote increases in flavour liking, is when we are deficient in those nutrients, which can be a risk factor for disease or malnutrition. For obvious reasons, it is difficult to conduct flavour preference studies in humans who are suffering from a specific nutrient deficiency. One situation in which nutrient, or at least energy, depletion can be studied in humans is, of course, as a result of hunger. As the wartime example above shows, the ability of ingested energy to promote a liking for flavours with which it is paired is most effective when we are hungry.[16] This is further evidence that interpretations of these effects in terms of the value of the nutrients to the body are correct. In fact, when conditioning is carried out when the participant has recently eaten, there is little evidence that liking for flavours changes when paired with nutrients that are valued when we are hungry.

Animal studies have enabled us to demonstrate in more detail how flavour preferences can be influenced by nutrient deficiencies. In a variety of species, increased liking for flavours can be seen when the flavour is associated with recovery from specific nutrient deficiencies, including those of proteins and amino acids.[17] Clearly, in such cases the flavour becomes a signal linked to the recovery from a situation that is potentially threatening to health. By contrast, ingesting foods that lead to a deficiency of specific nutrients in the diet, which of course may ultimately cause serious illness, leads to a dislike of those food flavours. This is true of all species, so far as we are aware.

Avoidance

Learning plays a crucial role in forming food dislikes, just as it does in food likes. I noted in chapter Three that innate responses to taste were a useful, but imperfect, signal for both calories and toxicity. Pairing a flavour with a bitter taste can, especially in the absence of ingested calories, lead to the flavour being disliked. However, we also need to learn links between flavours and their consequences when an obvious signal such as bitterness is not present. In both humans and other animals, the most extreme food dislikes stem from the pairing of food flavours with post-consumption gastro-intestinal upsets.[18] Such learning can be thought of as our final line of defence against poisoning.

Imagine – or perhaps recall – a situation in which you are not feeling too well and the idea of a typical meal is unappealing, so you decide to explore the fridge in search of something naughty but nice. Ah, here's that delicious mango ice cream, your favourite flavour. A few scoops cheer you up for the moment, but you still feel that you might be coming down with a stomach bug. It turns out that you are, and within the hour, you begin to feel nauseous, and then . . . It is hardly surprising that most foods under such circumstances lose their appeal until you are feeling better. But without knowing it, you have also triggered a built-in system for protecting you once again from the dangers of being an omnivore. Instinctively, your brain has linked the gastrointestinal upset with the most likely environmental cause on offer, namely the food that you had just consumed. In the same way that associations are made between a flavour and a valued nutrient such as sugar or fat, flavours also become bound to the experience of illness. In effect, the brain now interprets the distinctive mango flavour as a signal of something that should not be eaten. This can lead to an intense dislike and persistent avoidance of that flavour.

For many, even those who have never encountered a *taste aversion* such as this, the idea that our bodies somehow guide us to correct choices about what to consume and what to avoid makes intuitive sense. In a very gross way, this is of course true. If we are hungry, in part a function of blood sugar levels, we want to eat, and if we are very hungry we will even eat foods that are relatively unpalatable at other times. An even stronger view, though, is that the body has an innate wisdom in directing our appetites. This notion is allied to the concept that food is literally medicine, a view often identified with traditional Chinese societies. To a large extent, discussion of this idea about whether we are drawn towards needed nutrients is left to the chapter on craving (chapter Six), since this notion is central to defining a craving.

However, taste aversions, because they are powerful and sudden changes in flavour liking with a direct link to a bodily response, do provide an unambiguous example of the body's (apparent) wisdom. Like other learned responses to flavours, the taste aversion becomes what the term suggests – an aversion to the taste (or more correctly flavour) of the food. In the same way that a learned preference for a flavour becomes an incentive to consume foods with that flavour, the impact of a taste aversion is a profound reluctance to taste or even smell the offending flavour, which may previously have been highly liked. Indeed, a newly acquired dislike for mango ice cream may be strong enough to spread to other mango-flavoured foods.

Taste aversions are unique among learned likes and dislikes. They are both very rapidly learned from a single pairing of illness with a flavour, as well as being extremely long-lasting, typically still present years if not decades after a single flavour–illness pairing. As the hypothetical mango ice cream example indicates, though, the associative process lacks intelligence. It is irrelevant to the formation of the aversion whether or not the food itself was actually the cause of the illness, or even if you are aware that there was not a causal connection. This tells us that this learning process is a coarse, but ultimately effective, means of making sure that any foods that could potentially have contributed to illness are avoided in future. In this sense, it can be seen as highly adaptive. In the same way that bitterness is innately aversive, even in the context of something that is not toxic, so taste aversions operate conservatively to ensure survival. In nature, when foraging for food, surviving a bout of illness is an important lesson to learn, since the presence of toxins in plants and animals used as foods is a genuine risk.

Taste aversions rely on quite specific associations. In humans, the classic taste aversion (but also see below) is formed via an association built on the experience of a flavour that is followed by gastrointestinal upset, typically nausea. Pairing a flavour with pain or discomfort or a nasty taste will not produce an aversion, nor will pairing with some other unpleasant effects of foods such as an allergic reaction. For example, if I am lactose intolerant I know that milk products may lead to an unpleasant and, in some cases, life-threatening allergic reaction. However, because this reaction is not based on nausea, the flavour of milk products such as ice cream do not become intensely disliked as they do in taste aversions.

Much of the scientific research on taste aversions has been carried out with animals, and these studies reveal the importance of this specific flavour–nausea pairing to the development of taste aversions. The crucial finding from these studies is that, although aversions are found in very many animal species, the particular pairing seen in humans and, for example, rats reflects the importance of the different senses in food selection. Thus rats (as do humans) use their senses of smell and taste in finding and recognizing food. On the other hand, for birds such as quail, sight is a much more crucial sense. This is reflected in what each of these species will develop an aversion to. Rats will associate tastes and odours (flavours) with illness to produce an aversion; quail, by contrast, will develop an aversion if a visual signal such as a food colour is followed by nausea.[19] The importance of this distinction is that it strongly indicates that such aversions are based on learning to avoid those sensory properties or signals that are most critically related to food selection. Food aversions perform an adaptive function – keeping us alive by helping us to avoid those foods that have made us ill in the past. Their evolutionary significance is illustrated well by the exception to the rule. This is the intriguing finding that there is one species of mammal that does not develop taste aversions – the vampire bat – in whom an aversion to blood (its only food) would have disastrous consequences.[20]

How prevalent are human taste aversions? Studies on population samples in the USA have suggested that at least 40 per cent of us develop an aversion at some time in our life, although some other estimates are higher than 60 per cent.[21] The differences between studies may reflect differences in deciding what constitutes an aversion, as distinct from a strong dislike. A characteristic of aversions is our extreme reluctance to expose ourselves to the offending flavour, in anticipation of the nausea that may be triggered. Thus developing a liking for the flavour once again becomes problematic.

Not all foods are equally vulnerable to the development of taste aversions. One survey of US consumers found that meats and fish, particularly in a main course meal context, accounted for up to 30 per cent of all aversions. Intermediate rates of 12–14 per cent were found for vegetables, desserts and alcohol, with potatoes, bread and rice all showing low rates (3 per cent) of aversions.[22] What do these different rates reflect? One possibility is that the proteins in meat or fish are the target of most aversions because of their potential for inducing illness if spoiled or infected with dangerous microorganisms such as *Listeria* and *Salmonella*. Proteins also take longest to digest, so perhaps it is easier to associate their flavours with illness. The most likely reason, though, is the fact that proteins and vegetables can be considered to have much more distinctive flavours once prepared in different ways within a meal (see the section on flavour principles in chapter Nine) than staples such as bread, potatoes and rice. Hence it may be that differences are related to flavour distinctiveness of target foods. Just such a conclusion is supported by studies in which animals are fed proteins and other nutrient-based foods directly into the stomach before illness is induced. Without being able to experience the flavour of the food, the likelihood of a taste aversion is the same regardless of the food's composition.[23]

As we have seen with the neophobic response to foods, unfamiliarity is a signal for potential danger that can only be resolved by experiencing the positive or negative consequences of both the food's flavour and its consumption. So it is not surprising that taste aversions are much more likely to occur when illness follows the experience of a relatively novel flavour. Foods that are highly familiar are, of course, those to which you have had multiple prior exposures, and therefore you have learnt that they are safe to consume. The example of highly liked mango ice cream becoming the target of a taste aversion is therefore less likely – although still possible – than a flavour that was both distinctive and unusual. In effect, once you have experienced no negative consequences from a food on a number of occasions, this inhibits the learning of a taste aversion.

The illness-based taste aversions are prototypical in the sense that they are both the most common and they are also found across very many species including humans. However, there are other types of events that produce aversions. Only recently has another type of taste aversion been recognized. In both animals and humans, food flavours followed by a bout of exercise can become highly disliked.[24] Two potential reasons for this seem obvious. Firstly, some sort of gastrointestinal distress may be produced by undertaking exercise following food consumption. Alternatively, perhaps the exercise itself is unpleasant enough – as it would be for many people – to become as powerful as an illness in its links to the flavour. However, neither reason turns out to be a correct explanation. Whether or not you experience a gastrointestinal upset following exercise appears to have no relationship to whether you will develop an aversion. Moreover, the aversion is produced even without maximum exertion. So, what is producing the change in liking? The most plausible explanation so far is that, since exercise results in a net loss of energy (calories), the body may be seeking to protect itself by avoiding any signals – in this case, flavours – that might predict such energy loss. As we have seen, humans are predisposed to link flavours to their consequences – correctly or not. This is certainly consistent with ideas about how learned responses to flavours seek to promote energy intake and minimize exposure to toxicity.

Humans also – and presumably uniquely – experience taste aversions that are essentially *cognitive* in nature.[25] That is, they involve associations between foods and either feelings of disgust or negative information about the food. For some, reactions to certain foods are clearly sufficiently potent to produce an aversion without the food having been consumed or even without direct contact with those foods. In such cases, modelling others' reactions to the foods or being emotionally upset by some aspect of a food are involved. Estimated at around 20 per cent of all human aversions, cognitive aversions are thought to be even longer-lasting than traditional, nausea-based aversions. One other difference between cognitive and nausea-based aversions is that, for most of us, nausea will reliably induce an aversion to a recently experienced flavour. In contrast, a characteristic of cognitive aversions is that the same experience of a food can be disgusting to one person and not to another. Thus a visit to an abattoir might be traumatic for you and an exciting day out for me. Such food-related emotional trauma, and the resultant aversion, have been linked to instances of 'moral vegetarianism', in which the idea of killing animals is so unpleasant that the flavour or even odour of meat can become highly unpleasant.

Relative to the numbers of times we eat, taste aversions are rare. The vast majority of foods or meals are not followed by illness, and those with aversions typically have them for a single food. So what is the overall importance of taste aversions in determining our food choices? It is difficult to generalize. Depending on your diet and your culture, avoiding mango-flavoured ice cream or other similar flavoured foods may not be an inconvenience. But if you develop an aversion to a staple meat or vegetable, under conditions in which food variety is limited, then the implications for a nutritionally balanced diet could be substantial.

One group that we know is severely affected by taste aversions comprises patients undergoing treatment for cancer. Severe nausea is often an unfortunate consequence of chemotherapy treatments and, as a result, aversions to foods eaten prior to treatment sessions are common, particularly in children. Even in adults, it has been estimated that as many as 50 per cent of those receiving chemotherapy will develop an aversion to one or more foods, with the most common targets being meats.[26] One approach to dealing with the problem is to artificially provide a target for the development of an aversion. Sweets/candy with a distinctive, novel (that is, unfamilar) flavour, eaten between a meal and the chemotherapy, have been successfully used as 'scapegoats' in children. The aversion develops to the flavour of the particular sweet and not to the food that the patient needs to consume to assist in their recovery.[27] As a young man, a friend experienced much the same effect by consuming a glass of milk immediately after prolonged exposure to whisky while on a rough ferry trip. For a Scotsman, the need to drink his coffee black in the several decades since has been a small price to pay for a continued preference for his national drink.

FIVE

Too Much of a Good Thing

It is now 7.00 pm and I am having a little glass of wine (and quite a nice one, too). In itself, this is far from noteworthy, but an analysis of the reasons why I chose to have a drink is very relevant to the question of how our food (and drink) preferences shape eating itself. The first thing that is evident is that none of those reasons relates at all to a physiological need such as thirst. My list included: appropriate time of day, or at least not inappropriate; to reward myself for writing for hours; and to experience the pleasure of a well-made wine. Of these reasons, only the last one matters since the first two are really about giving myself permission to indulge my preferences.

Human and other omnivores survive because they have been able to select foods based on instinctive and learned motivations underpinned by preferences. But one additional consequence of the way in which our flavour preferences arise is that they are responsible to a significant degree for why we start and stop eating (and of course drinking). Once again, an adaptive purpose is evident. Pleasure-driven eating is linked to energy requirements at that time (but see chapter Twelve for a discussion of the consequences when this is not true) and also helps to maximize sensory, and therefore nutritional, variety. Of course, physiological signals from the gut as well as stomach and liver enzymes are crucial too in initiation and termination of eating, but our concern here is for the role that food preferences play in appetite, satiety and the ways in which we eat.[1]

Learned flavour preferences are an important part of the processes that promote the body's use of nutrients in food. The world remembers Ivan Pavlov's drooling dogs mainly because of what they tell us about our ability to learn to use sensory cues to predict the arrival of biologically important food. But originally, Pavlov studied the gastric and salivary secretions that occurred in the presence of the food itself. The sight of food, and the experience of taste and flavours in the mouth, all act to initiate physiological processes that promote digestion and use of the energy and other nutrients provided by foods. This includes not only increases in salivation and gastric juices, but also secretion of enzymes from the pancreas and insulin into the bloodstream. Again, palatability is important. Thus, although all tastes – and particularly sourness – can elicit salivation, glucose absorption in the gut is triggered optimally by sweet tastes, and the secretion of pancreatic enzymes by both sweet and umami tastes. Sweetness is also especially effective in influencing the body to burn calories by increasing *thermogenesis*, the generation of heat by the body.[2] The existence of such responses has led to studies that suggest that it may be possible to enhance digestion in pre-term infants by providing a sweet taste on their pacifier. Effects of palatability are also seen with fat metabolism, since more preferred fats decrease the rise in lipids in the bloodstream seen following the taste of fat-containing foods.[3]

Eating for Pleasure

Much of the time, we do not start eating because we are significantly depleted of energy. In affluent societies at least, this state is relatively rare. We eat because of cues that tell us that sufficient time has passed since our last meal, or we eat to experience the sensory pleasure of foods, or because we are bored. Eating initiation can be learned and modified just as preferences can. In particular, eating is stimulated by our preferences for smell and flavour cues that signal the presence of energy, even if we do not need it. One can imagine that such opportunistic eating would be useful in those circumstances in which food availability is inconsistent.

Sensory pleasure continues to be an important influence on eating throughout a meal. Everyday life provides us with various demonstrations that how much we eat is controlled by the hedonic properties of foods at least as much as it is by our initial hunger and

subsequent fullness, or by the composition of a food. Most fundamentally, when food is palatable – regardless of its nutrient content
– we eat more.[4] Therefore our responses to the sensory properties
of the foods are playing an important role in determining amounts
eaten within the meal. In fact, this influence is evident even prior to
meals, as illustrated by the commonly given advice that it is unwise
to shop for food while hungry, since purchases will be driven by
anticipated pleasure rather than nutrition or dietary needs.

Once you start to eat, palatable food provides increased motivation to continue eating. This has been termed an *appetiser effect*, and
approximately corresponds to the everyday idea of some foods being
moreish (that is, 'you can't just have one'). Even following a generous
meal, further eating can be stimulated by sampling, or even just the
presence of, liked foods. Moreover, while a sweet dessert encourages
eating following a meal, so can a savoury food if it is liked enough
(see also the section below on *sensory-specific satiety*). Palatable foods
also increase our *rate* of eating, at least initially.[5]

The impact of sensory preferences on eating can be better understood by reference to a distinction, recently made by some researchers,
between *liking* and *wanting*.[6] Although it is clear that wanted foods
are often liked, and vice versa, there are times when wanting
might be influential independently of whether or not a food is liked.
In particular, the idea of wanting involves the central idea of motivation or desire to consume. One, perhaps obvious, example would
be that, if we were exceptionally hungry, we might be strongly
motivated to eat foods that were unpalatable. Conversely, chocolate
is typically consumed in relatively small amounts – as a treat – even
though it is consistently rated as many people's most liked food.

It is possible to distinguish between liking and wanting, and
in recent research this has been done using ratings of liking as
compared to ratings of desire to eat. One other way is to observe facial
expressions. As was obvious with the babies and infants illustrated
in chapters Two and Three respectively, such expressions are often
very clear signs of likes and dislikes. But they are not always an indi-
cation of how much of a food will be eaten. In Julie Mennella's study
in which the infants were given a novel food, green beans, she found
that the repeated exposure to the beans generally increased how

much was eaten. However, she observed that facial expressions only became more positive in those infants who had been fed peaches after the beans. This, therefore, is a clear example of how liking (facial expressions) and wanting (amount consumed) do not always occur at the same time or under the same circumstances.

The learning that follows pairing flavours with tastes that signal nutrients, or directly with the ingestion of those nutrients themselves, reflects both of these processes. Following conditioning, the odour of a food may not only be more liked, but can also act as a cue that increases appetite for the associated food, or for eating in general. For instance, soup flavours that had been repeatedly paired with added MSG later not only became more liked, but were able, on tasting, to stimulate an increase in both hunger and consumption of the soup, even without the added MSG.[7] Thus the soup flavour became a cue that motivated the desire or want for consumption of the soup. Such effects correspond to the common experience of being stimulated to eat by the sights or smells of a food. In fact, palatable foods in general seem to increase the desire to consume.

Just how powerful learned cues that signal nutrients can be in motivating eating is shown by the fact that, via conditioning, the cues come to have their own value. That is, the cue itself can be an object of desire or wanting. This is nicely illustrated by studies of animal learning. Pigeons, for example, can be easily taught that a light coming on means that food will be automatically dispensed into a slot below the light. The birds 'know' that the delicious bird-seed will be presented after the light comes on since they will almost immediately reach into the dispenser and eat it. But first – and this occurs only after learning has taken place – they will peck at the light itself, even though this has no impact on whether or not the food arrives. The cue, in other words, appears to have become something that the bird wants to eat. A human equivalent may be the pleasure that we often get from simply inhaling the smell of freshly baked bread, even if we have no intention of eating any.

Our worlds are filled with a multitude of cues to wanting that occur without our being consciously aware of them. These are not just odours or flavours, but sights and sounds associated with eating and drinking. We might ask, for example, to what extent advertising, particularly television advertising, is geared towards the stimulation of wanting generally. One study of such processes had participants performing a computer-based task during which either angry or happy faces were flashed on the screen for periods so brief that participants were unaware of their presence. They were then given a novel drink to try. Those exposed to the subliminal happy faces not only liked the drink more, but drank more of it, and would have been willing to pay more for the drink than those exposed to the angry faces. The implication here is that the happy faces had engaged wanting for the drink, without any awareness by the participants of how this had arisen.[8]

Why Stop?

As we continue eating, we eat more slowly as our hunger decreases and then we stop, frequently before everything is consumed, as we experience *satiation*. The question of why this happens in the continued presence of food is not as straightforward as it might at first seem. Imagine that you are hungry and have access to an unlimited quantity of your favourite food. How would you know when to stop eating? The most obvious reason for stopping might be the feeling of satiation, or fullness, accompanied by gut tightness. However, we all know of occasions when such internal signals are ignored, especially if the food is delicious. Perhaps our favourite foods make us more tolerant of feeling full, but there is no evidence that this is true.

It has recently become apparent that satiation is far more complex than has previously been thought. A purely biological view of satiation implicates not only feelings of fullness but the activity of several 'satiety hormones' (these include cholecystokinin, glucagon-like peptide and leptin) stimulated primarily by nutrients contained in foods. But it is now clear that non-biological factors, including our expectations of the satiating properties of foods, and indeed how we eat, are just as crucial to influencing when we stop eating.

It has been known for some time, initially through studies with animals, that we learn to associate certain sensory qualities with the satiating ability of the energy associated typically with those qualities. Sometimes such learned expectations are evident in humans as well. A striking illustration of expectations regarding the satiating power of a food comes from a study showing that apple juice is far more satiating when served as an 'apple soup' in a bowl.[9] Similarly, certain textures are reliably associated with greater satiation – thicker foods are judged more satiating, for example, no doubt because increasing thickness is very often a signal for higher energy in food.[10]

The importance of cognitive factors in satiation, relative to signals from the gut, are evident in a remarkable published case study of two men, both severely amnesic due to brain damage, who participated in a study about the effects of memory on eating. While both men had normal intellectual abilities otherwise, neither was able to recall events more than around a minute earlier. On three separate occasions, the researchers provided both men with a meal consisting of several foods that the men considered palatable, taking hunger ratings before and after the meal. For one of the men, in particular, hunger ratings did not change substantially following the meal. But most surprisingly, on each occasion both men consumed a second meal offered 10 to 30 minutes later. A third meal, again offered after a similar break, was consumed entirely by one of the men and partially eaten by the other.[11] This is a strong demonstration that, while the body's absorption of nutrients may be involved in a subsequent willingness to eat, psychological factors such as the ability to recall what we have eaten can also be crucial. Even in everyday eating situations, cues that remind us of how much we have consumed – one example is the presence of food wrappers – tend to lead to lower intakes of food.

Researchers from Cornell University in the USA conducted an ingenious study to demonstrate just how necessary in everyday circumstances such cues are to our perceptions of being full. As part of the study, two groups of students were given bowls of soup for lunch and asked to consume as much as they liked. Without knowing it, one group ate from a bowl that self-refilled using a hidden tube. This group consumed 73 per cent more soup than the group of students using an ordinary bowl. Despite this, these students not only felt that they had eaten about the same amount as those who ate from the regular bowl, but they rated themselves as feeling no more full.[12]

Food sensory properties also play another, unlearned, role. A consistent finding has been that liquid foods are far less satiating than solid foods, even if the energy and other nutrient contents are equal. The reason for this seems to be that liquids are commonly consumed far more rapidly than solids. Studies on the rate of eating have shown that the longer that a food is held in the mouth, the more satiating it becomes. This points to the fact that sensory stimulation is an important determinant of satiation. The mechanism appears to be the link between sensory stimulation and the variety of physiological processes – salivation and the release of enzymes from the pancreas and gut – that prepare the body to use a food's nutrients. Liquids are far less effective in initiating any of these.[13] By contrast, liquid foods are much better at producing a rapid rise in blood sugar, followed by an early decline, at which point appetite once again starts to increase.[14]

These findings may have profound implications for understanding weight gain. Those who are obese have been found to ingest food more quickly and to chew it less. In turn, fewer chews are associated with lower release of the hormones associated with satiation.[15] Clearly, just as mother suggested, chewing your food properly and not gulping your drinks is likely to be a helpful approach to make sure that you do not consume too much.

It has been generally thought that satiety, defined as the period *after* a meal during which we have a reduced desire to eat again, is determined both by the amount eaten and by the composition of the meal. A large, high-energy breakfast, for example, will be compensated by a lower energy intake at lunch. However, once again, sensory properties seem to be important. One study in human volunteers found that the pleasantness of a salted soup increased as lunchtime approached, presumably as hunger increased. After administration of naltrexone, an opioid-blocking drug that reduces the pleasantness of foods but has no impact on other aspects of hunger, the increase in the soup's pleasantness was not seen. The drug's effect also included a reduction of the amount that these volunteers ate at lunch, compared to when they had consumed an inactive placebo drug.[16] This suggests that the impulse to eat again is substantially under the control of the changes in the pleasantness of the soup rather than changes in the body's needs.

An important scientific contribution to understanding how sensory and metabolic factors interact to influence motivations to cease eating was made in the 1970s by Michel Cabanac of Claude Bernard University Lyon 1, France. Cabanac showed that consumption of a glucose solution could render subsequent sweet tastes less pleasant, particularly when this occurred after fasting. The effect, which he named *alliesthesia*, was said to reflect the effects of a decline in the body's need for the energy provided by glucose, as signalled by a sweet taste. In keeping with this interpretation, the onset of the decrease in sweet liking was gradual, in parallel with the body's absorption of the glucose over the 45 minutes or so following ingestion. Cabanac suggested therefore that the degree of sensory pleasure derived from a food is related to our physiological need for the food's nutrients.[17]

This is what we might call a *homeostatic* view of food preferences. *Homeostasis* is the term used for the suite of automatic processes that the body uses to regulate itself via feedback mechanisms. Thus shivering and perspiring are homeostatic processes for temperature regulation that act to increase and reduce, respectively, body temperature. Similarly, Cabanac's concept of alliesthesia is that it is a homeostatic process in which our bodies provide us with feedback about nutritional needs that modulates the pleasantness of food qualities. In turn, the degree of pleasantness guides our behaviour in deciding to eat or not.

Subsequent research extended these findings to a variety of other sensory properties, including a reduction in liking for food odours following a meal. Conversely, the need for energy or nutrients can influence sensory qualities to make them more palatable. Since it is generally not possible to manipulate essential nutrients in human diets, animal studies have been very useful in providing evidence for tastes and flavours reflecting internal needs. One such study showed that rats fed a diet deficient in the essential amino acid lysine subsequently preferred to consume foods containing lysine, even though they normally find its taste unpalatable (incidentally, a good example of the distinction between *liking* and *wanting*).[18] In humans, we know that the preferred level of salt in foods increases following salt depletion and the desirability of salty foods goes up. This effect has also been shown for amino acids in cases of malnourished children and the elderly, where the addition of an otherwise unpalatable amino acid mixture to a soup increased the amount consumed.[19]

The apparent significance of alliesthesia is that, eventually, following consumption, food flavours lose some of their appeal and this contributes – along with feelings of fullness – to why we stop eating. But this explanation does not complete the story and it is clear that factors other than the influence of ingested nutrients must also be important. Consider the 'I'm full, but . . .' phenomenon, which most of us have experienced. The main meal is complete, we feel that we could not eat any more, but . . . 'Did you say chocolate mousse?' In other words, the extent to which a decline in liking for foods and their flavours is able to influence what we eat seems to be specific to those particular qualities of the consumed foods, and not those of non-consumed food items. Following a main course of meat and vegetables, additional portions of these items may be unattractive, relative to something such as a dessert that is both highly palatable and different to what has already been eaten.

The Drive for Sensory Variety

Following Cabanac's findings, Barbara Rolls, then of The Johns Hopkins University, and colleagues, including Edmund Rolls of Oxford University, demonstrated that liking for the sensory qualities of foods can actually decline within a few minutes following consumption. In *sensory-specific satiety* (sss), as this effect was termed, the perception of sensory characteristics themselves is not altered – flavours do not become less intense, for example. Rather, sss seems to act only on the hedonic value of a food's sensory qualities, reducing its pleasantness and making it less likely that the food will continue to be eaten.[20]

Central to the notion of sss – and what distinguishes it from alliesthesia – is that the decline in liking begins within too short a time frame for the effect to be due to gastric signals or the absorption of nutrients. Nor does it reflect the nutrient content, including the amount of energy, of foods. Thus there is an equivalent reduction of liking with low- and high-fat, but similarly flavoured, versions of a food, and with the sweetness produced by a non-nutritive sweetener such as aspartame as compared to glucose, with the calories that the latter delivers. Therefore the extent to which SSS to one food generalizes to another food reflects a similarity of sensory properties in the two foods, but not the similarity of their nutritional make-up.[21] Most distinctive of all, though, is that SSS can be demonstrated without consuming food. If you chew a food, you will experience decreases in liking for its sensory properties, even if the food is not swallowed.[22]

Sensory-specific satiety is, as the name suggests, much more specific than alliesthesia, and the pleasantness of individual, distinct qualities can be reduced by consumption or exposure. For example, hard-textured foods become less pleasant following the consumption of other hard foods, but not following foods with a different texture. Similar findings have been reported for many other characteristics, including the colour and shape of foods. Consume a handful of red Smarties or M&Ms, for example, and this colour will become less appealing than the orange, blue and yellow ones. The shape of penne pasta will undergo SSS if eaten, while leaving the dissimilar shape of spaghetti relatively preferred.

A variety of SSS studies have estimated that, on average, there is a 15–20 per cent decrease in liking of consumed foods, compared to foods that are not consumed, regardless of whether the foods were snacks, confectionery, cola beverages, fruit drinks or dairy products. On the other hand, staples such as bread seem less vulnerable to reduced liking.[23] Although a 20 per cent reduction in liking may not seem particularly large, particularly for foods that start out as highly palatable, it appears to be sufficient to be a cause of whether or not we continue eating. Both our speed of eating and the ability of a palatable food to stimulate saliva decrease in parallel with the decline in liking during a meal. Moreover, in studies that allowed *ad libitum* food consumption, and asked participants their reasons for stopping eating, the explanation 'I just got tired of eating that food' was found to be just as common as 'feeling full'.

One implication of SSS and its effects on the palatability of what we are eating is that foods with different sensory properties are subsequently more likely to be eaten, presumably because of the difference now in the relative palatability of the eaten and uneaten foods. While readers are free to use this fact to suggest that we have an inbuilt mechanism to allow us to eat more chocolate mousse, the implications are somewhat broader. Barbara Rolls and others have argued that sss represents an adaptive strategy to ensure adequate nutrition through food variety.[24] A mechanism that discourages continued consumption of one food to the exclusion of others should lead to dietary variety, thus maximizing the possibility that we will consume all the nutrients necessary to maintain health.

This hypothesis has been borne out in a number of studies. When participants ate meals containing foods that varied in their sensory properties – be it flavour, colour or shape – total consumption was greater than when only one version of each sensory property was provided. Thus you will eat more sandwiches if the fillings are varied than if they all contain ham, or cheese, or any other single ingredient. Importantly, from the point of view of this explanation of the significance of sss, the proportional increase in intake (15 per cent on average) that providing variety within a meal or a food type produces matches quite closely with the decline in liking for a single food seen with sss.

How might sss influence everyday eating? Most obviously, it will be an important influence on how we consume different components of a meal. There is no strong nutritional reason, for example, why, when faced with a plate of different vegetables and meat, we should not consume all of each item in turn – that is, the carrots first, followed by the potatoes, and then the chicken. But this is not what we do. Eating small portions of the different food items such that we finish everything at more or less the same time ensures that the degree of sss for each item is minimized. Also, liking for the individual meal components does not decline substantially, and so this is therefore a good strategy to reduce the effects of sss and maintain interest in everything on the plate.

This explanation of sss implies that we may therefore be predisposed to seek variety in sensory properties and, ultimately, foods, and that this is achieved via modifying preferences for these properties. This may also underlie the popularity of foods that exhibit sensory contrasts, often in food textures, during eating. Ice cream and chocolate, for example, both melt during consumption, providing changing mouthfeel experiences over time. Combining very distinctive qualities in foods, especially opposites, in textures (crunchy and soft) and tastes (sweet and sour) is a common enough practice to support the view that contrasts are valued for their ability to enhance palatability.

Boredom

The corollary of the fact that variety within meals produces greater intake is that reduced variety should lead to lower intakes. If this effect is repeated across a whole diet, rather than just a meal, then there are substantial implications for situations in which promotion or restriction of intake are important for health reasons. Hence to eat less one should reduce dietary variety. Does something like SSS occur over longer time frames than a single eating occasion? If so, it may be that many of the effects of various weight-loss diets can be attributed to reduced enjoyment of food if there is low variety within the diet.

In fact, there is good evidence that a monotonous diet does reduce food acceptability, leading to less being eaten. One study, in which volunteers consumed a bland, monotonous liquid diet for seventeen days, found that the amount of liquid consumed each day decreased over the period of the study, resulting in weight loss.[25] In a less drastic intervention, US army personnel were given either the same lunch every day for a week or, alternatively, the same lunch at the beginning and end of the week, with different lunches in between. In the latter, variety condition, the acceptability of the meal overall and of individual meal components increased somewhat across the week. In the monotony condition, liking overall for the meal, and for some meal components, declined, and the amount consumed decreased over the same period.[26]

Other studies of US Army personnel, undertaken this time while they were 'in the field', have been important in illustrating the practical impact of monotonous diets. In such situations, meal acceptability and intake has shown a clear relationship with increased variety, with both increasing when compared to a diet of monotonous meals. Variety of the components within the army's field ration, the MRE (Meal Ready to Eat), shows a similar impact on the overall calorie intake. In situations such as active duty, where adequate food intake will be crucial for the proper functioning of army personnel, it may be that understanding and addressing the impact of food variety is a vital component of the army's ability to perform.[27]

Monotonous diets tend to be bland. An important question is whether it is the blandness of the food that is disliked, or whether the lack of variety by itself reduces interest in food. Thus the introduction of variety into a diet may stimulate appetite, as might making the food more interesting – it is difficult to say definitively. Most of the world's population has a diet consisting of a limited range of protein sources, usually in combination with a staple food based on rice, corn, wheat or potatoes. Such staples, although bland, are highly resistant to the effects of monotony, as they are to the impact of SSS. Even in affluent, Western societies, the one food item that resists the effects of monotony is bread. All this tends to suggest that blandness by itself does not produce monotony. One explanation for such resistance to monotony is that there is an expectation that staple foods will be a daily part of the diet. Traditionally, they will have been foods that are, relatively, more freely available, compared to scarcer high-protein or high-energy food sources.

Perhaps we only become bored with unvarying, but distinctive, flavours. More likely, though, is that we become bored if our diet does not contain variety and its associated sensory stimulation. Certainly, this is suggested by the high uptake of highly stimulating spices such as chilli in countries in which a major source of calories is a bland staple such as corn (Mexico) or rice (South-east Asia). Similarly, a study of Ethiopian refugees who had eaten a monotonous diet for six months rated new foods as much more pleasant, in contrast to a comparable shorter-stay group (two days), who found both the regular and the new foods equally palatable.[28]

Monotony is not always seen as a problem for food acceptability. We often opt to stay with the same foods for particular meals or occasions, perhaps after an initial period of 'exploration'. Breakfast choices provide excellent evidence of this. Of course, the choice to consume breakfast cereals, toast, eggs or ham and cheese each morning may be related more to convenience or the need for ease of preparation at that time of day than anything else. Nevertheless, we can clearly sacrifice dietary variety in the face of a busy schedule in a way that we would not when competing external demands are less, such as during the evening meal.

One essential feature of becoming bored with foods is the extent to which our choices are limited. Knowing that we could have bacon and eggs for breakfast if time permitted seems to reduce the impact of monotony of, for example, the same breakfast cereal day after day. In a similar vein, perceived self-control over what to eat may be important in maintaining interest. While restricting the number of foods available might be expected to reduce the acceptability of a diet, such restrictions have less impact if we are able to control the planning of what to eat.

Are there ways to insulate specific foods, or even our whole diet, against boredom? In situations in which neophobia is unlikely to be important, for example in the case of a novel flavour in a familiar food, novelty may actually be associated with increased liking. The Japanese ice cream market is well known for introducing a range of entirely new flavours each year, an approach that aims to maintain interest in a familiar product. In the US army context, novel MRES stimulate intake. Whether this persists over time, though, is likely to reflect the sensory complexity of the product. It is thought that, generally, simple foods do not maintain interest, whereas complexity is more resistant to boredom.[29] The degree of complexity might refer to flavours or texture combinations or could also reflect the degree of variety in a sequence of foods. But the conclusion is clearly that, so far as our foods are concerned, variety is the spice of life.

SIX

Consuming Passions

In 1940, medical researchers Lawson Wilkins and Curt Richter reported in the prestigious *Journal of the American Medical Association* the case of a three-year-old boy (identified only as 'D') who had been hospitalized with adrenal insufficiency. Among other things, the adrenal glands regulate sodium in the bloodstream, which in turn controls blood pressure and volume. When the glands malfunction, the body suffers from a lack of sodium, which can be overcome by increased salt consumption. The Wilkins and Richter report was, however, not about the causes of the infant's disease, but was instead a detailed history provided by his mother of her son's eating behaviour. Even prior to D's first birthday, his mother noted that her son would lick salt off crackers. By eighteen months of age, D not only demanded salt with all meals, but also would eat it directly from the salt shaker, if allowed. Foods that were not salty themselves, or to which salt had not been added, were rejected. Breakfast cereals were only consumed when salt was sprinkled on top. Surprisingly, perhaps, D's diet was varied, but saltiness was always a feature of what he ate.[1]

Unfortunately, D's story did not end well. Following hospitalization, he was given a regular hospital diet with no access to additional salt, and died suddenly as a result. While this example of a bodily need dictating both preference and behaviour is extreme, it is nevertheless important as a well-documented and easily recognizable account of craving for a specific taste. The account both conforms to the popular idea that food cravings such as this are somehow the body's way of letting us know about needs for particular nutrients, and also seems to act as a warning of the potentially dire consequences of ignoring cravings.

At some time, most of us have experienced a craving for a specific food – something that we must have now, and which we will go out of our way to obtain. It is as if the body is insisting that we must have that food. As a survival mechanism, craving makes complete sense as a response to a nutritional need. But while there is much anecdotal information about craving and physiological needs, hard evidence of sudden irresistible appetites for specific foods is sparse. It is clear that we get hungry and thirsty, clear signs of a strong desire for food or drink, but does the body really crave particular nutrients if we are deficient in them? Such specific desires would require us to propose the existence of internal needs that, via a signalling mechanism involving food pleasure or food wants, direct behaviour towards food ingredients. This notion is reminiscent of the homeostatic processes in alliesthesia that act to reduce the pleasantness of food qualities we explored in chapter Five, except in reverse. So is craving part of a homeostatic process that ensures that we consume enough essential nutrients?

In the case of salt, the answer is yes. Intense desire for salt is not confined to rare clinical case studies. Not only have other patients with adrenal insufficiency subsequently reported craving for salty foods, but even in the absence of this disorder, the one incontrovertible specific hunger that all humans (and other mammals) possess is for sodium chloride, common salt. Salt is metabolically essential and this need is primarily met through the diet. As the case of D illustrates so tragically, without dietary salt, death is inevitable. How does the body let us know it wants more salt if dietary levels become insufficient? Clinical studies have demonstrated that in cases where humans (and many other animals) are depleted of salt, we develop strong appetites for the taste of salt, which increases in palatability. The same increase in palatability for salty foods is found in studies in which volunteers are fed low-salt diets.[2] Hence it appears that changes in the hedonic value of salt underlie the increased intake when depleted – just as a homeostatic explanation would suggest.

The underlying physiological mechanisms of these hedonic changes are suggested by studies of animals deprived of salt.[3] When recordings are taken from individual brain cells of these animals during the experience of salty tastes, it has been found that those cells in the brain that typically respond best to highly palatable sweetness also start to respond to salty tastes. This suggests that these cells are now sending a signal to other parts of the brain resulting in a perception of increased salt palatability. Under the same conditions, facial responses such as licking that are typically seen while consuming sweet tastes are seen when the animal is given a salt solution that it would normally find unpleasantly strong. All of this is consistent with the idea that, during depletion, the motivation to consume salt and thus restore normal salt levels is driven by an increase in salt's palatability.

Innate Wisdom?

Beyond salt appetite, however, there is little evidence that other specific appetites exist, or at least none that can be easily explained using the idea of homeostasis. This is surprising given the range of nutrients – amino acids, vitamins, minerals – that are required in the diet to maintain normal health. One distinct possibility is that salt craving stands out because of the unambiguous link between a physiological need and the familiar taste of salt.

Yet despite the limited scientific evidence, the idea that the body has an innate wisdom that directs specific nutritional needs via preferences is a popular belief. Many arguments for such an innate wisdom draw upon the pioneering work of Clara Davis who, during the 1930s in the USA, studied groups of post-weaning infants aged six to eleven months for more than six years. Davis provided the children with a broad range of foods, both raw and cooked, and allowed them to select and consume whatever foods they wished each mealtime. What followed appeared to demonstrate an extraordinary ability among these infants to select a balanced diet. On average, their diets consisted of around 17 per cent protein, 35 per cent fat and 48 per cent carbohydrates, with these proportions judged at the time to be 'within nutritional standards'. Davis suggested that

> such successful juggling and balancing of more than
> thirty nutritional essentials that exist in mixed and different

proportions in the foods from which they must be derived suggest at once the existence of some innate, automatic mechanism for its accomplishment, of which appetite is a part.[4]

As one example, Davis noted an increase in the consumption of three foods – raw beef, carrots and beetroot (beets) – when the infants were recovering from illness, again apparently pointing to the body's quest for particular nutrients in a time of need.

If the infants' food choices were indeed driven by an innate 'wisdom of the body' as expressed in food preferences, then we would expect that, like D, the infants would be drawn to specific tastes or foods. But, in fact, what Davis noticed was that initial food choices were largely random, with all foods tried at least once. In other words, the innate drive, if there was one, was towards variety, rather than towards nutrients based on metabolic need. Preferences for particular foods and, as a consequence, a reduction in dietary variety, emerged as the infants re-selected foods that they had tried and liked. The final message from Davis's research was that, given a selection of foods that, overall, provided a nutritionally balanced diet, it was generally difficult not to eat in what adults would consider a healthy manner. This was true even if sometimes the infants' food selections and meal compositions were not typical of what adults would choose. One infant, for example, enjoyed pairing their breakfast orange juice with liver!

It goes without saying that such a large-scale, intrusive manipulation of infants' food intake would be difficult, if not impossible, to carry out today. In particular, the real test of what an infant would choose given unfettered access to foods really requires that the infant also has access to 'junk' foods. Thus it is crucial to know what we would observe on the first occasion an infant was faced with a choice between a carrot and a chocolate bar and, more importantly perhaps, having tasted both, what they would choose on the second such occasion.

An apparent link of a different kind between taste preferences and nutritional needs comes from observations of the consumption of specific non-foods.[5] This phenomenon, known as pica, is named after the alleged indiscriminate food habits of the magpie (Latin species name: *Pica pica*). Noted since antiquity across very many cultures, pica is commonly observed as a craving for, and consumption of, substances such as earth, clay, starch and even ice. That pica might be driven by nutritional deficiency is suggested by the high prevalence of this behaviour – often greater than 50 per cent – among pregnant women, particularly those in poor, rural communities where nutritional disorders are relatively commonplace. Pica is also observed among children, and in some clinical populations, including those suffering from kidney or coeliac disease. Animals, too, have been known to show pica.

The most common explanation for pica is that it is directed by a need to consume minerals in which the body is currently deficient. However, while pica does, in fact, occur frequently in those with iron, zinc and calcium deficiencies, it has been difficult to show that these deficiencies actually cause pica. Not only do many of the substances consumed not contain significant amounts of the required minerals, the consumption itself does not seem to correct the deficiency. Neither does treating the deficiency necessarily reduce the pica. There are also some indications that eating substances such as earth may *produce* mineral deficiencies in the eater. Therefore, despite pica's widespread prevalence, its origins remain a mystery.

Everyday Craving

Craving, in the sense of a strong desire to consume a food, seems remarkably common, at least among young adults (it is less common in the elderly). Even if specific, pathological eating such as that shown by D or cases of pica was guided by metabolic needs, 'normal' human cravings appear to be far more common than could be explained by nutrient deficiencies. Surveys have found that as high as 90 per cent of the sample experience cravings at some time. Lower figures are sometimes reported, but most estimates are high enough to suggest that craving is quite normal. Moreover, for those that report cravings, experiencing them more than once a week is common.[6] Cravings of this frequency are typically defined as strong desires for specific foods in absence of hunger. They may therefore be of an entirely different character and have a different underlying cause than, for example, D's salt craving.

Why does this form of craving occur, if not because of a physiological need? A picture of the most commonly craved foods provides some clues, even if not a definitive answer. In one survey of a large group of students in the USA, the overwhelming majority reported having cravings at some time.[7] Of these, over 70 per cent reported that they primarily craved carbohydrates, in particular, chocolate, followed by pasta, desserts, confectionary, potatoes, ice cream and, finally, bread. The cravings of the remaining students were focused mainly on proteins, especially beef, then chicken, seafood, cheese, pizza, vegetables and milk. Only 2 per cent of students reported that they craved foods that were specifically high in fat. While all of the foods nominated might be considered palatable, there is clearly no obvious relationship in the specific foods, or their place in the hierarchy of desires, to sweet taste or fat content. This is relevant if the craving was related to energy needs or even just to the degree of palatability. In most students' list of food favourites, for example, pizza will never come second to chicken.

The few studies of 'everyday' craving in different cultures reveal some interesting commonalities, as well as differences. In several US/Canadian studies, women report that they crave chocolate most, while men tend to crave savoury foods. The same gender difference in chocolate craving is also seen in Spain, but men and women there both report cravings for savoury foods approximately equally.[8] Similarly, studies in Egypt find that savoury cravings are most common in both men and women.[9] That there would be both cultural, as well as gender, differences in reported cravings should be expected since all craved foods are by definition part of the usual diet (with the exception of pica), even if they are not the most common foods eaten.

Craving is particularly associated in the popular imagination with the hormonal changes in pregnancy and the menstrual cycle. This is perhaps one of the key reasons why the idea of craving related to altered physiological states remains strong. Although public knowledge of the link between craving and pregnancy is mostly gathered via popular media, especially films and television, it turns out to be quite true. Surveys from 1930s Britain report a variety of cravings during pregnancy, including for fruit, vegetables, confectionery, pickles (presumably with or without ice cream) and cereals. A subsequent 1961 British survey reported that cravings, especially for fruit and strongly flavoured foods, were experienced in 75 per cent of a pregnant group. In the USA, pregnancy has been reported to be accompanied by craving for foods high in fat or sugar, as well as fruit.[10] This apparent link of cravings with pregnancy suggests the possibility that either hormonal changes or changes in nutritional needs might underlie the cravings.

Chocolate craving, in particular, has been linked to the hormonal changes that occur during the menstrual cycle and in pregnancy. A survey of US college undergraduates found that about 50 per cent of female cravers show a peak of chocolate craving around the time of menstruation. Such a pattern of craving tends to implicate hormonal variations as a cause. If so, we would predict quite a substantial decrease in craving following menopause. In fact, chocolate craving does decrease, but not to the degree one would expect if hormones were really responsible, and particularly since craving decreases with age anyway. Neither hormonal influences nor nutritional needs as causes of cravings in pregnancy can be completely dismissed. However, it is worth noting that food aversions – especially to meat, eggs and fried foods – appear to be at least as common as food cravings during pregnancy. Thus all we can say with certainty is that a woman's normal food likes and dislikes are commonly disturbed during her pregnancy.[11] An alternative explanation is based on the observation that negative moods are sometimes associated with increased desire for, and consumption of, palatable foods (see section below). An important reason, therefore, why cravings are so often associated with pregnancy and menstrual cycle variations may also be the mood changes that are commonly experienced with hormonal fluctuations.

An important question to consider is whether cravings are increased during periods of dieting and, if so, what this might mean. If cravings are an attempt at fulfilling nutritional needs, we would expect that, at the very least, foods high in sugars or fats would be craved during diets. Once again, though, this has been difficult to show, and the strongest statement that can be made is that the relationship of craving to dieting is inconsistent, or at least more complex than we might expect. Craving (as distinct from simply hunger) is sometimes reported during dieting, but not always. One apparently paradoxical fact about craving is that it tends to become less frequent during extreme reductions of food intake (fasting), just as, eventually, hunger also declines.[12] Whatever the reason for this, it does tend to support the view that craving does not arise automatically from energy depletion, as does the failure of exercise to be associated with craving. Even the fact that craving tends to increase during occasions when blood sugar is low can be explained by the fact that thinking about food also increases with low blood sugar, and craving may therefore be secondary to food thoughts.

The Chocolate Fix

If nutrient deficiencies do not underlie cravings – or at least, if we have little evidence that they do – then the question of what produces cravings remains. Attempts to explain food cravings have often used craving for addictive drugs as a model. It is clear that with alcohol and nicotine, and opioid drugs such as heroin, regular usage builds tolerance for their effects – that is, the subjective and physiological effects of a given dose decrease. At the same time as tolerance develops, states of intense discomfort and 'wanting' are experienced if the drug becomes unavailable. If foods do contain addictive substances, it is possible that processes similar to drug cravings explain food cravings.

Can foods be addictive in this sense? There have been some intriguing pointers towards an addiction view of food craving. Animal studies show that administration of morphine leads to an increase in food intake, but only for palatable foods, whereas drugs such as naloxone, which blocks the action of such opioids, leads to a decreased preference for normally palatable foods that are high in sugar and fat.[13] Brain imaging studies in humans, too, have identified common brain areas activated by addictive opioid drugs and craved foods.[14] Given that environmental cues trigger food cravings (see below), they have some things in common with drug cravings. Cues such as familiar environments, drug-using friends and the drug injection paraphernalia are known to induce craving for the effects of the drug in habitual users.

Chocolate is the single most commonly craved food in Western societies. It makes sense therefore to examine the idea of foods as drugs in relation to chocolate, particularly since chocolate does contain many pharmacologically active compounds. Because the cocoa base of chocolate includes caffeine and theobromine, which are stimulants, and phenylethyamine, which potentially has mood-enhancing properties, there is at least the possibility that an addiction-like process could operate to produce intense desire for chocolate. First, of course, it is important to know if chocolate does have drug-like effects that influence the experience of a craving. If it does, it is also crucial to work out which aspect of the chocolate influences the craving: its flavour or the active compounds that it contains?

The most well-controlled study to date that has examined this possibility asked volunteers, all of whom were self-confessed chocolate cravers, to rate the intensity of their next experience of a craving.[15] Immediately following this rating, separate groups of these volunteers were asked to consume from a box they had been given either capsules containing cocoa (and thus all the pharmacologically active ingredients in chocolate), or pieces of milk chocolate, or white chocolate (which contains no cocoa, and therefore none of the active ingredients), or white chocolate pieces together with cocoa capsules. Other groups consumed either nothing or placebo capsules, containing no active ingredients. Ninety minutes later, the volunteers once again rated the intensity of their craving. There was little evidence that the compounds in cocoa were important in reducing craving. Craving was most reduced by consuming milk chocolate, which of course does contain the active compounds. However, adding the active ingredients in the cocoa capsules to white chocolate consumption produced no greater reduction in craving than white chocolate alone, while the cocoa capsules by themselves did not influence craving intensity any more significantly than the placebo capsules.

The results of this study imply that milk chocolate reduces craving most effectively via its sensory qualities rather than any psychoactive compounds that it may contain. Craving for chocolate is related to craving for other sweet foods, suggesting that it is its palatability, based on an optimal combination of sugar and fat, that is most important. After all, not only is chocolate treated like a special food to be enjoyed as a guilty pleasure, but each experience of chocolate flavour is paired with sweet tastes and the energy provided by the sugars and fats to guarantee a strong, conditioned preference for the flavour. Why milk chocolate is better at reducing craving than white chocolate may simply be that it has a stronger conditioned preference, since it is both more commonly consumed and has a more distinctive chocolate flavour.

Although pharmacologically active compounds such as caffeine may play some role in chocolate craving, they are likely to do so by promoting preference for the flavour, rather than acting as addictive substances to which we experience withdrawal. Moreover, tolerance is seldom, if ever, seen with respect to foods. That is, chocolate does not become increasingly less pleasant the more that we consume it, so that we require more and more to achieve the same degree of pleasure. In fact, craved foods are often those that are described in terms of 'moreishness'. Although foods described as 'moreish' are those for which 'one bite/piece/slice is never enough', they also tend to be consumed in small amounts.[16] Often their consumption is subject to restraint. Even if you are not dieting, you may want another slice of cake, another piece of chocolate or another potato chip, but you will tend to hold back. Because of the typically small portion sizes, moreish foods may be an example of the appetiser effect seen in the last chapter, which occurs when the initial consumption of palatable foods produces a desire for further eating.

Many foods are palatable, so why do we show restraint only with certain select items such as chocolate? Clearly, this is related to what is deemed appropriate. Chocolate is an indulgence. Whereas chocolate manufacturers may use this word in advertising to enhance the appeal of their product, indulgence has another, negative connotation – that of greediness or lack of self-control. Of course, it is perfectly possible to come up with a rational explanation for restraint when it comes to chocolate. Apart from anything else, regularly consuming large amounts is likely to lead to a substantial weight gain. But this does not address the question of why some palatable, high-energy foods are seen as indulgences, while others such as pizza or other 'fast foods' are not.

How does this issue of indulgence and restraint relate to that of craving? Psychologists studying the way in which behaviours are shaped by the reinforcers that follow the behaviour have, for many years, argued over the question of what constitutes a reinforcer. Obviously, if you are hungry, you will act in a way that results in access to food ('No dinner until you have cleaned your room!'); if you are thirsty, water will similarly act as a reinforcer for any behaviour that gives you access to the water. But, the question also has a more abstract aspect – in general, just what *sort of thing* are reinforcers? The *response deprivation hypothesis* has been proposed in an effort to provide a unifying concept to explain reinforcers.[17] This hypothesis proposes that the key to understanding those things that act as reinforcers is that they are restricted. In a typical animal learning reinforcement experiment, the reward (for example, food) is not given until the hungry animal has pressed a bar a certain number of times, or run a maze, or lifted its paw to shake hands. In other words, the reinforcer is restricted until the response is performed. Conversely, if access to food is already unrestricted, it will not work as a reinforcer, since it is unlikely that the animal will perform any of these behaviours in order to gain food.

This admittedly rather theoretical view of reinforcement is relevant because it may provide some insight into why a substance like chocolate is so commonly the object of craving. The prevailing view, certainly of most parents, is that such a highly palatable food should be eaten only with restraint – that is, as a special treat. Viewed within the framework of the response deprivation hypothesis, it may be that it is this restriction of consumption that heightens the reward value of chocolate, making it so commonly craved. There is some evidence to support this view. While those on diets do not always show cravings, when cravings are seen, it is mainly for those foods that were most recently restricted.[18]

Hedonic Hunger

The idea of the restriction of access to foods as a mechanism for craving tells us why some foods rather than others tend to be craved. But we are still left with trying to understand why craving occurs at all. The scientific evidence outlined so far in this chapter suggests that cravings tell us little about the body's nutritional needs, beyond the fact that craved foods are often highly palatable and also often high in energy.

Recently, it has been proposed that there exists a drive towards food pleasure-seeking – a sort of *hedonic hunger* – that coexists with the more traditional hunger for food that is driven by energy needs.[19] If you have not eaten for twelve hours, then your body's need for energy will act as a powerful motivator to eat. However, the fact that your stomach rumbles when passing a bakery two hours after lunch has little to do with energy needs. Instead, your responses, both physiological and subjective, are much like those of Pavlov's dogs – that is, driven by prior experiences with the pleasures of freshly baked bread or croissants or pastries. That we can occasionally miss a meal when our attention is heavily engaged by what we are doing is a good indicator that learned responses to food-related cues are crucial as determinants of wanting to eat.

An essential feature of hedonic hunger is that it is under the control of food cues in our environment. It leads to eating that is initiated by desire, rather than need. By definition, it is a hunger that is satisfied only by highly preferred foods. In other words, it is eating that is reinforced by the pleasure derived from the food, rather than the provision of any particular nutrient. In this context, feeling hedonic hunger even *while* you are eating is not impossible. So, for example, a low sensory impact meal of raw vegetables might be good for the waistline, but it is likely to leave the need for sensory pleasure from eating unsatisfied. This distinction is consistent with our willingness to consume palatable foods such as desserts, even though we would refuse further helpings of meats or vegetables.

One way, therefore, of thinking about food cravings is as examples of hedonic hunger that are elicited by the presence of foods or cues for foods. One experimental study of craving demonstrated how this might work. Student volunteers were first provided with a large lunch, thus removing any possibility that they could still be hungry in the traditional sense. Two equally palatable foods, pizza and ice cream, were then shown to the participants, who reported high levels of desire for consuming them. When allowed, the students in fact consumed significant amounts of these foods, despite previously reporting that they did not feel hungry. Moreover, since equal amounts of both of these foods were consumed, this effect cannot be seen as an example of leaving room for the ice cream as a dessert. Rather, it seems that the presence of the food itself stimulated further eating.[20]

Of course, cravings also occur without foods being physically present. It is unsurprising that craving is commonly accompanied by vivid images of the craved substance. But which is the (delicious, mouthwatering) chicken and which is the egg? Craving could induce thoughts of food, just as the thoughts might lead to craving. Asking volunteers to imagine liked foods can produce cravings when, previously, they were not present. In addition, the strength of that craving is determined by the vividness of the imagery. This suggests that it is those often uninvited thoughts of food that lead to the craving, rather than vice versa.

What a majority of diets have in common is that they are both monotonous and low in sensory pleasure, and it is under such circumstances that hedonic hunger will emerge. Given the wide variety of triggers for thoughts about food in most of our environments, it is easy to see why cravings might occur. Precisely because dieting is associated with lowered sensory pleasure, in the same way that low blood sugar triggers hunger, dietary monotony triggers hedonic hunger and craving.

Connections between sensory pleasure and craving are demonstrated, too, in the relationship between craving and mood. In particular, a link has been made between craving for carbohydrates and negative moods. Carbohydrate cravers report that feelings of anxiety, fatigue, tension and depression are commonly experienced prior to craving. Especially for sweet foods, the strength of the craving appears to be associated with these negative emotions. Conversely, after consuming the craved foods, the most common feelings were relaxation, happiness and increased energy.[21] Such observations have led to the notion that craving arises from negative emotions and that the pleasure derived from eating the craved food is a form of self-medication that counteracts the unpleasant moods. Consistent with this idea of self-medication are studies that show that when negative moods are induced in dieters, they overeat.

Since cravings may be frequently followed, and therefore reinforced by, improvement in mood, it is not surprising that they persist. And because craved foods are often high-energy foods, there is the potential for craving to be a major issue in attempts to maintain a healthy diet. This raises the question therefore of how normal cravings – as opposed to those of the type experienced by D – can be 'treated' to ensure that the cravings do not become a health issue. The most obvious, and obviously easy, strategy is to give in to cravings. Satisfying a burning desire for chocolate once or twice a week is hardly going to ruin an otherwise nutritionally balanced diet. If this approach elicits just too much guilt, then an alternative solution has been provided by those learning psychologists studying reinforcers. The demonstration in psychological research of a *value-discounting function* for reinforcement means that the longer we wait for a reinforcer, the less valuable it becomes. So exercising short-term willpower by waiting an hour before consuming a craved food will mean that the food's appeal may drop substantially during this time. Willpower, under such circumstances, is likely to be much more effective in helping you refuse the tasty snack. Recognizing the cues that lead to craving and limiting their impact will mean that their power to induce craving is lessened. As noted earlier, food imagery is a very common accompaniment to subjective feelings of craving. There is some evidence that interfering with these images by directing attention elsewhere reduces craving. Similarly, engaging in other pleasurable activities unrelated to food may short-cut the link between negative emotions and craving.[22]

Finally, it is crucial to recall the distinction between hunger based on bodily needs, which necessarily requires energy input, and hedonic hunger, which can be satisfied with sensory pleasure. In other words, hedonic hunger requires a hedonic solution, not necessarily a calorific one. About a year ago, one of my colleagues had a stomach operation that has left him with a chronic loss of appetite and, as a consequence, loss of weight. He still has no interest in eating and frequently needs to remind himself that a mealtime has arrived. Despite this lack of appetite, though, from time to time he still experiences cravings. This is not for a food that he wishes to eat, but merely for the experience of its sensory pleasure. His most craved food is curry, and even though he has absolutely no desire to eat such a spicy treat, he wants to experience it in some way. His approach to dealing with his cravings is nothing if not inventive. He found that his craving could be relieved by entering his favourite curry restaurant and inhaling deeply to experience the rich, spicy aroma. Satisfied, he then leaves without eating. While this does provide an excellent example of hedonic hunger completely isolated from a desire to consume food, it is probably not a strategy that those of us with intact appetites should try. Being in the presence of food while being denied access – for example, by waiting in a queue – is an excellent way to encourage the body to respond to the sights and smells by increasing salivation, gastric juices and appetite generally.

SEVEN

Just Disgusting

The diners at the next table are in no doubt that something is wrong with your meal. Without making a sound, you have let them know that the dish in front of you will not be eaten. Your face says it all: your mouth is gaping, your nose is wrinkled and your top lip is drawn back over your upper teeth. You also seem to be physically drawing away from the plate in front of you. The signs are unmistakeable – something about the food has disgusted you. The feeling may even be a little contagious, leading your fellow diners to poke and prod at their own food in case something is amiss.

Enough of them – what have *you* experienced? A perfectly respectable restaurant has just served you a plate of grilled field mushrooms, which you expect will be delicious. Your food is not too bitter or sour or too spicy. Cutting a piece to consume, however, you notice that the underside seems a little, well, squishy. There is also some . . . movement! With mounting horror, you look more closely, to find the mushroom underside crawling with maggots.

To accompany your all too apparent facial expression, you are now experiencing a sense of revulsion, or an overwhelming 'yuckiness', and probably feelings of nausea. What would otherwise have been a tasty food is now rendered inedible, something that is disturbing to even contemplate. Were I measuring your blood pressure, heart rate or sweat gland activity, I would also notice that all of these had decreased. So a quite specific emotion – subjectively and physiologically – is being experienced. There is also the possibility that you will develop an aversion to mushrooms, but even if not, you will undoubtedly never look at a mushroom in the same way again.

Despite the literal meaning of *dis-* (bad) *gust* (taste), it is not just an extreme dislike for an unpalatable food. Disgusting foods are more than unpleasant: they are offensive. And this ability to give offence has a complex relationship with the expected sensory properties of the food. Foods may taste unpleasant without inducing disgust. Many people dislike Brussels sprouts, mainly due to their bitterness, but they are not disgusting. In contrast, we might accept, in the abstract, that sheep's eyeballs (a food in some cultures) could conceivably taste good, but the idea of eating them is quite likely to disgust many used to a Western diet. Similarly, a roasted rat might taste delicious, but once you find out what it is, may still cause disgust. So what accounts for the sense of revulsion, feelings of nausea and posture of withdrawal? It is not simply a matter of inappropriateness (although this can play a part – see below). The cardboard box in which a food is packed is not seen as food, but the thought of eating it, though hardly appealing, does not evoke the intense emotional quality associated with your maggot-infested mushrooms.

The characteristic facial expression associated with disgust is very much a clue to its distinctiveness and meaning as an emotion. Some of the earliest observations of the features of the disgust face were made by Charles Darwin in his book *The Expression of Emotions in Man and Animals* (1872).

Darwin's writings on disgust illustrate a number of its key characteristics. These include its universality. Darwin believed, and it is still generally accepted, that disgust is an emotion shared by us all, in the same way as emotions such as sadness, happiness, fear or anger. In what was then considered the furthest reaches of the earth, he recognizes this distinctive emotion in another despite a vast cultural gulf:

> In Tierra del Fuego a native touched with his finger on some cold preserved meat which I was eating at our bivouac, and plainly showed utter disgust at its softness; whilst I felt utter disgust at my food being touched by a naked savage, though his hands did not appear dirty.[1]

More recent studies on the characteristic disgust face have supported Darwin's idea of disgust as a universal emotion. More than

A New Guinean Fore tribesman photographed during the 1960s responding to a description of a situation likely to elicit disgust. Despite little interaction with Western societies at this point, the expression contains all the same features recognizable as disgust across a variety of cultures.

forty years ago, studies of emotional expressions in New Guinean Fore tribesmen included presenting them with a series of imagined scenarios, and the facial expressions that these elicited were recorded. Included in these scenarios was one in which they were asked to imagine a situation in which they come across a pig that has been dead for some time. The resultant expression shares significant similarities with Darwin's descriptions of disgust and to disgusted Western faces photographed more recently.[2] The choice of the Fore tribe for this study was deliberate in that, at the time, they had only been in contact with Westerners for around a decade. Thus the opportunity for this group to learn to express disgust in a Western manner was extremely limited.

Another sign of the universality of the disgust expression is the widespread ability of people to recognize this emotion accurately, irrespective of their culture. In cross-cultural studies in which participants were shown a photograph of a disgusted face, a majority of those asked in 21 cultures as diverse as the USA, Japan, Chile, Brazil, Ethiopia, Indonesia, China and Estonia correctly identified the emotion expressed.[3]

Disgusting Objects

Harm-minimization is a key role that our taste preferences perform, as shown by our innate reaction to bitterness. We can learn, too, to avoid flavours and odours associated with gastrointestinal upset. But that still leaves a large category of potentially harmful substances that could be consumed. Imagine if cockroaches tasted nice. For most of us, this would still not be much of a dilemma because of the 'uncleanness' of the cockroach. There is something about its habitat and its habits that we feel certain is likely to make the cockroach unsafe to consume. There are thus objects or situations that pose a very real danger of contamination, in particular via consumption, and which might provide a serious risk even in tasting. In such cases, the experience of disgust provides the necessary motivation to avoid any possibility that contamination might occur.

Although disgust – or what is sometimes called *core disgust* – appears to be universally associated with foods (or at least things that could be consumed), the specific sources of food disgust vary from culture to culture. Consumption of certain insects is perfectly acceptable in some cultures, but not in many others. Part of the prohibition against eating certain animals in some religions is related to their alleged unclean nature or behaviour, raising the possibility of real or symbolic contamination. Some things by themselves can be disgusting (for example, faeces, worms or blood), with feelings of disgust increasing dramatically if consuming them is contemplated.[4] But some otherwise innocuous items become disgusting *only* in the context of possible consumption. The idea of eating a plastic bag or a piece of (unused) toilet paper can, for some, be quite disgusting. In both of these examples, a fear of symbolic contamination might be behind the disgust. However, it is also possible that the disgust reflects neophobia for something that is unexpected as a food. This is seen sometimes in the ability of novel combinations of actual (and acceptable) foods – for example, ice cream and ketchup – to generate disgust in children.

In chapter One, texture was identified as a common reason for rejection of certain foods, for example, oysters. This is at least partly because some textural properties are able themselves to evoke disgust. In fact, one study has suggested that textures might be a key feature of all food disgust. The researchers presented to participants a series of written scenarios about consuming foods under different circumstances. In these scenarios, there were a variety of reminders of both food *animalness* (descriptions of blood and viscera) and of textures (slimy, mushy). When asked to indicate the degree of disgust that was evoked, the participants rated the textural properties as more important in producing feelings of disgust than the degree of 'animalness' (although this was still important).[5] The likely reason for this is that textures such as sliminess are often associated with decay and spoilage in foods, irrespective of whether the food is animal- or vegetable-based. Consumer surveys support this interpretation, finding that possession of qualities such as sliminess, slipperiness and fattiness are major reasons why a food is rejected. In the case of Darwin's curious Tierra del Fuegan, the meat's softness was clearly a source of disgust.

Animals Behaving Badly

So why have we all evolved – genetically or socially or both – to feel disgust? The most influential interpretation of disgust has come from the food-choice psychologist Paul Rozin. He has suggested that disgust, when related to food, is 'revulsion at the prospect of oral incorporation of an offensive substance'.[6] Rozin argues that disgust originates as a rejection of bad-tasting food. In this, it shares some aspects of the facial expression associated with bitterness, particularly the mouth gape. In order to analyse what the different facial expression components of disgust might reflect, Rozin presented a group of university students with descriptions of potential disgust-eliciting situations and asked them to match these with photographs of different facial gestures, including those that occur in disgust.[7] Gaping and tongue protrusion were recognized as being associated with the expulsion of food from the mouth, as one might with something that is spoiled ('rotten meat') or contaminated ('an apple with a worm in it'). The characteristic nose wrinkle strongly suggested a response to a bad smell ('rotten eggs') or a bad taste ('something sour'), both of which we also associate with food spoilage. When the students were asked what the other typical disgust face feature, the raised/retracted upper lip, might reflect, the most common situations selected related to interpersonal contamination ('sleeping in an unclean hotel bed') or moral offence ('a 15-year-old and a 90-year-old having sex') or reminders of 'animalness' ('an apple with a worm in it'). Clearly, some aspects of these aspects of disgust are unrelated to food, and this will be considered briefly below.

Rozin suggests that a major part of the origin of disgust is as a way of protecting ourselves from our own essential 'animalness', which uncomfortably for many of us includes the inevitability of death. Reminders of death such as rotting flesh or obvious signs of disease are disgusting for just this reason. Consider the worst things that you could possibly imagine eating and your shortlist will no doubt include the prototypical disgust substances. Body waste products such as faeces seem to be universal disgust items, as are many animal products such as blood or viscera – at least when considered as foods. To some, the whole idea of a 'blood sausage' is far too much about the blood rather than the sausage. Rozin argues that reminders of these 'animal' aspects of ourselves are unacceptable when considered in the context of eating primarily because of the common belief that 'you are what you eat'.

This belief may also be behind the fact that meats are very frequently given names that separate what we are eating from the animal that provided it. We eat pork and bacon rather than pig, for example, and veal rather than cute baby cow. And sweetbreads sounds so much more acceptable than 'various internal organs'. Such renaming serves to put some distance between what you are eating, its animal origins, and the fact that it had to be slaughtered to end up on your plate as a nice fillet. Note, also, how meat is often served: chopped or sliced in such a way as to disguise obvious signs of anatomy. When this does not occur, for example serving a pig's head or trotters, it can elicit disgust.

As a young man, a friend, Neil, travelled in Italy and was confronted while dining in a family home with a leg of wild boar, complete with skin, hair and trotter. Neil admitted that he found being served slices of ham from this all too real limb was . . . challenging.

Decades later, he still has pride in the ability he showed at the time to suppress his gag reflex. My own response as a twenty-something-year-old to being served a sausage made from pig's intestines at a restaurant in rural France was not dissimilar. I lacked the necessary French language skills to know what le plat du jour was, but the obvious 'anatomical-ness' of what I was served set alarm bells ringing immediately. I suspect, too, that many of us might have difficulties with dining on the Ecuadorian delicacy 'cui'. These fine little animals, guinea pigs to you and me, are roasted and served whole, with dried eyeballs, little teeth and sharp nails intact.

There are other reasons, too, why the most common disgust elicitors are meats and meat products. Signs of spoilage in meat are far more indicative of the potential for food poisoning than they are in vegetables or fruits, given the risk of the presence of harmful bacteria. Neophobia is also strongest for novel foods of animal origin, as we saw in chapter Three, and this is sometimes due to the disgust these foods elicit. These are rejected because they are not only thought to be bad-tasting but also potentially dangerous.

Contaminated

In a classic cartoon, a waiter removes a fly from the soup he has just served, but reassures the diner that it will not have drunk much. The cartoon is (or was) funny precisely because the waiter has missed the point: the soup is now inedible. This illustrates a key feature of many disgust items, especially those associated with animals or waste products. This is their ability to contaminate food, rendering an otherwise acceptable food inedible merely by being in contact with it, no matter how briefly. Once in contact, the impact of waste products and other unacceptable items such as insects on food can never really be undone. So . . . once in contact, always in contact, and your mushrooms will not suddenly be made edible once the chef removes the maggots. Darwin's account of the contact with the Tierra del Fuegan also reveals not just the social values of his day, but also the feeling of contamination that his touch would bring. Note that it is not a worry about the food being unhygienic as a result, since he notes that the man's hands do not appear to be dirty. Instead, there is the implication that contact with his mere savageness could make the meat unfit for eating.

Contamination contact can even be symbolic. Foods can be made undesirable when they have some superficial similarity to something that *would* elicit disgust if eaten. Hence, given a choice, we are more likely to want to eat a chocolate in the shape of a rabbit than one shaped like a cockroach. Similarly, ketchup on a sterile bandage or apple juice in a sterile bedpan are able to elicit disgust even though, rationally, there is no danger of either a bad taste or genuine contamination.

While contamination through consumption may be the origin of the emotion, disgust may be too important and useful to be confined to foods. Sitting next to someone on a bus whose standards of personal hygiene are low, especially if body odours are evident, can be a potent elicitor of disgust. How else would we express our feelings of repugnance at our smelly travelling companion? By themselves, neither sadness nor anger nor fear feel suitable. The same is true of our responses to someone showing obvious signs of injury or disease, or someone engaged in a behaviour that is morally or sexually unacceptable. None of these examples fit within the concept of core disgust – that is, associated with the consumption of something offensive. Therefore the emotion that is core disgust may have been co-opted through social evolution as a way of registering and conveying to others situations, people or behaviours that are offensive in general.[8] This function may also be part of a broader means to preserve moral values within a culture.

Food-related and other forms of disgust do share common features. The idea of contamination is still important. A smelly person may be unwell and contagious, as may someone with skin lesions. The fear of contamination may not necessarily be rational. Many people will be reluctant, for example, to wear an item of clothing that once belonged to a mass murderer, no matter how convinced they are that the garment has been thoroughly cleaned. There are nevertheless differences that suggest perhaps that the core disgust is a purer expression of this emotion. From the point of view of subjective feelings, core disgust seems to exist as a central, emotional 'gut' response that occurs automatically. Items that induce moral disgust tend to be associated with a range of emotions, including sadness, anger and contempt, that may require some evaluation and consideration of information: 'Is that politician really telling lies? If so, I am disgusted.' The only other emotion reported to be associated with core disgust is fear, which makes sense in terms of perceived dangers of contamination.[9]

Dis-gust and Dis-ease

The notion that disgust might signal danger underlies another interpretation of the significance of this emotion. The central idea of disgust is as a response to the oral incorporation of something that is offensive. But this is essentially a descriptive explanation that does not reveal an adaptive purpose for the emotion itself. If this emotion is universal, then the experience and expression of it must convey some advantage that aids survival. One such view is that disgust has evolved as an emotion that engages behaviours that help to protect us against disease. The most potent elicitors of core disgust – faeces, blood, vomit, urine, spoiled food, dead bodies, obvious signs of disease – also represent a risk of contracting disease. It therefore makes sense to feel revulsion and seek to avoid such risks.[10]

This interpretation of disgust has been useful in explaining a number of different aspects of disgust, especially the observed gender differences. Women are not only more sensitive to disgust than men, they are also more able to recognize expressions of disgust in others. The ability to know in advance if a food is contaminated by observing the expression of others obviously confers a degree of protection both to the mother as well as to young children in her care. Heightened sensitivity to disgust occurs during the first trimester of pregnancy, especially with respect to foods. Arguably, such sensitivity confers protection to the foetus at its most vulnerable stage. Disgust as an aid to reproductive success is seen in the increase in disgust sensitivity around the time of ovulation, but only for sexually related activities. The argument here is that some more 'unusual' sexual activities are those that are less likely to be related to reproduction, and it is these activities that will elicit disgust.

It is also observed that disgust is especially potent when the source of the disgust is a stranger. This is nicely illustrated by surveys that ask about how disgusted you would be by using another person's toothbrush. This produces very high levels of disgust for complete strangers, and relatively low levels with partners, decreasing the more familiar you are with the toothbrush owner.[11] This effect of familiarity can be explained by the risk that strangers pose in spreading disease to which you have no pre-existing immunity. This is a blunt instrument, but being conservative to avoid disease is a good survival strategy if you have little actual knowledge of whether or not a stranger does represent a risk.

Most intriguingly, the disease hypothesis seeks to explain that signals of disease – and especially textural cues, whether visual, tactile or auditory, that accompany disease or contamination – should be the best elicitors of disgust. So, for example, visible signs of disease may involve changes to skin texture. Thus sores are often associated with moist secretions that might suggest the type of slimy or soft textures that can be associated with disgust in foods.

Development of Disgust

Like other apparently universal emotions, disgust is recognized across cultures. This raises the question of its origins. Is disgust innate, like the positive emotions generated by sugar in the newborn? This question really has two parts. First, is the disgust *expression* innate? The answer to this question appears to be yes. This is illustrated by the fact that the characteristic disgust face can be observed in people who are congenitally blind, and thus have had no opportunity to learn how to respond. It is also strongly indicated by both Darwin's observations in Tierra del Fuego and the studies of Fore tribesmen in New Guinea. Hence it is not unreasonable to suggest that the expression of disgust is genetically programmed. Its adaptive value will have been as a way of communicating within social groups the potential danger in foods, perhaps even dating from prior to the acquisition of language.

Second, we can ask if there are certain things that elicit disgust innately, in the same way that bitterness produces the same expression of rejection in newborns and adults alike. That disgust is elicited in similar ways and to a similar degree in parents and their children could indicate a genetic inheritance of disgust sensitivity. However, the weight of evidence points to a primary role of learning in deciding what will elicit disgust. A number of studies have clearly outlined the developmental pathway in children and shown that it involves transmission by parents of the conditions under which the expression of disgust is appropriate.

The development of core disgust seems to occur some time after about the age of two. This is around the same time we can observe the start of the development of dislikes to odours that reflect decay. There is some debate, though, about how early the notion of contamination develops. In one study, children were told a story in which disgust items (faeces and an insect) are placed in a drink.[12] Children younger than seven years old were not willing to accept a drink that contained either item, and were aware that when the item was in the drink, it might make it both bad-tasting and harmful. However, they indicated that they would accept the drink once they had been told that the item had been removed. This suggests that they are unfamiliar with the idea of residual contamination. Above this age, though, the idea that such a drink might still be unsuitable to consume is increasingly expressed. In contrast, a study with three-year-olds found that they were able to reason that a drink from which a cockroach had been removed might still make them sick.[13] If the identification of disgust items and the notion of contamination are learned from parents, however, it is easy to account for such variation in terms of different degrees of disgust sensitivity in the parents.

Irrespective of whether it is associated with notions of contamination or not, we can see that core disgust to food and disgust to other items develop at different rates. Parents presented with a series of short stories containing disgust items and asked to report their own children's degree of disgust identified the presence of core disgust at around three years of age. Other types of disgust, for example those related to animalness or unacceptable behaviours, are seen later, on average at the ages of four and seven respectively.[14] This strongly supports the notion that we learn to apply the emotion first to foods, and then broaden it as we are taught to recognize other offensive items or behaviours.

A subsequent study provided a clear illustration of how the learning might occur. Taking children aged two to sixteen and their parents, the researchers presented actual items that they expected to elicit disgust, recording and coding the facial expression of both parents and children. Disgust stimuli included not only items related to food (ice cream covered in ketchup), but also those related to a number of other probable disgust elicitors, including those related to contamination (a potty in which they placed a sweet), animals (a jar of worms) and body products (faecal and urine-like odours). The parents' disgust faces were most pronounced with the youngest children, suggesting that they were deliberately exaggerating their own expressions of disgust as a form of explicitly assisting their child to attach the expression to the item. The outcome of such emotion modelling is seen in the presentation of a (new) potty containing the sweet. Each child was asked if they would be willing to take out the sweet and eat it – a clear test of their ability to understand the idea of (symbolic) contamination. Parents whose children refused to take out the sweet showed much greater expressions of disgust than those whose children were willing, as did the children themselves.[15]

This process of the socialization of disgust can be seen as a way for the parent to protect their child once they have reached an age (from two to three years onwards) where they are likely to come into contact with potentially harmful substances. In this regard, disgust functions much like neophobia. In addition, though, it builds upon the fear of novelty. How else can a child learn to reject a familiar and delicious food that has fallen into the gutter? At this stage, when the child largely inhabits the orbit of the parents, only simple rules are needed – if it contacts the ground, it is no longer food. The regular pairing of the disgust face, perhaps with loud exclamations of 'Yuk!', with now filthy biscuits or sweets or fruit provides the toddler with a rule by which the food can change, but the principle remains the same: contact with the ground or dirt or anything else is yucky. Older children can grasp the more abstract concept, namely the idea of contamination, as this allows them to deal with novel scenarios that they might encounter at school or elsewhere.

In essence, there appears to be an innate preparedness to experience and express disgust. However, those things that elicit disgust are learned from parents, who in turn reflect, to a large extent, cultural norms. That there are apparently some 'universal' disgust items such as faeces and rotting flesh does not mean that learning does not occur. Rather, it more likely reflects that there is universal recognition that such items carry high risk of disease, particularly if there is any possibility of consumption through contact with foods. Learning also allows for flexibility regarding what might be rejected as disgusting. Disgust and neophobia are intimately connected precisely because it makes sense to fear those things that might possibly result in contamination. Increasing experience, on the other hand, allows us to refine the list of items that might be genuinely concerning versus those that merely seemed 'gross' initially. Neil, for example, has no problem these days eating meat cut from a leg to which the skin is still attached because he is now aware that this method of food presentation is culturally based. He has embraced, in other words, his inner animal.

EIGHT

You Eat What You Are

A Bitter Taste in the Mouth

Oliver likes food. This twenty-year-old student will happily accept invitations to dine at ethnic restaurants, and does not shrink from trying odd-sounding dishes that may contain strange animal parts. In fact, his favourite restaurant advertises itself as offering 'dining from nose to tail'. Obviously, for him, neophobia is not an issue. Nevertheless, his food preferences have their limitations. He is reluctant to eat very spicy dishes, no matter how much his curry-mad friends try to persuade him. He has tried coffee, but finds it just too bitter, even with some sugar added. Cheese is fine, if it is mild in taste, but olives are off the menu. Other food items on the reject list include anything that is too sour or tart, too bitter or just very strongly flavoured. He quite enjoys a few kinds of beer, but many more bitter beers and ales such as Guinness are out of the question; vodka, Scotch or other spirits have simply too much 'bite' to be palatable.

It is not that Oliver has not been exposed to a wide variety of foods at home and elsewhere – his parents love to cook and also took him to restaurants from a very early age. What distinguishes Oliver from many of his friends is his taste anatomy. He has an unusually large number of taste buds, contained in the fungiform papillae on his tongue. In addition, he has a particular version of a specific taste gene (known as TAS2R38). This gene can be expressed with three distinct structural variations, and Oliver has the one that is present in around 20–25 per cent of Western populations. In recent years, those with combinations of this gene structure and a high density of taste buds have come to be called *supertasters*.[1]

Prominent taste scientist Linda Bartoshuk, of the University of Florida, has for some decades been researching the nature and implications of individual differences in taste perceptions. She and her colleagues initially identified those supertasters like Oliver – as well as the complementary non-taster and medium taster groups – based on tasting and rating the intensity of two compounds with similar chemical structures, phenylthiocarbamide (PTC) and 6-n-propylthiouracil (PROP).[2] For many of us, and in particular for those who are supertasters, PTC and PROP are extraordinarily bitter. For non-tasters, at the other end of the taste spectrum, they have little or no taste at all. Bartoshuk's conclusion was that we do not all inhabit the same taste worlds. If we use a colour analogy, if I am a supertaster and you are not, it is as if when you see pink, I see red.

It has long been known that we vary from one another in taste sensitivity. Almost 200 years ago, the French philosopher of food and eating Brillat-Savarin noted in his The Physiology of Taste (1825) that 'anatomy teaches that all tongues are not equally provided with these papillae, and that one tongue may possess three times as many as another . . . the empire of taste also has its blind and deaf subjects'.[3]

But the existence of these relatively insensitive non-tasters – also around 25–30 per cent of Western populations – was accidentally discovered in 1931 by A. L. Fox, a chemist with the Dupont Company who was synthesizing PTC.[4] Fox's discovery prompted widespread testing of the ability to taste this compound, including studies of the heritability of this taste trait. It was thought that the inheritance pattern was Mendellian, like eye colour. However, the fact that non-taster parents can have taster children means that the mechanism is somewhat more complex, and still incompletely understood.

The non-taster's experience of taste qualities is overall less intense than 75 per cent of the population. By default, then, around half of us are medium tasters, sitting between the non-taster and super-taster extremes. In reality, classifying everyone into one of three groups suggests stricter divisions in terms of what is perceived than in fact exist. The 'typical' medium taster is simply relatively more sensitive to tastes and other oral sensations than the non-taster – PROP can still be moderately or even strongly bitter – but much less so than a supertaster. But the differences can still be dramatic. In my university classes, I often include a demonstration of PROP sensitivity. Recently, one student thought that the PROP solution was plain water. In the same class, another student took the solution into his mouth, a second or two passed, and suddenly his eyes bulged and his face turned red. Without waiting to rate how strong the taste was, he ran to the sink to spit out the offending liquid and spent the next five minutes rinsing and re-rinsing with water. Needless to say, his subsequent rating of the PROP bitterness identified him as a supertaster.

So why is the bitterness of these compounds interesting? Neither is contained in the foods we eat. However, different sensitivities to PROP or PTC are a straightforward way of identifying both variations in taste bud numbers and the presence of different variants of the TAS2R38 gene. In particular, the density of taste buds on the tongue varies quite substantially from person to person. The picture below shows the densely packed fungiform papillae (structures that contain the taste buds) of a supertaster contrasted with the sparse, widely distributed papillae of a non-taster. Increasing numbers of taste buds mean that all tastes are increasingly intense because our perception is based on the total number of taste receptors stimulated. While a classification of supertaster or non-taster might typically be defined by the intensity of PROP or PTC, it relates to overall sensitivity to taste because sensitivity to the bitterness of these compounds and number of taste buds are reliably associated. Hence, someone who rates the taste of PROP as very strongly bitter will also typically have a large number of taste buds that are responsive to all taste qualities.[5]

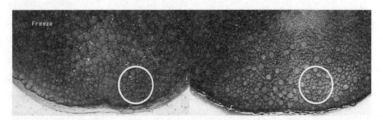

Photographs of human tongues after the application of blue food dye. Since the circular papillae that contain the taste buds stain less well than the tongue surface, they become easier to see against the background. The circles drawn on the tongues are of the same area but enclose far more papillae on the tongue of the PROP supertaster (left) than of the non-taster (right).

PROP tasting can also be used to identify those who are most sensitive to tactile sensations in the mouth, as for example in different food textures or different degrees of heat in spicy foods. This is because nerve fibres within the tongue that are responsive to pain, heat and touch tend to be present wherever there are the fungiform papillae that contain the taste buds. PROP supertasters are therefore also more sensitive to the burn of chilli, the bite of sharp cheese or strong alcohol, and even the bubbles in fizzy drinks and the creaminess and thickness of desserts. The more intense such tactile sensations become, the greater the differences seen between the different taster groups.[6] We can expect, therefore, that highly pungent foods – typically those containing chilli or other hot spices – will be perceived as dramatically different, depending on your taster group.

So far in this book, we have considered the mechanisms by which foods come to be liked. In doing this, an assumption has been made that everyone is pretty much like everyone else in what they perceive in foods. Why then, when you and I are more or less equally exposed to a particular food, do you develop a strong preference while I remain uninterested, or perhaps even have a dislike of that food? A major part of the answer to this is that, while mechanisms of exposure and learning may operate on us all to influence food likes and dislikes, we are not all influenced to the same extent. The reason why genetic variations in the expression of taste receptors, and in numbers of taste buds, are important to understanding food preferences is that these variations to perception translate into differences in food likes and dislikes.

The ways in which bitterness sensitivity or sensitivity to strong sourness or pungency influence food preference are complex. Most obviously, foods that are high in these qualities may simply be unpalatable. Oliver and other supertasters will find a variety of foods unpleasant to begin with that non-tasters, and perhaps even many medium tasters, will not. As a result, the more sensitive you are to PROP, the more food dislikes you are likely to have. Those with high sensitivity will be particularly reluctant to consume any food that is significantly bitter or intensely flavoured. This includes beer and other alcohols, coffee, grapefruit juice, and even Brussels sprouts, broccoli and spinach. The bitter taste of these green, leafy vegetables, as well as that of some other vegetables and fruits, is the main reason why they are rejected by some people. Even in children as young as three years old, dislike of vegetables such as raw spinach and broccoli is predicted by the ability to taste PROP.[7] The impact of this can be seen in the fact that, given a choice of vegetables to consume, non-taster children will eat a larger range of vegetables, including those that are considered bitter. In effect, there are fewer hurdles for the non-taster to overcome in accepting foods that are bitter, sharp or burning.

Lower taste bud numbers will also make you a less fussy eater overall, since you are also less sensitive to *variations* in taste qualities within foods. But is this really an advantage from an evolutionary standpoint? Since it is adaptive to be maximally sensitive to bitterness to avoid toxic plants, why have the non-tasters not all died out? The most obvious explanation is that taste sensitivity is always a trade-off with food availability. Since not all bitter compounds in foods are toxic, or at least not at the levels at which they are found in the food, being less sensitive opens up more potential food sources. In some environments, this may have been crucial to survival.

Beyond such distant considerations, are there still advantages in being a supertaster? Do they make great chefs, or product developers, or wine judges? There has certainly been an increasing recognition in the food industry that PROP-tasting might be a worthwhile screening process for the expert panels that make judgements about the sensory properties of different product formulations. A recent finding that wine experts tended to rate PROP as more intense than do regular wine consumers suggests that those in occupations where ability to detect or discriminate tastes and other oral sensations is crucial may 'self-select' such occupations partly because of their abilities.[8] Whether such sensitivity would make a better chef, though, is debatable. It seems unlikely that a chef's success could be attributable to cooking with more subtlety than could be appreciated by a majority of their diners.

PROP tasting may also underlie the strength of feelings of disgust. In chapter Seven, I discussed the idea that core, visceral disgust may have 'evolved' from our innate responses to bitterness. Support for this notion has come recently from a study revealing that increasing scores on scales of visceral (as opposed to moral; see below) disgust are associated with sensitivity to the bitterness of PROP.[9]

In a diet that contains very many alternative foods, fundamental variations in taste sensitivity will dictate to some degree which foods get selected. In a choice between eating a bitter, leafy green such as cabbage or spinach and an alternative such as beans or peas, a super-taster will likely choose the latter. On the other hand, those less sensitive to bitterness might be just as likely to choose one or the other. In circumstances where a dietary choice is more limited, say in a culture with relatively few protein or vegetable sources available, such variations may be less influential. For instance, if I am a super-taster living in a culture that consumes chilli every day, avoiding chilli may not be an option, no matter how sensitive I am to the burn. Nevertheless, I can moderate the amount of chilli I consume, and it is certainly the case that even among very regular chilli-eaters, there are variations in how much heat is preferred.

Even so-called 'moral vegetarians' – those who reject meat because of concerns about animal welfare – may be doing so unwittingly because of their sensory responses to vegetables. Recent research has suggested that this group may in fact be less sensitive to the bitterness that is present in some vegetables such as spinach and Brussels sprouts. Moral vegetarians appear to like and consume bitter vegetables more than non-vegetarians, but there are no differences between these groups for other vegetables.[10]

Some of the consequences of variations in bitterness sensitivity are seemingly paradoxical, but in fact reflect the complexity of the interactions of tastes with one another. For example, sensitivity to PROP is associated with increased salt intake, even though salt taste is more intense for supertasters. One explanation for this is that, in foods, salt is very good at suppressing bitterness, in just the same way that a sweet taste makes lemon juice less sour. Supertasters' enhanced salt preferences are therefore really about helping to reduce bitterness in many foods.[11]

All this does not necessarily mean that your taster group – whether non-taster, medium taster or supertaster – entirely governs your food preferences, or ultimately your diet. The first time that Oliver tastes many of the more 'serious' beers is unlikely to be a pleasant experience because of his sensitivity to their bitter taste. But he may persist, motivated by the sense of belonging to his peer group that drinking beer provides. He might also be willing to be persuaded to suffer the pain of a curry for much the same reason. We would then expect that the effects of exposure and post-ingestive learning will operate as usual to produce a liking for these flavours, despite their bitterness or pungency. But if sensitivity to bitterness is a hurdle to be overcome, as we might expect with supertasters, then it is probable that many others might simply decide after sampling once or a few times that beer is not for them. Numbers of taste buds are therefore not an absolute determinant of food preferences for any given individual. However, when we consider whole populations, it is evident that these taster groups are associated with different patterns of food preferences.

In the scientific literature on the determinants of what we eat, there is a vast amount of published research about the various influences on food *choice*. Socio-economic status, education, age, sex/gender, biochemistry and genes are all shown to be influences, to greater or lesser degrees. Aspects of your personality will also shape your behaviour in relation to food. Hence the extent to which you are adventurous in your diet (that is, whether or not you continue to be highly neophobic after childhood) will determine those foods with which you come into contact.

But, increasingly, we are discovering individual physiological differences that, like PROP sensitivity, are likely to be important reasons why we vary from one another – and perhaps from culture to culture – in the foods we like. Just how important is as yet unclear, but it is certainly possible that these individual differences may help to explain not just preferences but also susceptibility to obesity.

It may be that the intensity of a taste that is considered ideal is essentially the same, regardless of whether I am a non-taster or a supertaster. But if this is true, then I will need a different formulation (more fat or less fat, for example) to achieve the same perception depending on my PROP status. This has important public health implications. If, as a non-taster, my preferred level of sugar or fat is relatively high, then this is clearly an obesity risk.[12] This has been borne out by studies showing a relationship between PROP intensity and body mass index (BMI), the standard measure of weight relative to one's height. The less intense I find PROP, the higher my BMI. Simply put, tasters, especially supertasters, tend to be thinner than non-tasters. However, while that seemingly puts the supertaster at lower risk of obesity and its health consequences, the news for them is not all good. The sensitivity of the supertaster to bitterness means that they will tend to avoid not just bitter coffee, for example, but also those leafy green vegetables such as spinach.[13] These contain antioxidant flavonoids, thought to be protective against a range of cancers. Moreover, if, as a supertaster, I reduce my intake of vegetables because I find many of them bitter, then my replacement might be a higher consumption of meat, with an associated higher fat intake, or carbohydrates.

The Sweet Tooth

As noted earlier, the reason why variations in sensitivity to tastes and odours is important is that there is very often a relationship between how intense a food quality is, and how much we like it. This is the main reason, for example, why PROP tasters have more food dislikes than non-tasters. It is also generally assumed that the relationship between the intensity of a taste and the hedonic response to it is relatively uniform. Thus, liking for positive qualities such as sweetness will grow as their intensity increases, while liking for negative qualities such as bitterness will decline. Certainly, as far as we know, this is true at birth.

By adulthood, however, individual variations in the patterns relating intensity to pleasantness emerge for both saltiness and sweetness. It is not surprising that our food experiences over time modify our liking for particular qualities within foods. As adults, many of us have the experience of finding at least some foods *too* sweet. Thus, you may enjoy sweet wines, whereas I find them too rich. The same is true for very many foods. By asking a large number of people to taste and rate their liking for increasing levels of sucrose in water from very weak to very strong and combining their ratings, we will see a pattern of increasing liking up to about 10 per cent sucrose, followed by a very gradual decline at higher levels of sweetness. In other words, the most liked concentration is revealed to be 10 per cent sucrose, around the same sweetness as ripe fruit. As noted in chapter Two, this is part of the argument that the fixed responses to basic tastes are innate, because they were highly adaptive to our ancestors.

At least when we measure preferred sweetness intensities in adults, though, this figure is somewhat misleading. Citing the same most liked level for everyone gives the impression both that sweetness is universally positive, and that everyone's ideal sweetness level is about the same. However, because we are producing an average response, much the same pattern would be evident if some people continued to like increasing levels of sweetness above 10 per cent sucrose, while others found such levels increasingly too sweet. This division is essentially what is found if we look at each individual response to sweetness, rather than an averaged, or combined, response. As a result, a distinction in terms of sweet likers and sweet dislikers has been made.[14] The distinction is relative, of course, since individuals who actively dislike sweetness at any level are rare. Rather, if we look at liking ratings for increasing sweetness either in solutions or foods, some find their preferred level at lower degrees of sweetness, while others continue to find increasing sweetness palatable.

It is well known that only some of us have a sweet tooth. If you do not eat sweet foods very often, for example, any sufficiently rich dessert may seem very sweet. Importantly, however, and unlike responses to PROP, the sweet liker/disliker distinction does not appear to be associated with different degrees of sensitivity to sweetness. Instead it seems to be a consistent response to the pleasantness of sweetness. Presented with a particular intensity of sweetness, a sweet liker will typically find that level very pleasant, while a sweet disliker may either be neutral or show a dislike. The origin of these differences is yet to be properly determined. There is evidence to suggest that liking for strong, sweet tastes, and for sweet foods generally, is partly inherited, and a particular genetic basis for sweet liking has been proposed.[15] By contrast, such heritability does not appear to be true for responses to salt, even though we can identify individual differences in liking for different salt levels. Since, though, the sweetness hedonic response is not completely heritable, it does suggest that previous food experiences are also important.

Genetic variations such as PROP sensitivity and sweet liking exert an influence on food preferences through directly determining which food qualities will be acceptable. In addition, though, these variations influence how food preferences are *formed*. Consider, for example, that one of the ways that preferences for flavours arise is via pairing with already-liked qualities such as sweetness, as discussed in chapter Three. This assumes that sweetness is always positive. But the sweet liker/disliker distinction means that pairing with sweetness may, for some, not be quite as positive.

A study in which a novel flavour was repeatedly paired with the artificial sweetener saccharin showed exactly this.[16] Sweet likers developed a liking for the flavour, as expected, whereas sweet dislikers either showed no change in liking or actually came to dislike the flavour. Development of a dislike was especially evident in those individuals who were *both* sweet dislikers *and* PROP supertasters, primarily because the supertasters were especially sensitive to saccharin's slight bitterness. So, for the supertasters, the flavour was actually being paired with both sweetness and bitterness. The implications of such a finding are substantial because, while the mechanisms behind learned likes and dislikes are the same for us all, we cannot really predict the outcome of pairing tastes and flavours until we know something about a person's individual perceptual and hedonic responses to the tastes. So, not only may you and I inhabit different taste worlds, we may also follow distinctive pathways to food preferences.

Inheriting Your Menu

That a propensity to perceive tastes and tactile sensations as intense, or to find sweetness more positive, or to be more or less neophobic, can all be partly inherited raises the broader question of just how heritable food preferences are generally. In chapters Three and Four, we covered the mechanisms of food likes and dislikes from a mainly environmental – exposure and learning – perspective. But how could we determine if, for example, your liking for olives and that of your mother was due to shared experience of the flavour, perhaps even while you were in *utero*, or a genetic inheritance? On the face of it, the former seems much more likely, particularly given the substantial evidence for the effects of exposure and modelling on food preferences. In fact, studies often show that many of the food preferences of parents and children are not strongly associated. This is most likely for the good reason that the preferences of the parents have been modified by many more years of experience with foods.

Nevertheless, there is evidence of a genetic basis for preferences for specific food groups. One illustration of this came from a study of four- to five-year-old female twins, both monozygotic (MZ, or identical) and dizygotic (DZ, or non-identical).[17] The twins' mothers were asked to rate their daughters' liking for a range of 77 foods, grouped into fruit and vegetables, desserts and protein foods (fish and meat). Since MZ twins share both identical genetic make-up and an identical environment, while DZ twins share only an identical environment, it is possible to estimate the extent to which genes determine preferences. A key finding was not just that there was an inherited component to the preferences of these children, but that it differed according to type of food. The degree of heritability for desserts was smallest and quite modest, while that for fruit and vegetables was higher, but still only moderate. The protein foods, however, showed a strong heritability. In other words, the shared environment of the twins – and ultimately those learning and exposure factors already discussed – was most influential on the development of liking for fruit and vegetables and desserts. While this perhaps suggests that if your child eats only sausages, there is little you can do, it does also carry the message that preferences for fruits and vegetables (and desserts, too, if that is a concern) are open to influence through exposure and learning.

Heritability for specific foods was also evident in a study of a large sample of adult female MZ and DZ twins in the UK.[18] Based on questionnaires of the consumption frequency of a range of different foods, the most heritable food preferences were fruit and vegetables, garlic and coffee. This seemingly odd group can perhaps be best explained by considering whether the genetic inheritance in this case may have been related to taste (for example, inheritance of different variants of the TAS2R38 PTC/PROP gene or in the genetic control of taste bud numbers). Another instance of where the preferences of parents and children appear to coincide regularly is in liking for black olives. Bitterness is a component of coffee, olives and many fruits and vegetables, while garlic contains several pungent compounds that would be more intense to those with a high density of taste buds. While this is only one possible explanation for these and other inherited preferences, it is plausible given what we know about the impact of genetic differences in taste perceptions.

Genetic variations in taste sensitivity may not only explain person-to-person differences in food likes, but they could also be responsible for some of the differences seen between men and women. Surveys in both the US and UK show that sex differences in food preferences are evident prior to puberty, with girls showing greater liking for fruits and vegetables than boys, who in turn show greater preference for protein foods, particularly meats.[19] Again, though, the extent to which these differences reflect modelling, for example of the eating habits of same-sex parents, as compared to genetic inheritance, is not clear. However, it has been consistently shown that PROP supertasters are more common among women than men, again suggesting a plausible explanation for at least some gender differences in preferences.

How Do You Smell?

Since food flavours are distinguished from one another mainly by the odour rather than the taste, we might expect that sensitivity to odours varies from person to person as well. The wine judge may make some decisions based on taste or other oral characteristics – sourness, sweetness, astringency, for example – but what distinguishes a Cabernet from a Shiraz, or a Bordeaux from a Burgundy, is mainly the wine's 'nose'. Such experts seem to us to be far more sensitive to odours than the rest of us; the same also seems true of food or restaurant critics, and indeed expert tasters of any kind. This may be true, but before returning to this issue, we can consider the ways in which odour perceptions might vary among the non-experts among us.

Our sense of smell is quite sensitive to insult and injury. Whereas complete loss of the sense of taste is quite rare, there are estimates suggesting that around 1 per cent of the population in Western countries is *anosmic* – that is, totally without a sense of smell.[20] Anosmia can be produced in different ways, but chronic sinus or respiratory infections and head injuries are the most common.[21] Anosmic individuals can perceive tastes and textural food qualities. They may also still be able to detect some 'smells'. For example, the smell of peppermint is only partly produced by an odour; the cooling sensation it produces is due to the activity of tactile receptors in the nose and mouth that respond to menthol. Nevertheless, any pleasure derived from foods is dramatically reduced for the anosmic individual, and reduced food intake is often the result. Those who strive to cope with anosmia often try to compensate by increasing the sugar or salt or spice content of their foods to overcome food flavours' lack of impact.

While anosmia affects a relatively small percentage of the population, there are still a variety of ways in which the sense of smell can vary from person to person. Those in occupations in which exposure to certain chemicals is common often have some smell loss.[22] One of the more common 'environmental insults' to our sense of smell is, unsurprisingly, smoking. It is well established that smokers are less sensitive to smells and that the more you smoke, the less sensitive you are.[23] There is therefore truth in the idea that, for smokers, foods tend to taste more alike. Fortunately, those who quit smoking tend to improve in their sensitivity to smells, and presumably in their enjoyment of foods.

Somewhat less amenable to intervention is ageing. We do lose sensitivity in our sense of taste as we age, but it is much more pronounced for smell, and therefore for flavour. A study of a large group of Americans varying in age from 5 to 100 years old showed that our ability to recognize common odours will, for most of us, remain intact until about the age of 70. Thereafter the decline becomes steep.[24] Until recently, this sort of picture of decline might not have seemed particularly worrying. However, in many affluent countries, the average lifespan now exceeds 80 years. In addition, the over-70s will be both increasingly healthy and increasingly demanding in their wish to enjoy foods. While the causes of age-related smell loss remain unclear, the need to help ageing consumers maintain an enjoyment of food is now being recognized. This is especially critical in the institutionalized elderly or those living alone, where a lack of interest in foods due to smell loss means that weight loss becomes a significant risk for illness and injury.

One approach has been to try to enhance food flavours for at-risk elderly groups. The improvements in flavour due to increased umami taste increase acceptability and intake in those foods to which glutamate has been added. Because of this, the ability of glutamate to enhance palatability has been employed therapeutically to enhance food intake in elderly patients and improve their nutritional status as a result.[25] Even in healthy elderly consumers, the addition of glutamate to foods has been shown to promote both satisfaction with foods and increased food intake, and as a result improvements in overall health.[26] Of course, as with those who are anosmic, self-selected strategies that are less benign may be used. Increasing the use of salt, for example, may enhance flavours but may also increase the already high risk of high blood pressure in the elderly.

The changes with age in our ability to recognize odours and flavours has two slightly less depressing aspects. The first of these is that, as average age increases, so does the variability in smell ability from person to person. You may be fine therefore, while your friends continue to sniff without reward. In addition, though, the loss of smell as we age is less for women than for men – consistent with the commonly held view that women of all ages are in general more sensitive than men to odours. This view is based on more than anecdote. Women are, on the whole, better at both detecting and identifying odours. They also tend to find odours more intense than do men.[27] All of these findings apply equally well to both food and non-food odours. What this might mean for food preferences is not certain. As I discussed in relation to taste sensitivity, it may not be an advantage to be more sensitive to food odours. This seems to be the case, since women are also more likely than men to report many odours as less pleasant.

Are the differences between men and women in smell ability due to hormonal differences? This would seem a reasonable explanation, but even prior to puberty, girls outperform boys in odour identification. Moreover, while smell sensitivity fluctuates during the menstrual cycle, a consistent pattern has been difficult to pin down. Many women believe that they become more sensitive to odours during pregnancy. Certainly, the number of food dislikes and aversions does increase at this time, but there appears not to be an overall increase in sensitivity that applies to all odours.

One explanation for the greater odour sensitivity of women is that they may be more exposed than men to a variety of odours, and in particular food odours. This is because of the enhancement in sensitivity to a smell that occurs simply by repeatedly experiencing it. Thus, exposure improves our ability to detect and identify odours. One very intriguing finding has been that women benefit far more than men from this enhancement . . . but only for those women of reproductive age.[28] This suggests that both hormones and experience are important. It also makes evolutionary sense. The sense of smell is crucial in bonding to newborn babies and perhaps to reproductive partners as well.

There is little doubt that there is a wide range of sensitivity to smells overall. The National Geographic Smell Survey was conducted in 1986, with approximately 1.5 million respondents, each providing information on their ability to detect and identify the six 'scratch and sniff' odours included in the survey. Only two of these odours were food-related (banana and cloves), but the survey did reveal considerable variation from person to person in both odour ID and detection. Two of the other odours included in the survey provided strong support for previous observations that there are specific anosmias to particular odours. Such anosmias have been shown for a range of musky smells.[29] One musky odour used in the survey was detected by only around 70 per cent of US participants, compared to 98–9 per cent for some other odours such as rose. Another compound, androstenone, is well known to smell researchers and to pork eaters alike. It is the *animally* odour, generally considered unpleasant, often present in pork (including bacon) from male pigs. It can also sometimes be detected in truffles. Referred to as 'boar taint', androstenone smells like urine to some, like musk to others, and has no smell at all to around a third of those who sniff it.

Such specific anosmias are genetically based. Anosmia for adrostenone is, for example, found more commonly in both MZ than both

DZ twins.[30] But it probably has relatively little impact overall on food preferences, except perhaps in your degree of liking for pork. Yet there is certainly the possibility that your sensitivity to a wide range of food odorants does reflect genetic variations and ultimately influences what foods you choose. Our sensitivity to different odours varies quite considerably from one another, and even if you and I can both detect a smell or flavour in food, we probably differ in just how strong it is to us. A good example of this is cork taint (aka trichloranisole or TCA). TCA is responsible for the damp cellar smell that wine sometimes has, and its presence is the reason why wines are sometimes said to be 'corked'. This compound is undetectable for some, while others at the same table may turn their noses up even when the wine is being poured for someone else.

Repeated exposure can also be effective for those with a specific 'anosmia'. So, even for those who normally cannot smell androstenone, smelling it repeatedly can, at least for some people, 'restore' their ability to detect it.[31] This may not sound like a tremendous advantage, especially if you are a pork-lover. However, it does illustrate the important effect that experience with odours has on awareness of the odour's presence. Such experience has another effect as well. Since the vast majority of odours that we encounter in foods and elsewhere are mixtures, odours often have complex characteristics sometimes called notes. The notes sometimes reflect the specific odours in the mixture and sometimes are generated by the combining of the different odours in the mixture. Our wine experts, through experience, are much more able to tease apart these different qualities. In a sense, the wine flavour becomes more complex the more you are exposed to it.

There is a well-established philosophical viewpoint that our perceptions are shaped by the words we use to describe them. Certainly, we can see something of this in the other key aspect of food or wine expertise, namely the rich vocabulary that is used to describe odours and flavours. For the wine expert, learning to apply labels to odour or flavour notes in a wine enables those notes to be more evident and more identifiable when that same wine is encountered again.

Does this sensitivity and descriptive ability lead to greater pleasure in eating or drinking? Is it better to taste a nice red wine or a flavour redolent of ripe berries, chocolate and tobacco, with hints of sweaty saddle? There are good reasons for thinking that detailed analysis of a complex flavour might be incompatible with simple, direct pleasure.[32] Of course, wine and food enthusiasts may derive pleasure from the analysis itself. In current gastronomy, stellar chefs from the world of haute cuisine earn their reputations not from merely dropping something delicious on to your plate, but by dazzling the diner with wit, imagination and food combinations worthy of scrutiny (see also chapter Ten). It is pleasure of a more intellectual sort, but pleasure nonetheless.

NINE

Diner in a Strange Land

'Foreigners' certainly do eat a lot of strange foods. Anyone who has travelled off the beaten track will have odd, often disgusting, and sometimes frightening, culinary tales to tell. Consider the following account:

> In Chile, they love sea urchins that contain a lot of iodine. These preferred animals grow at the mouth of rivers that feed plants that use a lot of iodine. Here, sea urchins grow with a parasite spider that stays over their feeding tube or 'mouth'. To prove that the urchins when served are fresh (alive), the spider must still be around the mouth . . . moving and alive. I was invited to have lunch with a group of locals. Immediately I was offered a sea urchin and prodded to eat the spider first . . . While everybody was watching I had to taste and swallow the bitterest morsel I have ever had in my mouth! I was so disgusted that I asked for a bottle of wine, hoping that it would erase the taste . . . it didn't, so I asked for another bottle. When I finished I wasn't in any shape to tell whether the bitterness had subsided or not! *

What's so odd about this plucky traveller's experience is not just that sea urchins and spiders are Chilean delicacies, but rather that many of us would never consider consuming either of these – they

---

* With thanks to Andrea Marcello Ottolenghi for allowing his suffering to be used in a good cause.

are simply not recognized as foods. When we compare the differences between our own diets and those of cultures elsewhere – particularly those of different ethnic origins – it is obvious that food likes and dislikes are not merely variations on a universal theme. That is, culture does not merely specify whether you eat chicken or beef, or fish, or which vegetables you grow. While being omnivores allows us to select different fruits, vegetables and meats from an available range, it also allows us to decide what fauna and flora actually constitute foods. Few Westerners consider a walk along the seashore or riverbank as an opportunity to gather up delicious seaweed or tree root fungus. Yet both are a notable part of the Japanese diet. Similarly, a forest may contain potentially dozens of edible plant species, yet only a subset are likely to be recognized as foods in any particular culture. But, of course, the foods we eat can change, particularly as cultures interact with one another. This issue will be taken up later in this chapter.

The differences in food preferences between ourselves and those around us *within* the same culture are almost always less pronounced than dietary differences *between* different cultures. Paul Rozin, the well-known researcher in the psychology of food choice, has noted that if we want to understand any individual's food likes and dislikes, then knowing their culture would be the one piece of information that would tell us the most.[1] So what accounts for the sometimes dramatic cultural differences that we see in food selection? Decisions about what constitutes a food and which options are selected for consumption are, of course, overwhelmingly determined by availability, which in turn is a function of differing climatic conditions and physical geography. In cultures where protein has traditionally been relatively scarce, 'dining from nose to tail' is more than just a restaurant slogan. Such cultures frequently maintain as part of their cuisine an appreciation of animal parts – brain, lung, heart, intestines – that would be rejected elsewhere.

Nutritional needs play a part in food selection, in that the food sources highest in energy and protein can be expected to be selected, all things being equal. However, even given availability and nutritional demands, there are substantial determinants of what is appropriate to eat that are entirely cultural. Some of these are based on religion

– Jews do not regard shellfish as suitable foods, Muslims do not eat pork and Hindus refuse to eat beef. At one time, such restrictions may have had a practical or health-related rationale, but they have now been incorporated into cultural and religious practice, as a way of signifying that one is a member of a particular group. However, the complex interactions of all of these cultural and geographic factors over time means that it is impossible to completely trace the hows and whys of the cuisine that seems to be characteristic of any culture.

Ethnic Sources

Are cross-cultural differences in cuisines, then, nothing more than the fact that coriander grows wild in your country and parsley in mine? A starting point in trying to account for cross-cultural differences in preferences is to ask whether there is something about the food perceptions or sensitivities of different ethnic groups that allows either a greater tolerance, or, alternatively, promotes avoidance of specific food qualities. Perhaps if you eat bitter spiders, for example, you are not (among other things) particularly sensitive to bitterness to begin with. Or if, like many Japanese consumers, you are easily able to recognize a food that is high in umami, then it is reasonable to ask whether the Japanese palate is somehow naturally more finely attuned to this quality. We know that ethnicities vary in different ways that are primarily controlled by genetics, including skin colour, facial features and tolerance for certain edible substances such as milk and alcohol. Are there innate, genetic factors that determine differences between cultures in what is eaten or in the ways in which food preferences develop?

In chapter Eight, the variations between individuals in sensitivity to tastes, odours and textures that might lead to variations in food preferences were discussed. At least in the case of responses to the compounds PROP and PTC, often used as proxy measures for taste sensitivity generally, we know there are differences between cultures. In fact, the bulk of research on these compounds during the 1940s and '50s was conducted by anthropologists interested in how this genetically determined taste sensitivity could be used as a genetic marker for different ethnic populations. While this led to some unusual study topics, including comparisons of bitterness sensitivity in Koreans and Australian aborigines, most of these studies failed to shed light on culturally determined food preferences. More recently, studies conducted by food researchers and sensory psychologists indicate that the relative proportions of those who are insensitive and very sensitive to PROP bitterness can vary ethnically. Compared with population samples from Western countries (25–30 per cent), higher percentages of non-tasters have been reported in samples from India (50 per cent or higher), and lower percentages from China and Japan (10–20 per cent).[2] On the face of it, this *could* mean that a higher proportion of one culture may be more accepting of bitter foods than another, although it is too early to conclude just how influential this difference is. But such examples of genetic differences are un-common. As far as we know, most aspects of taste and smell *ability* are not highly variable across ethnic groups.

There is also a major issue of determining whether ethnic differences cause differences in the perception of foods or food qualities, leading to different likes or dislikes, or vice versa. Although it is plausible that major differences in diets lead to variations in sensitivity to the particular foods or food ingredients consumed, this does not appear to be the case with innate hedonic responses to basic tastes. Studies of groups of Australians, Taiwanese and Japanese consumers found that, despite their substantial dietary differences, all give very similar ratings to solutions of compounds representing the basic tastes – sweetness, sourness, bitterness, saltiness and umami. Across all these groups, liking for sweetness increases up to a point (around 10–12 per cent sucrose in water) and then gradually declines; by contrast, all groups show a steep decline in liking once the bitterness of caffeine, and to a lesser extent the sourness of citric acid, exceeds a very weak concentration.[3]

Overall, there is little evidence that people in different cultures innately perceive the majority of foods or food qualities in different ways. Or at least, it is unlikely that the differences between ethnic groups in the extent to which they are more or less sensitive to food qualities is the major determinant of what they eat or do not eat. Much more likely to be crucial for why cultures vary in their food preferences is their differing experiences with foods. Since exposure to food flavours, from in utero onwards, shapes our preferences, cross-cultural variations in consumed foods will also be crucial in shaping preferences in different directions. In turn, our experience with foods changes both our expectations for their taste, flavour and texture combinations and our ability to recognize and respond to those qualities. Thus experienced consumers can be really very sensitive to product variations, even if they have difficulty in saying why. As a consumer, you will know, for example, if the manufacturer has changed your favourite chocolate bar, even slightly. This almost certainly accounts for the apparent ease with which Japanese consumers can readily identify foods high in umami, just as it does a wine-lover's ability to reliably pick up subtle notes of 'slightly medicinal, reminiscent of cough syrup' in a wine. In other words, it is probably more likely that experience shapes sensitivity, rather than vice versa.

Illustrative of this is a study of the taste preferences of labourers from the Indian region of Karnataka, who frequently chew the very sour tamarind fruit as though it were confectionary. Their preferences also extend to levels of sourness (and also bitterness) in other foods that would be unpleasant for most of us. One explanation is that this group is innately less sensitive to taste overall – and therefore could tolerate the high levels of sourness. However, in this particular case, this hypothesis was not supported due to the finding of very similar responses to sweet and salty tastes to those shown in Western populations.[4] It is most plausible, therefore, that their tolerance for sourness and bitterness in their diet is a consequence of their frequent consumption of tamarind, rather than a cause of it.

Differences in prior experience with particular types of foods and the ways in which dishes are composed leads to quite different expectations cross-culturally about ingredients and food characteristics. For example, bean paste is often used as a sweet filling in Japanese and Chinese cakes. In many Western countries, this would be viewed as inappropriate, or at least surprising, since it is expected that bean will be a savoury, not sweet, filling. Even between cultures with similar ethnic backgrounds and cultural histories, the effects of experience are evident in sometimes subtle but crucial preferences for different versions of the same food. Hence whether you think eggs should be brown or white, butter white or yellow and pumpkin sweet or savoury, or whether or not you accept that cheese can be orange and without flavour, is a reliable indicator of whether you were raised in the United States or a variety of other Western countries.

In other cases, because of different histories of exposure, liked flavours in one culture may be perceived as unpleasant in another. The odour of lamb and mutton are highly liked in many Western countries but rejected in some parts of Asia. In China, the odour of these meats while cooking is often described using negative terms that translate as 'sweaty' or 'sour'.[5] The question here, though, is not why Chinese consumers dislike these odours but rather why anyone likes them. Smelled outside of the context of food, the fatty acid compounds responsible for the distinctive flavour of lamb, and especially mutton, are quite unpleasant even to lamb-lovers. It is therefore easy to see why such negative terms are used. But, if you experience these flavours from an early age, perhaps partly masked by herbs or the sauces that often accompany lamb, a preference for the overall flavour of lamb develops.

The differing experiences across cultures also shape just how sweet or sour or crunchy or spicy particular foods should be. For all of us, there is an ideal level for food qualities, sometimes referred to as a 'bliss point', determined once again by the level at which you have received most exposure. Above and below this point, liking drops away. In addition, our food experiences strongly shape the degree to which we find a quality to be weak or strong. Such context effects mean that, if our food is generally very spicy, or salty, or garlicky, then a food lower in these qualities is seen as bland and unappealing. To someone from another culture whose use of strongly tasting ingredients is more moderate, the weaker versions may still be experienced as intense. Similar context effects are commonly experienced when, for health or other reasons, we reduce our salt or sugar or fat intake. After only a couple of weeks without sugar in coffee or tea, even a small amount makes the drink unacceptably sweet.

Adding Spice to Life

Even if it amounts only to adding salt, food seasoning of some sort is practised in all cultures. This appears to be primarily driven by a desire to improve food flavour, rather than any practical reason such as food preservation. Some salt intake is physiologically necessary, and it was once used as a preservative, but this does not account for the fact that a majority of cultures use far more than is required to maintain health. In fact, most of us like to consume about twice as much salt as we need, elevating this common substance to the world's number one food additive. Intriguingly, salt preference in non-human animals is also known. One well-known instance involves macaque monkeys living on the Japanese island of Koshima. A particular monkey troop learned, largely by watching one of their members, that washing their favoured sweet potatoes in seawater rather than fresh water was preferable. That the macaques repeatedly washed the potatoes between bites led to the conclusion that the added salt was used to improve the flavour.[6]

More intense spices such as chilli are thought to be generally confined to humans, although there are also anecdotal reports of dogs learning to accept food containing chilli in cultures such as Mexico. Regular consumption of chilli, too, is a very obvious difference between cultures. Although chilli arrived from the New World via Europe, its uptake was much greater in countries throughout Asia, particularly in South East Asia. Now, at least 25 per cent of the world's population consumes chilli every day.[7] Are there good reasons for differences in preferences for the burn of chilli that are observed across cultures? Why was Thailand so keen to incorporate such a fiery ingredient into its cuisine and much of Western Europe not?

We know that regular chilli eaters – that is, those who consume chilli at least a few times a week – become less sensitive to the burning sensations. This decreased sensitivity, known as *desensitization*, occurs in all of us following consumption of very spicy foods. Eat something spicy, wait 30 minutes, and then the same food will be far less hot. Given that chilli is a daily condiment and ingredient in the cuisine of counties such as Mexico, Korea and Thailand, perhaps the consumers in these countries more easily become insensitive to the burn, whereas the delicate European palate continues to scream with pain.

A couple of lines of evidence suggest that this is not the reason for the differing uptakes of chilli. First, Western consumers increasingly love chilli. Adult Americans of European descent now consume more spicy salsa annually than they do ketchup. Moreover, our common view of Western cuisines as traditionally uniformly bland does not stand up well to scrutiny. It will be recalled that the planned destination of Columbus's voyage of discovery was to the East Indies, the source of highly valued black pepper, amongst other spices. It is a grand irony that he discovered the far more pungent chilli by accident in what became the West Indies.

And the Mediterranean cultures were not alone in valuing something spicy in their food. A French traveller, reporting back to those at home on English eating habits during the middle of the nineteenth century, commented that 'A man of substance will serve a salmon or sturgeon at least a metre long, with various sauces and peppery relishes in the English taste. Their flavour, to us, is most like swallowing a lighted firework.'[8]

While few would take the view that English food is currently one of the world's spicier cuisines, we can still see vestiges of a fondness for spiciness in the intense bite of English mustard. Recently, too, Britain's most popular dish was named: no, not *rostbiff* (a label for the English once disparagingly used by the French) but Chicken Tikka Masala, a curry dish with an entirely British heritage.

The other reason why differences in sensitivity to chilli burn are unlikely to be the factor that determines why only some cultures consume chilli in quantity is simply that chilli consumers do not dislike the burn. On the contrary, surveys of both Mexican and American chilli consumers have indicated that chilli is consumed *because* of its ability to add a 'kick' to food flavours. In getting to like food with chilli, it seems that we come to like the burning sensation even though it might have been initially unpleasant.[9] So spicy food is liked because of the burn, not despite it. If they have to replace chilli as a condiment, American consumers choose pepper rather than a non-spicy alternative. For those Western consumers who become regular chilli eaters, its pungency becomes an essential meal component. Foods that lack chilli spiciness are bland and unappetizing, perhaps due to a contrast between high-impact, spicy foods and foods that lack this impact. It may seem like masochism, but for some, a dish is not truly satisfying unless they are in pain and perspiring profusely.

Even those whose diet is relatively bland by 'hot food addict' standards would miss the enhancing effects of pungency were it absent from the diet. Part of the reason why low-salt foods are unappetizing is that they do not have the 'bite' that is produced by higher levels of salt. Similarly, low-alcohol beers and wines have failed to attract a wide following for their taste, primarily because of their low flavour impact. Like regular chilli consumers, the majority of alcohol drinkers consume because of the 'sharpness' of the alcohol, not in spite of it. Ginger, pepper, cinnamon, wasabi, garlic, onion and vinegar are crucial flavourings in very many cuisines, at least to some extent because they all add some form of pungency to food.

Even the very hot spices are finding a home in Western cuisines, partly due to the rapid expansion in the availability of a wide variety of Asian and Mexican cuisines. Adding to the long-standing and near ubiquitous Chinese (mainly Cantonese) foods in many Western societies has, in recent decades, come the chilli-infused cuisines of Thailand, Vietnam, Laos, Malaysia, Singapore and Korea, as well as regional cuisines from Chinese provinces such as Szechuan and Hunan.

Flavour Principles

While the cuisines of many different cultures are linked by their use of chilli, they are often substantially different from one another in ways that make each cuisine distinctive. This is, of course, very apparent to regular consumers of different Asian foods, even when similar meats and vegetables are used. A south Indian curry is very different from a Thai curry, even if they both include chicken and some hot spices. The reasons for this lie in those ingredients that add specific flavours. The Indian curry might include the flavours of ginger, cardamom, cloves, turmeric, whereas the flavour of the

Thai curry is often built on ingredients such as fish sauce, galangal and kaffir lime.

The use of characteristic ingredients reflects something more fundamental than merely varied cooking styles. In the early 1980s, Paul Rozin and his wife Elizabeth Rozin, a food writer, recognized that different cuisines could be described in terms of culturally specific *flavour principles*. They defined these as unique combinations of specific ingredients used across a variety of foods within a culture.[10] For example, a characteristic combination of ingredients in Japanese cooking is soy sauce, *mirin* (sweet rice wine) and *dashi* (a stock made from flakes of the bonito fish, which is high in umami taste). While Korea is geographically close to Japan, its flavour principles are very different, with the intense flavours of garlic, chilli, sesame and soy dominating many dishes. In Moroccan cooking, cinnamon, cumin, turmeric, ginger, paprika, coriander, saffron, anise, cardamom and other spices are combined into Ras El Hanout, a universal blend that renders the chicken, beef or lamb that it flavours characteristically Moroccan.

Each flavour principle is likely to have arisen through a combination of borrowing from other cultures together with availability of particular ingredients. But the end product is a description of the uniqueness of that cuisine. Preparation methods, too, are an essential part of a flavour principle. Fermentation, browning, smoking, marinating, stewing, frying in butter or oil, or burying in gravel for weeks are all methods of modifying the flavour of foods in distinctive ways. The combination of different ingredients prepared in different ways provides a characteristic flavour that unites foods within a culture, and identifies them as originating from that culture.

A key role of flavour principles is as a point of distinction from other cultures, even those that are neighbours. Flavour principles therefore not only define the national cuisine, but they also act as an expression of the individuality of the culture. As such, a cuisine can define a culture as much as vice versa. The importance of flavour principles to maintaining cultural identity is evident whenever there are significant movements of different cultures from country to country. Any Western city with a significant Chinese population (for example, London, San Francisco, Toronto and Sydney) will always have a Chinatown whose most prominent feature is its restaurants. The same applies wherever there has been substantial Italian, Greek, Lebanese, Indian or Korean immigration. Preferences for specific flavours can act, therefore, as a cultural bind and a signal that you maintain your cultural identity.

A characteristic and preferred combination of flavourings may provide variety and interest in diets dominated by bland staples such as corn or rice. However, a greater importance lies in the role of flavour principles in allowing for expansion in the range of foods to be included within the cuisine. This can help to ensure dietary variety and an adequate intake of nutrients. In doing this, flavour principles also address the problem of any neophobia that might be induced when incorporating a new food source into a cuisine. Since neophobia is largely based on fear of a food tasting unpleasant (see chapter Three), flavour principles can be seen as one way to address this problem at the level of a cultural group. The Omnivore's Paradox – the fact that the broad selection of potential foods open to omnivores can increase the potential for consuming something toxic – hinges on a need for a way of assessing the safety of any food. Using characteristic flavours is one means of providing a set of safety signals. Thus if goat meat is not part of your normal diet, its consumption may be initially a source of anxiety. However, pairing with a recognizable and liked set of flavours offers the consumer anxiety-relief in the form of familiar indicators that a food can be eaten without fear.

This explains how whole cultures can successfully incorporate new food sources, if circumstances suddenly change. If your staple meat is chicken, which your culture fries with vegetable oil, garlic, chilli and lemongrass, becoming vegetarian is not the only option if chicken is unavailable for any reason. The flavour principle – that is, frying in this particular combination of spices – allows a newly chickenless culture to start to consider other sources of animal protein (perhaps to the extreme consternation of local goats). Cooking in the characteristic spices identifies the new meat as part of your diet and allows the effects of exposure and conditioning to operate so that this new meat becomes preferred over time.

Since we know that our exposure to flavours while in *utero* has consequences for food preferences as infants and beyond, it is clear that the impact of flavour principles in shaping our preferences is operating at this point as well. It may be that prenatal exposure operates to ensure that the infant's preferences are in lockstep with those of the parents and the broader cultural group. As the infant develops into a child, flavour principles once again become important. When a parent pours fish sauce or tomato ketchup or any other familiar condiment onto their child's vegetables, they are effectively making use of a flavour principle that is already in the child's (admittedly rather limited) repertoire. This is a worthwhile strategy, too, since, as we found in chapter Three, familiar sauces do increase the willingness of children to consume novel foods that they might otherwise reject.[11]

One Flavour Principle to Rule Them All?

Increasingly, the food industry operates in a global setting. The mostly giant food companies that produce the products that form your daily diet are likely to have manufacturing plants in the USA, the Netherlands, China or India. In each of these, they will produce a range of identical products, sometimes irrespective of the culture in which they are to be marketed. This means that those foods that are purchased in your local supermarket are, or soon will be, also available on the other side of the world, perhaps within a culture whose cuisine is vastly different to your own. What will this mean for distinctive, culturally based flavour principles? Will cuisine-specific flavour principles ultimately be diluted or replaced? Some evidence suggests no.

For instance, the Japanese food market has been one of the export markets of choice for North American and European food companies for several decades. As a result, Japanese urban populations have long enjoyed wide access to foods from other parts of the world. Yet while rice consumption has fallen and red meat and dairy food consumption has increased in recent years, there is little evidence that more traditional foods are disappearing. While their teenage children consume Western-style hamburgers, the Japanese salaryman and -woman continue to eat a lunch of noodles or another identifiably Japanese dish. The broader picture here and elsewhere is of cultures willing to incorporate aspects of different cuisines into their own, as a result of trade and other cultural interactions. That 'traditional' Japanese dish tempura is thought to have been borrowed from the Portuguese during contact in the sixteenth century. A willingness to borrow from other cultures may account for the fact that recent assessments of the level of neophobia in Japan have shown it to be low relative to some Western countries, indicating perhaps the impact of exposure to a wide variety of foods.[12]

Over a long time-frame, all cuisines can provide examples of borrowing, and this is likely to increase as trade barriers decrease. For purists, perhaps this is a pity. However, much like language, a culture's flavour principle can be seen as an evolving process, open to external influences. One outcome could be dilution of that flavour principle, but another could be that the foods incorporated into the cuisine and its flavour principle might expand and evolve.

This latter possibility is suggested by the fact that Western food companies wishing to export to those cultures whose cuisines are substantially different are learning that incorporating aspects of the flavour principles of those cultures is essential for producing acceptable foods that local consumers will purchase. Food manufacturers often have to alter the composition of their products – or be selective in which foods in their range they export – to be able to successfully market them in other cultures. One prominent example is fast food companies such as McDonalds, who pay attention to the sorts of flavours that might be suitable for their hamburgers in their non-Western markets, and tailor meat marinades and sauces to the local palate. In Japan, this might be use of a teriyaki sauce, in China, chilli garlic, and in Korea, a bulgogi (soy, sesame and garlic) meat marinade.

However, varying products for export to foreign markets may not be quite as easy as simply identifying the ingredients that constitute a flavour principle. One of the issues that product developers face is determining exactly what qualities are valued in other cultures. When we refer to qualities such as orange flavour or saltiness, there may be little by way of ambiguity, even across cultures. But if it is not exactly clear what the quality of umami consists of, as was the case two decades ago, how do you know whether this is a crucial quality for Japanese consumers? Much like a novice wine drinker who can really only distinguish two varieties, red and white, the developer of a product for another culture may need a deep immersion in a culture's cuisine before being able to recognize the major qualities within a flavour principle, much less understand its subtleties.

Western cuisines have been similarly open to influence. To the average Western palate of the early twentieth century, Chinese or Japanese cuisine must have seemed extraordinarily exotic. Now, consumption of raw fish or steamed dumplings has long ceased to be on the eating fringe in most Western urban areas. Also, the range of green vegetables now available in the supermarkets of Europe and USA far exceeds that seen even ten years ago. These new varieties – for example, bok choy, choy sum, samphire and rocket – were not invented in the 1990s. Rather they were adopted from Asian and other cuisines as ethnic cooking styles and ingredients became more popular. If any trend is characteristic of Western eating habits in the recent past it has been the willingness to borrow from other long-established cuisines, particularly those in Asia.

The most obvious beneficial outcome of this has been an increase in dietary variety. Has borrowing from other cultures changed Western cuisines in more fundamental ways? There is no reason why the characteristic flavours incorporated into your traditional diet may not evolve over time. Even that bastion of the traditional, French cuisine, has shown itself open to influence from former colonies Vietnam and Algeria. Some of this cross-cultural influence can be seen in the international dining trend that has emerged in its wake, namely fusion cuisine (sometimes known by its Italian name, *con fusione*). While skilled chefs have found that such interactions can produce successful synergies, it has also led to flavour combinations that appear to have no heritage at all. The extent to which dishes such as foie gras sushi are signs of a lasting trend is unclear – but we should not give up hope just yet.

TEN

Future Taste: Art and Science

Because food preferences are no longer needed to assist us in maintaining an appropriate energy intake, for many, food pleasure is now tempered by fears that the dangers of obesity lie just ahead. Yet the decoupling of pleasure from nutrition has had other fascinating effects that are far less concerning nutritionally. Both food manufacturing and cooking have taken new directions in thinking about how desirable food sensory qualities can be delivered to consumers/ diners directly rather than as a by-product of the need to provide nutrients. At least in the world of gastronomy, there is now a freedom to explore concepts of food released from constraints of nutrition.

Taste without Calories

Low-calorie foods have not been the great success that might have been anticipated in the fight against obesity. This is at least as much through low consumer expectations as genuine flavour-related reasons. This has not stopped the food industry, motivated by perceived marketing opportunities based on nutritional concerns within the community, continuing to devote major resources in the quest for scientific and technological innovations that can make 'unhealthy' foods 'healthy'. Fortunately, they have also applied industrial ingenuity in dealing with the need to maintain food palatability in the face of demands for 'healthier' alternatives. Some of this research has focused on developing or utilizing existing substitutes for fats, sugars and salt that have all of the taste and functional (for example, required for cooking) qualities of the real thing. These applications have met with mixed success. Thus, although sugar substitutes have been used widely for several decades, efforts continue to find a low-calorie sucrose alternative that is a close match to this 'gold standard' but without any unwanted qualities like bitterness (saccharin) or astringency (aspartame).[1]

Both the industry and food researchers have recently focused on a new approach to developing foods that have reduced salt or energy but do not compromise taste. In parallel with ingredient and process approaches to delivering flavours, there has been a recognition that sensory properties of foods are not simply a function of the chemistry of the food itself, but are rather perceptual and hedonic responses from humans to the food. What do we know about human perception and how can this knowledge be used to deliver flavours that evoke pleasure?

Knowing that our brains, rather than our sense organs, are the source of our perceptions, of food or anything else, has important implications. Recognizing this simple fact allows us to ask whether we can manipulate perceptions to respond to reduced levels of energy or salt as though the usual amounts were still present. To do this, researchers have attempted to take advantage of some well-known features of human perception. One such phenomenon is *perceptual constancy*. This is our tendency to assume consistency in what we experience despite apparent changes in the quality or intensity of something we know to be constant. Even though the appearance of the walls in our house change as the light changes, we assume, correctly, that the paint colour has not become darker or lighter. In perceiving the colour, we take into account the ambient light. Similarly, we can increase the number of odour molecules that reach our smell receptors simply by sniffing more deeply. The brain, however, takes this extra sniff effort into account and, as a result, the intensity or quality of the smell changes little.

Perceptual constancy can also be relied upon to perceptually 'fill in gaps' in a way that is consistent with our expectations. Imagine biting into a sweet snack that was homogeneous in composition and texture. Your expectation would, correctly, be that the sugar is distributed throughout the snack, stimulating your taste buds to produce a sensation of uniform sweetness. However, if the same snack was made in multiple thin layers with only every second layer containing sugar, your brain would most likely 'fill in' the missing sweetness. This could potentially allow the manufacturer to eliminate up to 50 per cent of the product's sugar. One recent study found evidence of this effect in both tasters' self-reports and in imaging of their brains. When the researchers led the participants to expect to receive a very sweet drink (and relative to a 'no expectations' condition), they gave enhanced sweetness ratings to a less sweet drink, as well as showing increased activity in the primary taste area of the cortex.[2] Our expectations, in other words, can dictate our taste perceptions.

Another means of manipulating perceptions draws upon recent research on the multisensory nature of human perception, including that of flavours. As discussed in chapter One, what we perceive and enjoy when we eat is not a collection of separate tastes, odours and textures, but rather an overall quality, a flavour. Orange juice flavour appears somehow more than the sum of its parts. That is, during normal consumption, the different flavour elements – the orange odour, the tastes of sugar and citric acid, and tactile and temperature sensations – are highly integrated with one another.

One implication of this integration is that we commonly fail to make a distinction between odour and taste qualities within flavours. To some extent, this is why we often use the words taste and flavour interchangeably. In studies of other sensory systems – vision and hearing, for example – such multisensory integration is inferred from the influence of one type of sensory information on another.[3] For example, in a crowded room, speech comprehension is improved if we see the speaker's lip movements. A visual signal helps to effectively enhance an auditory one.

Tastes and odours, when they commonly occur together as a flavour, influence one another in a similar way. The most obvious expression of this influence is the attribution of taste qualities to odours. When asked to describe the odour of caramel or vanilla, most people will use the term 'sweet-smelling'; similarly, 'sour' is used for the odour of vinegar. This is not just an example of imprecise language (since specific odour descriptors are elusive) or even metaphor, given that the odour name is likely to refer to an object, which might also be sweet or sour. Rather it is a genuine perceptual effect that has measurable consequences. These odours, when added to tastants in solution, can modify the taste intensity.[4]

Enhancement of tastes by odours can be seen by putting a liquid version of a sweet-smelling odour (for instance, caramel, vanilla or strawberry) that has no taste of its own into a solution of sugar in water. This solution will be judged overall as sweeter than the solution without the odour. This phenomenon is both taste- and odour-specific. For example, the sweet-smelling odour of strawberry will enhance a sweet taste, but the odour of bacon will not. Conversely, a non-sweet taste, for example, saltiness, will not be enhanced by strawberry odour.[5] Of course, odours contain no calories, no matter how sweet they smell. This same principle has been used to add salty smelling odours (for example, soy sauce odour) to salty foods. The combined effect of the salty smelling odour and the food's sodium chloride means that the actual salt content can be decreased without any loss of perceived saltiness in the food.[6] The potential, therefore, is for the exploitation of the multisensory nature of our flavour perception to be used to deliver flavour perceptions effectively while reducing energy or salt.

At the same time as the implications of perceptual research are being explored, there has been increasing interest in the psychology and neuroscience of emotions. Part of this research has focused on the neuroscience of pleasure elicited by flavours and eating, including several of the phenomena described in earlier chapters. Distinct areas of the brain associated with liking and wanting have been investigated in animal studies, while brain imaging studies with humans have revealed activation of brain areas associated with pleasant and unpleasant flavours, as well as changes in human brain responses during sensory-specific satiety.[7]

Each of these approaches is in its early stages of application, and it is too early to tell if knowledge of neuroscience or human perception and emotion can contribute substantially to consumer acceptability of foods or translate directly into food applications. Equally, it could mark a turning point in how questions about palatable food flavours are addressed, simply because the focus has been shifted towards understanding how we perceive rather than on modifying the chemical ingredients in the foods themselves. Either way, it is clear that a fundamental understanding of the basis of human hedonic responses to foods and their sensory properties will be crucial in successful delivery of food pleasure without calories.

Some of this science, and in particular research on multisensory processes, has also had an impact in another, seemingly rarefied, quarter. At the same time as food manufacturing has started to pay attention to human perceptions in a more sophisticated fashion, we have seen the rise of *molecular gastronomy*, which is a singular example of food as a rational enterprise informed and inspired by the laws of physics, chemistry and perceptual psychology.[8]

There's No Taste Like Foam

At Britain's three-Michelin-starred restaurant The Fat Duck, the diner can experience 'Nitro-poached Green Tea and Lime Mousse'. This egg white concoction, flavoured with powdered green tea, is accompanied by a fine mist of lime odour sprayed into the air above the diner. The Fat Duck chef, Heston Blumenthal, created this mousse 'to be as light as possible, a fragile, evanescent thing that registered in the mouth and then – puff! – was gone'.[9]

The hidden surprise in this dish is the effortless way in which the textural and taste sensory properties of the light-as-air 'mousse' are combined with the lime odour to produce an integrated flavour. The diner receives a dramatic demonstration of a simple, but genuine, multisensory experience. And while the overall effect is also delicious, it has no purpose beyond this and no real nutritional value. It is as close as most of us have ever come to experiencing a flavour without a food.

It is hard not to be struck by the coincidence of haute cuisine restaurants using the same knowledge of multisensory perception that is currently being applied to address the food industry's dilemma over how to create palatable, 'healthy' foods. In restaurants such as The Fat Duck, and the equally acclaimed (but now sadly departed) Spanish restaurant El Bulli, the science of cooking – or rather cooking as a science – appears to have reached its apogee. Molecular gastronomy in its current form is very much a twenty-first-century phenomenon. Thus the 2003 edition of the *Encyclopedia of Food and Culture* contains no entry on molecular gastronomy. Molecular gastronomy restaurants are the antithesis of *La Grande Bouffe*, the 1973 Franco-Italian film in which four friends meet to eat themselves – in the nicest possible way – to death. This is cuisine that addresses flavour with barely a nod to energy or nutritional needs. Dishes such as the multisensory mousse are not only unlikely to be fattening, they often contain very little energy at all. Other Fat Duck dishes – while being more substantial in terms of nutrients – are no less inspired by science, with advances in chemistry from the laboratory (formerly the kitchen) aimed at influencing the sensory and cognitive psychology of the diner. Sensory pleasure is an important consideration, but there is an additional strong rationale for their existence, namely an appeal to our aesthetic sense, our intellect, and to a broader palette of emotions than simple sensory pleasure.

Blumenthal's dish 'The Sounds of the Sea', for example, uses the sound of waves on the shore (via an iPod hidden in a conch shell) to accentuate the visual presentation of seafood on a tapioca-based 'sandy beach', with a vegetable and seafood based foam as the rolling waves. The result is a multisensory immersion in sights, sounds, odours, textures and tastes with contributions from memories and emotions that are simultaneously evoked. One clear aim is hedonic, but it is at least partly pleasure based in memory, the evoking of warm feelings of nostalgia. It is ironic that such science-based approaches serve much the same function as the comfort food we might cook ourselves with much less effort.

Other dishes are based on well-known perceptual biases. We are poor at identifying flavours and we use visual cues as much as olfactory ones when recognizing foods. Understanding this means that apparently simple tastes such as an orange-flavoured jelly coloured a deep red, paired with a beetroot-flavoured jelly coloured orange, can arouse surprise, if not confusion in the diner, because of the conflict between what we see and what is tasted.

It is easy to be sceptical about the whole idea of dining trends that are far removed from anything to do with nutrition or the way we might eat day-to-day. And fashions have lifespans in cuisine just as in any area of life. Many will recall the fruit-and-meat combinations of 1970s nouvelle cuisine that are now most often put in the category of 'What were they thinking?'

Is molecular gastronomy any different? Does it actually have anything to do with everyday eating or how we will cook in future? Who knows, if The Fat Duck's Heston Blumenthal has his way, the twenty-second-century diner may recoil at the thought that bacon and egg are flavours for anything other than ice cream. More likely, however, is that its effects will be felt indirectly. The recipes of the world's stellar chefs are often so complex that attempting them outside of a commercial kitchen is not feasible. However, such chefs are clearly influential in terms of their ideas of what foods are, or should be. Already, less renowned chefs experiment with aspects of molecular gastronomy. The use of foams rather than traditional sauces, for example, has spread even to the characteristically conservative French cuisine. In contrast to butter, oil or stock-based sauces, a foam is little more than flavour molecules suspended in air and water. Its nutritional value may be close to zero – the culinary equivalent of homeopathy – but its sensory impact is preserved and sometimes intensified.[10] While, in future, the foam may come to connote an amusing dining excess, it already signifies the idea of flavour as a discrete entity, divorced from the food itself.

Molecular gastronomy has a *deconstruct* and then *reconstruct* approach. A deep understanding of the chemical processes involved in mixing chemical compounds to produce foods, and of the impact that various heating, cooling, drying and mechanical processes have on those foods, potentially allows a chef to work from first principles to construct something new. And, ideally, the new something should be both delicious and interesting. Of course, cooking in which entertainment value or intellectual, sensory or emotional stimulation is a consideration is not new. The extravagant banquets of past European royalty ('four and twenty blackbirds baked in a pie' is not only part of a nursery rhyme) is a well-known example. So, too, is Japanese *kaiseki* cuisine, an approximate equivalent to French haute cuisine, at least in terms of its approach to eating and artistic presentation. Kaiseki is derived from traditional aristocratic banquets, and is elaborate in terms of the sensory stimulation it provides. Apart from an artistic form of presentation, it also specifies that the courses should contain five colours (blue/green, yellow, red, black and purple), five flavours (sweet, sour, salty, bitter and hot) and eight types of preparation (raw, grilled, boiled, stewed, steamed, salted, pickled and dried). Where molecular gastronomy is different (although see below) is not just in the complexity of its ingredients and execution, but rather in its conscious directing of science towards achieving aesthetic and hedonic goals in cuisine.

All this science just to cook a meal? It could sound a little dystopian and reminiscent of the mid-twentieth-century slogan, 'Better Living through Chemistry!' Perhaps the future will consist (in addition to flying cars) of nothing more than adequate nutrition via the homogeneous pastes eaten by the astronauts in the Stanley Kubrick film 2001: A Space Odyssey (1968). Or perhaps popping a pill for our nutrition and dining on foam for sensory pleasure. A brave new world of food dualism: separate, distinct foods for the body and the soul. But it is also quite possible that molecular gastronomy might lead to thinking about taste in new, purely aesthetic ways.

Could art be based on taste? Taste and smell have long been considered, in scientific terms, the minor senses for humans. This is understandable since we are visually dominant creatures, evolved to use our sense of sight as a principal means of finding food and avoiding danger. Hearing, too, provides long-distance information that aids survival. But we trust vision most and we are excellent at linking this sense to our language capabilities. This is in contrast to our sense of smell. If I hold up a common object, for example, a pen, no adult will fail to identify it. Yet, as I pointed out in chapter One, only 41 per cent of a group of students could identify banana flavour. On average, sniffing common food odours gives only around a 50 per cent accuracy rate. It is clear that vision wins as a way of analysing our environment.

What arises from visual primacy is the traditional dominance of vision in artistic endeavour. Art as a way of representing the world, actually or symbolically, naturally relies on the power of vision to communicate. We have already seen food as visual art in restaurants. Japanese kaiseki cuisine, already mentioned, is a good example, as are the artful presentations that are part of French haute cuisine.

Molecular gastronomy is clearly part of a culinary avant-garde, but is it possible to consider it a part of an artistic avant-garde? In the same way that visual arts can influence our view of the world, the work of molecular gastronomy chefs will influence the idea of what it is to dine and perhaps even what constitutes a food (hopefully beyond the application of foams). In addition, though, could we consider molecular gastronomy as the start of a new aesthetic, one informed by science, working in the new medium of flavour?

It has been suggested that molecular gastronomy is a culinary equivalent of the Modernist art movement from the early decades of the twentieth century. Like molecular gastronomy, Modernism rejected traditional approaches (in their case, to art) and drew inspiration from science and technology.[11] But a closer parallel, one showing that radical reconsiderations of food are not new, might be with the early twentieth-century Futurist movement. A theme of the 1909 Futurist manifesto was to elevate aesthetic ideas to prominence in a variety of areas of art and culture, including cooking. The founder of the movement, Filippo Tommaso Marinetti, actually advanced the idea of obtaining nutrition in the form of pills, while food itself should have only aesthetic functions.[12] In many ways a distant echo of molecular gastronomy, Futurism exhorted cooking to break with the techniques and flavour combinations of the past and incorporate music and other sensory experiences into dining. Marinetti's *La cucina futurista* (1932) specified that sounds and lighting should be manipulated in such a way as to be in harmony with the food flavours. Most strikingly, from our perspective, was his insistence that traditional cooking methods should be replaced by techniques that employed equipment from the scientific laboratory.

Well-known author of the classic *Italian Food*, Elizabeth David outlined some of the more radical (at the time) Futurist dishes: Pineapple with Sardines; Fish Poached in Liquorice; and Cooked Salami Immersed in a Bath of Hot Black Coffee Flavoured with Eau-de-Cologne.* She also gives a vivid idea of the multisensory

---

* Just to emphasize the parallel with modern molecular gastronomy, note that only two of these are Futurist dishes; the other dates from 2003 and its recipe is included in *The Big Fat Duck Cookbook*.

nature of *cucina futurista*: 'Meals were to be eaten to the accompaniment of perfumes . . . to be sprayed over the diners, who, fork in the right hand, would stroke meanwhile with the left some suitable substance – velvet, silk, or emery paper.'[13]

There is more than a hint of Marinetti's ideas regarding novel flavour combinations, the application of laboratory techniques, and dining as a multisensory experience in today's molecular gastronomy. Most crucially, though, the two approaches are alike in their notion that there could be cooking that was primarily, if not entirely, an aesthetic enterprise.

Art is meant to stimulate the intellect and emotions and appeal to our sense of aesthetics. It should also confront expectations and preconceptions. With molecular gastronomy, science and new technologies underpin new ways of cooking and presentation to create dishes that challenge traditional notions of food and dining. But the science is subservient to an aesthetic based on taste and flavour, rather than predominantly vision. To some extent, a model for taste as art already exists. While perhaps we seldom think about perfumery as an art form, this may be entirely because of our biases towards thinking about art in visual terms.

Like never before, except perhaps in the case of Marinetti and his followers, the forefront of cuisine is currently an intellectual exercise. But molecular gastronomy also has the potential to give rise to the first *intrinsically hedonic* art form through the direct innate and learned links that smell and taste have to pleasure. Will it succeed? Marinetti's manifesto for Futurist cuisine was notably unpopular in his native Italy, perhaps because he suggested pasta eating should be made obsolete. His radicalism may therefore have doomed *cucina futurista* to a historical footnote. By contrast, molecular gastronomy has excited interest even in those who would seldom visit restaurants applying its principles. Of course, this has a lot to do with media coverage of molecular gastronomy chefs and their often appealingly quirky dishes. But in affluent societies, there is also a growing feeling that taste itself is now a sense worth paying attention to.

ELEVEN

Beyond Survival: Uncoupling Taste and Nutrition

Perhaps it has been a surprise to discover that, not only are your food likes and dislikes not random, but they are in fact underpinned by processes that have ensured our survival as a species. It could be argued that they are therefore as important in our evolution as toolmaking, upright posture and the opposable thumb. Congratulations, your enjoyment of doughnuts deserves an award! Do not celebrate too much, however. In the preface to this book, I laid out the paradox that our food preferences entail: they have been essential to our survival as a species, but yet they now appear to contribute to our individual demise. According to most informed medical opinion, affluent countries in the West are in the midst of an obesity 'epidemic'. This epidemic appears, too, to be reaching newly affluent consumers in China and India, where until relatively recently the only reports regarding food consumption were of under-nourishment.

So, are our food preferences now maladaptive? In one sense, yes. In early environments, there was no advantage in limiting energy intake through limiting food pleasure. What mechanisms that we have to do this – alliesthesia and sensory-specific satiety (sss) – operate only over the very short term, and in the case of sss is really only about promoting dietary variety. As I have noted in many places throughout this book, we have evolved to desire dietary sources of high energy which were once much scarcer than at present. Indeed, as we saw in chapters Three and Four, the whole basis of food preference development relies on flavours being paired with signals for calories (sweet; fat taste) or the calories themselves.

It is not that palatability is no longer an important aspect of food. We still need to be motivated to ingest energy as well as protein and other nutrients to maintain health. One consequence of a failure to find foods palatable can be seen in elderly institutionalized patients whose lack of interest in food often reflects the decline in their senses of smell and taste. Unfortunately, the result is often weight loss that renders this group susceptible to illness and injury. A similar pattern is sometimes seen in those who, through injury or illness, have permanently lost their sense of smell.

The paradox is really about our changing food environment, itself a consequence of affluence. In the current environment, increasingly for substantial proportions of the world's population, foods high in energy are both freely available and low-cost. Moreover, the food industry has grown the range and variety of high-energy foods quite dramatically. Think about the confectionery, snacks or ice cream products that you ate as a child. Even if that was two or three – or more – decades ago, you will probably find many of these still on the market. But they have been joined by dozens, if not hundreds, of other products in each of these categories, the majority varying only in relatively superficial ways in terms of flavour or texture.

Of course, this is only one part of the story, since weight gain is a function of violations of the apparently simple equation of *energy in = energy out*. In other words, understanding obesity requires awareness of energy expenditure as well as food consumption patterns. Not unreasonably, though, given our increasingly sedentary lifestyles, much of the attention directed towards solving the obesity epidemic has been placed on the 'energy in' side of the equation.

Research on the impact of learned preferences also makes it clear that the flavours not only become liked by pairing with energy but also become cues that engage wanting for foods, in particular palatable (often high-sugar, high-fat) foods. It is understandable, too, why we give in when confronted by palatable food cues. The idea of a *value discounting function* was introduced in chapter Six. This is essentially the finding that, if we delay reward, the reward becomes less valuable. But put another way – rewards experienced *now* are more rewarding – it gives us a clue to why immediate gratification is so powerful. Our food preferences therefore work within a very different time frame than do the anticipated consequences of eating solely in accord with those preferences. We can appreciate that those fried foods contribute too much to the waistline in the long term, but they are delicious now.

Indeed, given these conditioned responses to food cues, is there any hope for us to be able to resist? In the early decades of the twentieth century, Ivan Pavlov and behavioural psychologists such as B. F. Skinner and John Watson saw humans as essentially programmable machines to be shaped by their environments. In their interpretations of behaviour, we are all merely the sum total of the conditioned responses that we have acquired in our lifetime. This rather fatalistic view is seldom voiced today, having been replaced by a belated recognition that humans can actually think about their own behaviour and its consequences and modify it accordingly. Nevertheless, it seems short-sighted not to appreciate that, of all the conditioned responses that we do acquire, those involving foods are likely to be among the most powerful motivators of behaviour. Pavlov's puppies had no control over their saliva in the face of dog chow, so what hope do we have with chocolate?

We now find ourselves highly responsive to cues for the pleasures that foods provide – that is, they motivate us to eat – very often in the absence of any real need for the energy and other nutrients that the food provides. What tastes good and what is good for us have, throughout our evolutionary history, been linked. However, the decoupling of pleasure and nutrition has produced a range of consequences. The first of these consequences is that, shaped by the view of nutritionists and popularized in the media, we are increasingly putting foods into one of two incompatible shopping baskets – one containing 'delicious but deadly' foods and the other foods that are full of nutritional goodness and promote good health.

Step Away from the Chocolate!

The view of preferences as a problem primarily because of a clash with today's food environment is seldom explored as a reason for the nutritional problems of our age. Instead, our food preferences are treated as urges that must be modified or controlled. But, to make sure that the damage is limited when you inevitably do give in to the urges, we will change the foods. So the nutritional emphasis in the media is all about the food itself: there are good foods and bad foods, foods that are healthy and foods that are not. The idea that some foods are inherently 'unhealthy' is thriving. It is impossible to read any newspaper or magazine article, or watch any TV programme, dealing with nutrition and not come across the idea of junk foods. Inevitably, these are the ones high in fat and high in carbohydrates, especially sugars such as sucrose or fructose, or both. They are free of 'goodness', contribute to (bad) cholesterol and quite possibly make you hyperactive as well. Headlines such as 'Sugary Drinks Linked to High Blood Pressure' are typical of the key message about these types of foods that are conveyed to the general public.[1]

Convenience foods such as high-sugar breakfast cereals, high-sugar content drinks, salty and sweet snacks, burgers and other foods 'to go' are identified as culprits that are responsible for the 'obesity epidemic' in Western countries. The food industry clearly recognizes these and other high-sugar/high-fat foods as a public concern, and so in response are keen to promote alternative versions of their foods – 'diet', 'low carb', 'only 3 per cent fat' and so on. But navigating alternative versions of foods is not necessarily easy. No matter what food companies do, it is very unlikely that they will sacrifice the pleasure that the flavour gives, and therefore the food's consumer value. Low-fat versions of foods are often high in sugar, as are foods that claim to contain 'healthy' ingredients. Most importantly, perhaps, the industry continues to promote foods on the basis of their palatability. Food advertising is all about using cues to make you desire their food.

There are some inherent contradictions in the whole idea of 'unhealthy' foods. The first of these is that it is impossible to demonstrate that a given food, irrespective of its fat, sugar or salt content, has a harmful effect. This is in contrast to genuinely harmful foods that are contaminated by bacteria or contain an allergen or toxin. No matter the energy content of a food, the body values it. Does it also need it? Well, that is a separate question. As we have seen with the phenomenon of alliesthesia, we have inbuilt feedback mechanisms to regulate the pleasure that a food provides based on metabolic needs.

To illustrate exactly why the idea of 'healthy' foods is suspect, an analogy with alcohol can be used. Is alcohol intrinsically unhealthy or harmful? The answer is clearly no, since if we are otherwise reasonably healthy we could each have a glass of wine or beer every day without undermining our health. In fact, the bulk of scientific evidence suggests that this level of intake will probably extend our lives as well as giving much pleasure along the way. But ten glasses of wine per day on a regular basis will have serious health consequences, including weight gain, increased risk of liver and heart disease, and a range of cancers.

This analogy is not precise: who eats ten chocolate bars a day? But the key message is that the body needs energy sources and it can get it from chocolate as easily as from fruit. However, if you do eat ten chocolate bars a day, in all likelihood you are probably eating little fruit and hence missing the other nutrients that fruit provides. You are also taking in a lot more energy than you are likely to use in a short space of time. Relax, though, since your body will store this for you in case of a lean winter when no food is available. Oh, wait . . . food is *always* available? In that case, either more exercise or more generous clothing is called for. In other words, the energy demands of modern industrialized societies are such that storage of excess energy intake is unnecessary.

If your chocolate intake is much lower – say, one bar per day – how would it be possible to quantify the alleged harm that it produces? It is still energy that needs to be used but perhaps your activity level takes care of that and perhaps your intake of proteins and other nutrients is adequate. The point is the same one that can be made with alcohol. That is, harm does not relate to the substance itself (wine, chocolate) but to how it is used. Put another way, it is perfectly reasonable to talk about a diet that is 'unhealthy', but it makes little sense to refer to 'unhealthy' foods since the impact of foods can only be seen in relation to one another (enough fruit, too little fruit) and over periods of time (ten chocolate bars on Christmas Day; ten chocolate bars per day throughout December).

The analogy with alcohol holds up in another way, too. There is often more than a whiff of moral judgement in many purely nutritional approaches to considering the foods we eat, and this relates to the central idea of this book. Should we really be getting that much pleasure from eating? Surely there is something a little bit wicked about having regular access to so much sugar and fat? Are not food pleasures really just 'pleasures of the flesh'? I discussed in chapter Six the idea of sweet foods as an indulgence to be consumed in small quantities, and how this restriction actually underlies their reward value. By denying ourselves, we turn perfectly innocent foods into chocolate Sirens tempting us to crash on the rocks of obesity.

Most classifications of supposedly 'healthy' foods also fall down when we consider 'dose'. Carrots, for example, fit neatly into the 'healthy' basket until too many are eaten, at which point carotene poisoning can occur. Because of the well-demonstrated link between dietary salt and high blood pressure, salt intake is a risk factor for a stroke. With few exceptions, every culture takes in more salt than is required, the excess potentially contributing to a high blood pressure risk. So, what is the solution? Cut out crackers? Ban bread? Stop seasoning stews? Certainly, each of these measures would contribute to positive health outcomes over the long term if they could reduce a reasonable proportion of our salt intake. Salt reduction in bread might well be a useful strategy given that it is a daily staple. But one cannot infer, therefore, that a properly seasoned dish is somehow 'unhealthy'. As the sad case of D illustrated, dietary salt is necessary for survival. If you need it for survival, salt is not 'unhealthy', but you can take in too much in your regular diet.

This is not the most common perspective. Surveys in the USA have shown that substantial minorities of the public feel that salt, sugar and fat are actually intrinsically bad for health, no matter in what quantities. For example, more than a quarter of respondents to one survey believed that a diet completely free of salt was healthier than one with salt.[2] Adopting simple rules about foods and food ingredients – fat/salt/sugar is bad for you, and so on – is understandable. Such rules may actually be a means of dealing with the complexity and rapidly changing nature of nutritional information. Even so, Americans still tend to worry a lot about food and its health consequences. This is (unsurprisingly) in contrast to the French, whose focus is more on the pleasure afforded by food.[3] Importantly, though, such easy food categorizations may actually be counterproductive. In a study of US college students who were given cookies to eat, the researchers assigned the students to receive information about the healthiness of the cookies. Those students who were told that the cookies were a 'healthy snack' ate 35 per cent more than did those told that they were unhealthy.[4] Since there exists no commonly agreed understanding of what 'healthy' and 'unhealthy' might indicate in this context, these findings could mean that health-related food labels actually contribute to weight gain, rather than assisting in controlling weight.

Even if it is not useful to classify individual foods in terms of their health consequences, there is still the possibility that, overall, our food preferences are making us fat or unhealthy in some other way. Perhaps our preferences allow our diet to be dominated by particular types of foods. In affluent societies, we do consume proportions of fat, sugar and salt in our diets that are well in excess of what we need to survive. More importantly, the levels of salt and dietary fat – for example, many Western diets contain 35–40 per cent fat – in the long term put us at risk for cardiovascular and other diet-related diseases.

Why is this happening, and why now? Why should sensory pleasure from food lead to a high energy intake? These questions are addressed in the next chapter.

TWELVE

Palatability and the Energy Crisis

In our evolutionary history, innate and learned responses to food properties were an adaptive response to real or potential energy requirements. These energy needs are still real, although reduced by our sedentary lifestyle, but what has changed is that sufficient energy is now always available. The same is true of other nutrients that the body values, such as salt. At the same time, our diets are still driven by the same pleasure-seeking processes that have always operated and we tend to resist reductions in those food ingredients that contribute to sensory pleasure. For instance, attempts to reduce our physiologically excessive salt intake by using low-salt versions of products typically fail due to their lack of flavour impact. A 50 per cent reduction of salt in bread might have quite a substantial impact on the amount of salt in our diet because bread is a staple. But this will mainly be due to a dramatically reduced intake of a product that now tastes like cardboard.

The main worry for the nutritionally concerned is that, if we let taste dictate what we eat, our diet will be unbalanced and oriented towards energy-dense foods. On the face of it, it may seem obvious, therefore, that our preferences are driving the tendency towards obesity. The same wisdom that sees our bodies maintain functioning through the palatability of energy and sodium sources and maintain nutrient variety through changes in palatability may be making us vulnerable to chronic disease now that food pleasures and nutritional needs have been uncoupled.

In particular, it is apparent that, for most of us, most of the time, eating is not primarily driven by energy needs because we seldom get to a point of even moderate energy depletion. Our meals are taken at times of convenience or at times determined by social norms rather than in response to those internal cues that signal physiological hunger such as blood sugar levels. Such normative external cues also provide information about how much we should consume on a particular occasion. As we saw in the previous chapter, beliefs about the healthiness of foods derived from food labels are normative cues because they can influence the amount eaten. Two other normative cues, portion size and the eating behaviour of others, have also been found to be important influences on the amount eaten.[1]

The impact of portion size is well illustrated by the ingenious study discussed in chapter Five in which a soup bowl was covertly refilled from beneath, resulting in increased amounts consumed. A study from these same researchers similarly showed that, when given a larger container of popcorn, moviegoers ate almost 50 per cent more – even when the popcorn provided was stale![2] We also eat more when dining with others, particularly so when the group is large. Plus, if our companions eat a lot, then so will we. But it appears that we are blissfully unaware of such effects. When asked about the reasons for amounts consumed, participants in these studies have attributed the amount eaten to the food's taste and their own hunger, not to the presence or behaviour of others.[3] Such lack of awareness of normative cues means, therefore, that the impact of these cues is difficult to resist.

Anything that signals the palatability of food – sights, sounds (sizzling, for example), smells and tastes – is also an external cue. This is in contrast to internal cues to eat – for example, feelings of hunger. How we respond to external cues is sometimes innate (the pleasure produced by sweetness, for example) but very often learned. In addition, there is also a huge number of indirect food cues in our environment, particularly in television advertising. As much as learned preferences for food odours, these can be re-minders of food palatability and thus powerful triggers for food wanting. In essence, the multimedia environment in which we are all immersed in affluent societies means that cues signalling food palatability are present for a high proportion of our waking hours.

We are all influenced to greater or lesser degrees by internal and external food cues. But the fact that cues can have such a powerful impact on eating has raised the question of whether those who have difficulty controlling their food intake are somehow more aware or more reactive or perhaps more vulnerable to external cues. Indeed, this question has a long research history. Some early studies suggested that the obese are less responsive to internal cues to eat than those of normal weight. If so, it is likely that greater control of eating will be exerted by external cues, both sensory and normative, for this group. One study from the 1960s that suggested this involved researchers allowing groups of overweight and normal weight participants access to a food while they filled in a questionnaire. Covertly, the researchers also manipulated the room clock to be either much slower or much faster than normal. In response to these time cues, the obese group increased their food intake when they thought that their mealtime had passed relative to when they thought it had yet to arrive. In other words, their eating was largely driven by their expectation of when they *should* eat, rather than sensations of hunger. In contrast, the time cues had no impact on the eating of a normal weight group who ate the same amount regardless of the apparent time.[4]

But, regardless of our weight, we will all tend to eat more of a palatable food than one that is not palatable. So, the key question is really whether some of us are more strongly controlled by external cues that signal food palatability in both what we eat and how much we eat. This appears to be the case, in that obese people respond to palatable foods by eating even more than do normal weight individuals.[5] Is it just that the obese find palatable foods more pleasurable? This is a reasonable enough conclusion, but may be confusing palatability and energy content. Recall that wanting – increased appetite and hunger – can be triggered by sensory cues that have come to signal energy. Thus, cues such as the odour and sight of food are not only appealing but they motivate us to consume. For the obese, the sensory cues for the presence of energy may be especially powerful in triggering the desire to eat.[6] Since wanting and liking can be quite separate, this helps explain, too, why overeating can take place even if the food being eaten becomes less and less pleasant during eating (sensory-specific satiety; see chapter Five).

The extent to which we rely on internal rather than external cues in initiating eating may help to explain cross-cultural differences in obesity. The so-called *French paradox* has received considerable attention by both nutrition researchers and the general media. The French have quite substantial meals, especially at lunch and dinner, with high-fat foods and wine both part of normal French eating habits. Nevertheless, rates of obesity are much lower in France than they are in many other Western countries, particularly the USA. What are the French consuming to maintain such weight control? Is there wheat grass in the mousse? Much more likely than any secret ingredient is the fact that the French are far more reliant on internal than external cues when it comes to regulating their eating. In the USA, it is just the opposite. In other words, while French food is highly palatable, what determines how much the French eat are feelings of satiation, rather than the presence of still more food to eat.[7] This is all the more surprising since, as I noted earlier, the French seem more focused on the pleasure that food provides than are Americans. One could perhaps speculate that this focus on pleasure allows much greater enjoyment of meals with a lower food intake. Alternatively, it may be that the combination of an unrestricted diet together with a reliance on internal cues means that external cues lose their power because hedonic hunger is less likely.

Restrain Yourself

Even if you find chocolate or desserts highly appealing, you may or may not give in to the temptation to indulge when either is present. If you are dieting, you will probably feel that this is a test of your willpower. However, the real picture is a little more complex. Much research attention has been given in recent years to the concept of the *restrained eater*, someone who habitually monitors and controls food intake for the sake of their health, to control their weight or for other reasons. This propensity to diet means more than simply wanting to shed a few kilos after the festive season. Measures of restraint show an inherited component: both identical twins are much more likely to be restrained if one of the pair is than is the case with non-identical twins.[8]

Restrained eaters appear to be more reactive to foods in a variety of different ways than do non-restrained eaters. Most importantly, food cues (the sight or smells of a pizza, or even thoughts about food) exert their greatest influence on desire to eat if you are a restrained eater.[9] Such cues become powerful in this group because they represent the sensory pleasure provided by the food. For example, much like one of Pavlov's hungry dogs, restrained eaters tend to produce more saliva in the presence of food. They are also found to be more impulsive when food is available, being less able to delay food gratification.[10]

The greater responsiveness of restrained eaters is also seen in differences in the way that they learn about the relationships between flavours and either pleasant tastes or calories. With either form of learning, the expectation is that preferences for flavours are greater when they are paired with the ingestion of high energy (more calories) rather than low energy, and also when a flavour is paired with a sweet taste more often rather than less often. Indeed, this is exactly the pattern seen with unrestrained eaters. A flavour consumed with high calories becomes liked more than if it is paired with low calories. The same is true of a flavour paired 90 per cent of the time with a sweet taste compared to the flavour being paired with sweetness only 10 per cent of the time. Restrained eaters, by contrast, show no such discriminations. Regardless of the relative calorie content or frequency of sweet pairing, flavours become highly liked.[11] This pattern of learning reveals a strong response to the presence of both positive taste qualities and calorie consequences, but an insensitivity to *variations* in reward and pleasure. One strong possibility is that it is the long-term dietary restriction itself that reduces sensitivity to variations in the energy provided by a food.

Perhaps all this suggests an image of restrained eaters as wild-eyed and salivating, forever battling with urges to eat, and madly devouring any food available. But of course restrained eaters as a group must include both those who are successful at resisting these urges – successful dieters – as well as those who succumb. To reconcile these different groups of restrained eaters with findings of heightened reactivity to food cues, another factor has recently been implicated. Regardless of whether you are a restrained eater or not, you may still be someone who tends to succumb to the temptations posed by the sight or smell of their favourite foods. This characteristic has been termed *disinhibition*.

Many of us have tried to lose weight at some stage. This will often involve a considerable effort to inhibit your desire to consume the palatable foods that you will encounter. If you are effective at doing this, then you can be said to be low in disinhibition (the failure of inhibition); conversely, if resistance is futile, then you can be seen as high in disinhibition. Disinhibition is thought to be an enduring individual trait, but whether or not this is determined genetically, or by experience, or a combination of both, is unclear.[12] Similar degrees of responsiveness to foods are present in mothers and their children, but this could be an effect of a child modelling the eating behaviour of the parent. Irrespective of its origin, when measured on the *Three Factor Eating Questionnaire* (the other factors are *restraint* and *hunger*), up to 50 per cent of women in the USA show high disinhibition, and this percentage is highest in young women. Estimated rates in men tend to be much lower, perhaps around 25 per cent, depending on age and other demographic factors.[13]

Disinhibition is not just about reacting to *all* foods at *all* times. It was noted in chapter Six that desire to eat is increased by food palatability. Those who show high levels of disinhibition are especially prone to 'wanting' highly palatable foods. They have a greater liking for sweet foods and beverages and food high in fat, such as butter, cream and ice cream.[14] And because of the nature of the trait, they tend to act on these desires when palatable food is available and consume more. Those high in disinhibition are therefore not simply gluttons who want to continue to eat, but individuals whose responses to sensory cues are exaggerated.

This exaggerated response is evident even when flavour preferences are developing. Martin Yeomans of Sussex University has shown that women who are high in disinhibition show greater increases in liking for a flavour that has been paired with a sweet taste than do those low in disinhibition, suggesting a 'heightened hedonic sensitivity' to sweetness.[15] Since learning produces liked food odours and flavours that also stimulate increased appetite, those high in disinhibition will be especially responsive to cues that signal the calorie content of foods. For these individuals, palatable foods are clearly both highly rewarding and potent signals that engage 'wanting' – that is, high levels of motivation to eat.

Needless to say, degree of disinhibition is thought to be crucial in determining successful dieting. It is highest among those dieters who have most trouble maintaining their ideal weight. Whether those high in disinhibition are those dieters who experience cravings is not known. It is quite plausible, though, since food imagery is a much more potent cue for this group, in that imagery induces cravings that lead to eating. It is, for example, associated with increased chocolate intake by those who identify themselves as 'chocolate addicts'.

High disinhibition is also associated with stress and unpleasant mood states such as anxiety, boredom, depression or sadness, all of which increase vulnerability to food cues, undermining dietary restraint and leading to eating binges.[16] As noted previously, one way of interpreting this effect is as self-medication in which the hedonic pleasure counteracts the unpleasant emotional state, at least in the short term. But, of course, unsuccessful attempts to control weight might actually be the *causes* of these negative moods. Once 'off the wagon', the sense of failure that disinhibition produces is interpreted in a way that suggests there is no point in continuing to limit what is eaten.

To be able to understand the impact of food cues on eating, disinhibition and restraint need to be considered together. If you are low in disinhibition, it is more likely that you will be a successful restrained eater. If you are not trying to restrain your eating, then your level of disinhibition might seem to be of less concern. But if you do not restrain your eating *and* you are high in disinhibition, then you will still be highly responsive to palatable food cues. Although this group does not appear to respond to stress or negative moods by overeating, there is evidence that, when in a positive mood, their intake of palatable foods is higher. Importantly, this group is especially over-represented among the obese.

How these interactions might influence reactions to palatable foods is illustrated by a recent study in which a group of women were offered their most tempting snack food which, for 43 per cent of them, was chocolate, followed by crisps (15 per cent), candy (15 per cent), M&Ms/nuts (12 per cent) and cookies (9 per cent). The women were firstly asked to taste a small amount of the snack, and then given the remainder to take home and asked to come back a day later. Half of the women were instructed not to consume any of the snack until they returned the next day (the *temptation* condition), while the other half of the group were given no instructions (the control group). On returning to the laboratory the next day, all women were offered their snack to eat and the amount they consumed was measured. Regardless of the group they were in, those who measured low in restraint or those high in restraint but low in disinhibition ate approximately the same amount as they had on the previous day. By contrast, those high in *both* disinhibition and restraint ate significantly more *if* they were in the temptation group.[17] The combination of restraint and a strong tendency to disinhibition therefore made these women particularly vulnerable to the temptation of a palatable food that had been restricted. This is, of course, exactly the set of circumstances that those who experience cravings report during periods of dieting.

It is not completely clear as yet whether eating restraint is a risk for weight gain if you are disinhibited or disinhibition is a risk if you diet a lot. Increasingly, though, studies are teasing apart the relative contribution of these factors. The trend that is emerging is that disinhibition is the important personality factor that predisposes to weight gain. Hence, studies of disinhibited eaters show that following a high carbohydrate meal they consume far more of an available snack than do those low in disinhibition. Interestingly, this was not seen following a high-fat meal. Moreover, this overeating was not driven by hunger. Ratings of hunger in these studies did not differ between inhibited and disinhibited eaters, and indeed were overall lower following a high-carbohydrate than a high-fat meal.[18] Eating was therefore driven by the hedonic properties of the snack, not by any internal need.

Self-defeating Diets

Diets are notoriously ineffective. This is reflected, as much as it is by anything else, by the fact that the number of different diets being promoted continues to increase. Considering dieters in terms of restraint and disinhibition has provided some clues as to why permanent weight loss is difficult, and it all hinges on our responses to innate and learned cues to food palatability.

Unsuccessful dieters appear to be trapped in a vicious circle that undermines their ability to lose weight. First, restriction of a desired food actually makes it more rewarding and therefore desirable – essentially the idea of the attractiveness of 'forbidden fruit'. As I discussed in chapter Six, this phenomenon is explained by the *response deprivation hypothesis*, which proposes that restriction itself increases the reward value of whatever is restricted. Even for those of a normal weight, with unrestrained eaters, the deprivation of a liked palatable food increases the desirability of that food. Hence we tend to be much more willing to work harder at a task to obtain a food that is both palatable *and* restricted, rather than for an equivalently liked, but unrestricted, food.

Restriction also elicits cravings specifically for those restricted foods. Restrained eaters' increased cravings means that food thoughts are ever present – they become preoccupied with food.[19] Some dieters even dream about particular desirable foods. And cravings are primarily for those foods that are *most* restricted – frequently highly palatable, often sweet, high-fat foods. The food thoughts and cravings of the restrained eater become yet more external cues to the pleasure that the food provides. In addition to the shift in focus towards food pleasure, the vulnerability of the restrained eater increases because, as any repeat dieter will attest, the whole process of dieting involves learning to ignore internal signals of hunger. But, in turn, this means that eating is even more likely to come under the control of external cues, particularly anything that signals food palatability.

One way to look at dietary restrictions is that they are, unintentionally, an exercise in limiting the pleasure derived from food. In turn, this makes restrained eaters vulnerable to hedonic hunger. While restrained eaters may, in fact, be physiologically hungry, their focus is not on the calories that the nice piece of the particular fruit allowed in a diet might provide. Rather, it is specifically for those items that you cannot eat in the diet. Hedonic hunger is a function not just of restraint per se but of the restriction of palatable foods – which of course, since these are often high in energy, are the ones that are most likely to be restrained. Diets do not work if the only things that are restricted are carrots and spinach. Some diets do contain palatable high-fat foods. For example, the Atkins low-carbohydrate diet can contain high-fat protein foods. But this diet still restricts other palatable foods, and the most common foods craved by Atkins dieters are those that are excluded, namely bread, cakes, confectionery and so on. Indeed, restrained eaters rate themselves to be food deprived, but this has no relationship to their actual calorie intake. They are clearly saying, therefore, that they are pleasure deprived.

The final part of the vicious circle is that restrained eaters do, in fact, succumb to sensory cues by eating, often to excess, and primarily those foods that they have been restricting. One study restricted intake of chocolate-flavoured foods in both restrained and non-restrained eaters for seven days. The subsequent availability of these foods led to an increased intake in the restrained eaters, who also reported chocolate cravings during the period of restriction. This was not evident with less palatable, vanilla-flavoured foods. Also, interestingly, the restrained eaters' heightened sense of wanting was evident during a task in which the participants had to solve anagrams before they could consume the previously restricted chocolate foods. Restrained eaters were observed to rush through the task, frequently not completing it, so they could get their chocolate 'fix'.[20]

Thus, restriction itself predisposes the restrained eater to experience hedonic hunger and increases their vulnerability to food cues. Yet we all restrict our intake at some time for some reasons, whether it is motivated by religious observance or perhaps periodic attempts to be a little healthier. Why this is done with relatively little difficulty is because the problems described here arise primarily when the restrictions are repeatedly and consistently self-imposed.

The effects of chronic restriction are increasingly a topic of interest to nutrition researchers. It is becoming apparent that the normal ability to control overall energy intake may be disturbed in those who find dieting difficult. From early infancy onwards, we will try to compensate for lower calories at one meal with increased consumption at the next, and vice versa. This suggests that we unconsciously monitor energy intake, and the most likely way we can do that is by drawing upon the learned associations between sensory properties and energy: if we ate something that was thick and sweet and rich, then it probably had more calories, and so on. Hence the expected ability of the food to make us feel full relies on learned association between the food's sensory properties and the food's energy content.[21] But the normal energy regulation that occurs through changes in food palatability appears deficient in restrained eaters. Usually, having a high-energy drink prior to eating a meal leads to a reduction in the amount consumed, primarily because of a decrease in pleasantness of the meal (alliesthesia; see chapter Five). However, this effect is not seen in restrained eaters. In effect, they tend to show negative alliesthesia – responding to energy intake by eating more rather than less. Janet Polivy and colleagues at the University of Toronto have proposed that, in general, inhibiting one's own behaviour such as by restricting food intake produces frustration that may predispose to excessive eating.[22]

While this may be the case, there is another possibility. The development of many foods aimed at helping us to reduce weight may actually uncouple energy from learned sensory cues. Through our years of food experiences, we learn that both sweet taste and viscosity or thickness (for example, with cream) are associated with higher energy. Paradoxically, the ability of the food industry to produce sweeteners and fat replacers that neither add calories nor change viscosity may disrupt our normal ability to use sensory cues to respond appropriately to energy intake. This is not to say that diet drinks, for instance, do not contribute to reduced energy intake. Rather, their use and the use of other diet foods may have an inadvertent effect. For those relying most on external, and especially sensory, cues, their ability to use these cues to estimate and control energy intake may be undermined by increasingly frequent experiences with foods where sensory properties and palatability provide inconsistent information about energy content. It is important to point out that this remains only a possibility. Nevertheless, it does mean that, plausibly, special diet foods and beverages are not the solution to weight control.

Overall, it is difficult to conclude anything other than that chronic dieting is at the very least counter-productive as a permanent weight loss strategy. It even remains possible that it may potentially be contributing to the increase in obesity rates. This may not always be true, but it seems to be true in the 'toxic environment' in which cues to food palatability are everywhere. Restricting liked foods does not lead to successful dieting strategies because it promotes hedonic hunger, especially in those who are most vulnerable.

Reducing Vulnerability

Do we really have any choice if our genes, our tendencies to react to palatability and our particular lifelong history of exposure and conditioning are pushing us towards particular foods? If we have a fatal attraction for cream cakes, is there any point fighting it? Interestingly, most people would not ask this sort of question if I were writing about the origins of preferences for clothes or perfumes. There is an underlying assumption that our food preferences are, or have the potential to be, a problem. Can you limit the impact of those biological and learned cues to palatability?

While chronically restricted eating is itself a risk, there is obviously a paradox in proposing unrestricted eating as a means of weight control. As we saw in chapter Five, dietary monotony decreases intake even with palatable foods. Conversely, increased food variety is associated with lower sensory-specific satiety and lower monotony and hence increased food intake. In turn, this suggests that the best way of reducing intake would be to reduce food variety. Can the apparent contradictory effects of reducing food variety and restricting foods be reconciled? The first way to think about it is to consider that increased food intake is not necessarily a bad thing. No nutritionist will complain if you are eating large amounts of different leafy green vegetables so long as you are also eating protein, some carbohydrates and some fat. In fact, the effect of variety on increasing overall energy intake may only operate when high-energy foods are a major component of what is eaten. Clearly, therefore, an important issue is dietary balance and not just variety by itself.

Variation, even in sensory terms, means that there is an opportunity for preferences to develop for a wide range of foods. This not only ensures that a diet will include all necessary nutrients but also that preferred foods will not be limited to those that are sweet or high in fat. Vegetables *can* become palatable, in other words. A varied diet will include *some* sweet, high-fat foods, but not so much as to exclude vegetables, fruit, meats, fish and dairy. The important point here is that a varied diet should not be dominated by energy-dense foods, but equally it should not only consist of just 'healthy' foods either. Too much lettuce is, in some respects, just as bad as too much confectionary (perhaps not quite). Restriction of any part of an omnivore's diet increases the risks of hedonic hunger, craving and, for restrained, disinhibited eaters, a cycle of 'stuffing and starving'.[23]

Of course, an ideal varied diet may not always be easy to achieve. A consideration of the implications of the so-called *obesogenic* environment present in affluent societies is beyond the scope of this book. However, there is considerable evidence that socio-economic factors often determine access to fruits and vegetables and lower-fat sources of protein. For some, especially those in socially or economically deprived circumstances, dietary variety may mean alternating Big Macs with Kentucky Fried Chicken.

Diets are primed to fail unless they recognize that innately, and through conditioning, we are predisposed to find foods that are sweet and high in fat or salt as highly palatable and highly tempting. Restricting these completely is unrealistic in the long term because it promotes vulnerability to food pleasure cues. Reduction of calories is possible if you consider your diet in terms of total energy intake, and this can be achieved by eating less overall. This presents some difficulties. Remember that some external cues influence the amount eaten. Cues for palatable foods induce eating to the extent that they override normative cues in the vulnerable eater, inducing overeating. But what if the normative cues themselves contribute to the problem of overeating? In fact, it does seem that attitudes to eating have also changed in a direction that does little to discourage obesity within Western societies in particular. Thus, if portion sizes are increasing and everyone around you is eating more, then all of us may be influenced to consume more. This is particularly true if there is less reliance overall on internal cues.

Once again, cross-cultural comparisons illustrate the issue. Typical French meal portion sizes are known to be smaller than those in the USA – yet another contributor to lower obesity rates in France. Cross-cultural differences in attitudes were well illustrated during the making of the American film *Something's Gotta Give* (2003). A prominent scene in the film involved the main characters sharing a meal in a well-known Parisian restaurant, Le Grand Colbert. To maintain authenticity, the regular kitchen staff and waiters appeared in the film, serving the restaurant's dishes as they normally would. During filming, however, the kitchen was asked by the film's director to substantially increase the portion sizes that were on view in the filmed scenes. It was felt that American audiences would otherwise find the size of French dishes disturbingly small!

Reducing one's vulnerability to those food cues that elicit hedonic hunger is especially crucial, although it might seem improbably difficult. How is it possible to insulate oneself from food advertising and from the constant reminders of food pleasures? Affluent dieters sometimes resort to 'health farms' or retreats for periods of effective weight loss. This is not only because they are places that control energy intake, and often encourage increased energy expenditure through regular exercise. In addition, diet retreats are also a retreat from the multitude of reminders of foods that surround us in everyday life. Hence, fewer eating triggers that may induce craving are encountered.

Cues have little impact if you are not hedonically hungry. Therefore, not only eating, but also restraint itself should be undertaken in moderation. The *value discounting function* discussed in chapters Six and Eleven implies that delayed rewards are less valuable, an idea essentially no different from the idea of short-term restraint. But this may be effective in a context in which no food is *absolutely* restricted at all times. Hence you should feel free to go ahead and have your cake. When temptation strikes tomorrow for another slice, short-term restraint will be easier to apply because of the knowledge that you will be able to enjoy another slice in a few more days.

A not uncommon idea is that some people can be addicted to high-energy foods. The drug (including alcohol) addiction field has for several decades been grappling with the problem of how to free those who are dependent from learned cues to the drug's effect. It was proposed, especially by groups such as Alcoholics Anonymous, that for some alcohol was a poison, the consumption of which inevitably led to a loss of self-control. More recently, it has been recognized that the smell and taste of alcohol can be viewed in terms of sensory cues to which some are vulnerable, perhaps in some cases precisely because of attempts to restrict intake totally. A more recent emphasis on vulnerability to sensory cues has led to successful outcomes for controlled-drinking treatments for many who have previously suffered from alcohol abuse.

Can we expect in future to see food cue exposure treatment programmes for restrained disinhibited eaters? It is possible to imagine that exposure to food cues under 'controlled' conditions – that is, without subsequent food consumption – might be a way of reducing the power of the cues, as well as an exercise in demonstrating the effectiveness of willpower. While such approaches have met with success in treating drug and alcohol dependence, one of the key problems is that it is a 'treatment' that has to be applied in real settings. Thus, it might be easy to resist cues in a clinical setting, but how effective is this when faced with an opportunity to eat the cake?

The sensory pleasure that has motivated us to consume high-energy foods has given us huge adaptive advantages in our evolutionary past. It is what has kept us alive as a species. The malleability of our preferences in being able to link smells, sights and other sensations to calories has allowed us to respond to changing environments with success. Of course, now we can choose to obtain all the energy we need from selecting from easily available 'healthy' low-energy foods if we wish. And this may be an adequate diet if our energy needs are low, perhaps because we engage in little physical activity. On the other hand, if our eating habits follow our food preferences with enthusiasm, we cannot blame these preferences if we do not use up the energy that they encourage us to consume. And, perhaps more to the point, we ought to give thanks to them for providing us with some of life's greatest pleasures.

References

Preface: Brussels Sprouts and Ice Cream

1 J. Prescott, O. Young, L. O'Neill, N.J.N. Yau and R. Stevens, 'Cross-cultural Differences in Motives for Food Choice: A Comparison of Consumers from Japan, Taiwan, Malaysia and New Zealand', *Food Quality and Preference*, 13 (2002), pp. 489–95.
2 A. Eertmans, F. Baeyens and O. Van den Bergh, 'Food Likes and Their Relative Importance in Human Eating Behavior: Review and Preliminary Suggestions for Health Promotion', *Health Education Research*, 16 (2001), pp. 443–56.
3 K. Glanz, M. Basil, E. Maibach, J. Goldberg and D. Snyder, 'Why Americans Eat What They Do: Taste, Nutrition, Cost, Convenience, and Weight Control Concerns as Influences on Food Consumption', *Journal of the American Dietetic Association*, 98 (1998), pp. 1118–26.
4 J. Prescott and A. Young, 'Does Information about MSG (Monosodium Glutamate) Content Influence Consumer Ratings of Soups with and without Added MSG?', *Appetite*, 39 (2002), pp. 25–33.

1 Taste Sensations

1 P. Rozin, '"Taste–smell Confusions" and the Duality of the Olfactory Sense', *Perception and Psychophysics*, 31 (1982), pp. 397–401.
2 D. G. Laing, 'Perception of Odour Mixtures', in *Handbook of Olfaction and Gustation*, ed. R. L. Doty (New York, 1995), pp. 283–97.
3 D. V. Smith and R. F. Margolskee, 'Making Sense of Taste', *Scientific American*, 284 (2001), pp. 26–33.
4 J. Prescott and R. J. Stevenson, 'Pungency in Food Perception and Preference', *Food Reviews International*, 11 (1995), pp. 665–98.
5 J. Prescott and R. J. Stevenson, 'The Effects of Oral Chemical Irritation on Tastes and Flavors in Frequent and Infrequent Users of Chili', *Physiology & Behavior*, 58 (1995), pp. 1117–27.
6 M. Zampini and C. Spence, 'The Role of Auditory Cues in Modulating the Perceived Crispness and Staleness of Potato Chips', *Journal of Sensory Studies*, 19 (2004), pp. 347–63.

7 P.A.S. Breslin, M. M. Gilmore, G. K. Beauchamp and B. G. Green, 'Psychophysical Evidence that Oral Astringency is a Tactile Sensation', *Chemical Senses*, 18 (1993), pp. 405–18.

8 T. Schemper, S. Voss and W. S. Cain, 'Odour Identification in Young and Elderly Persons: Sensory and Cognitive Limitations', *Journal of Gerontology*, 36 (1981), pp. 446–52.

9 G. Morrot, F. Brochet and D. Dubourdieu, 'The Color of Odours', *Brain and Language*, 79 (2001), pp. 309–20.

2 We Eat What We Like

1 J.-A. Brillat-Savarin, *The Physiology of Taste* [1825] (London, 1994).

2 J. Prescott, 'Comparisons of Taste Perceptions and Preferences of Japanese and Australian Consumers: Overview and Implications for Cross-cultural Sensory Research', *Food Quality and Preference*, 9 (1998), pp. 393–402.

3 J. E. Steiner, D. Glaser, M. E. Hawilo and K. C. Berridge, 'Comparative Expression of Hedonic Impact: Affective Reactions to Taste by Human Infants and Other Primates', *Neuroscience and Biobehavioral Reviews*, 25 (2001), pp. 53–74.

4 K. Keskitalo, A. Knaapila, M. Kallela, A. Palotie, M. Wessman, S. Sammalisto, L. Peltonen, H. Tuorila and M. Perola, 'Sweet Taste Preferences Are Partly Genetically Determined: Identification of a Trait Locus on Chromosome 16(1–3)', *American Journal of Clinical Nutrition*, 86 (2007), pp. 55–63.

5 P. Macinnis, *Bittersweet: The Story of Sugar* (Sydney, 2002).

6 A. Drewnowski, 'Energy Intake and Sensory Properties of Food', *American Journal of Clinical Nutrition*, 62, suppl. (1995), pp. 1081s–5s.

7 M. Fantino, J. Hosotte and M. Apfelbaum, 'An Opioid Antagonist, Naltrexone, Reduces Preference for Sucrose in Humans', *American Journal of Physiology*, 251 (1986), pp. 91–6.

8 E. M. Blass and A. Shah, 'Pain-reducing Properties of Sucrose in Human Newborns', *Chemical Senses*, 20 (1995), pp. 29–35.

9 J. Prescott and J. Wilkie, 'Pain Tolerance Selectively Increased by a Sweet-smelling Odour', *Psychological Science*, 18 (2007), pp. 308–11.

10 A. Drewnowski and M.R.C. Greenwood, 'Cream and Sugar: Human Preferences for High-fat Foods', *Physiology & Behavior*, 30 (1983), pp. 629–33.

11 R. M. Pangborn, 'Individual Variation in Affective Responses to Taste Stimuli', *Psychonomic Science*, 21 (1970), pp. 125–6.

12 S. S. Schiffman, B. G. Graham, E. A. Sattely-Miller and Z. S. Warwick, 'Orosensory Perception of Dietary Fat', *Current Directions in Psychological Science*, 7 (1998), pp. 137–43.

13 R. D. Mattes, 'The Taste of Fat Elevates Postprandial Triacylglycerol', *Physiology & Behavior*, 74 (2001), pp. 343–8.

14 A. Drewnowski, S. A. Henderson, A. Levine and C. Hann, 'Taste and Food Preferences as Predictors of Dietary Practices in Young Women', *Public Health Nutrition*, 2 (1999), pp. 513–19.

15 G. K. Beauchamp, B. J. Cowart and M. Moran, 'Developmental Changes in Salt Acceptability in Human Infants', *Developmental Psychology*, 19 (1986), pp. 17–25.

16 M. Bertino, G. K. Beauchamp and K. Engleman, 'Long-term Reduction in Dietary Sodium Alters the Taste of Salt', *American Journal of Clinical Nutrition*, 36 (1982), pp. 1134–44.

17 I. J. Brown, I. Tzoulaki, V. Candeias and P. Elliot, 'Salt Intakes Around the World: Implications for Public Health', *International Journal of Epidemiology*, 38 (2009), pp. 791–813.

18 J. Stamler, 'The INTERSALT Study: Background, Methods, Findings, and Implications', *American Journal of Clinical Nutrition*, 65, suppl. (1997), pp. 626s–42s.

19 G. K. Beauchamp, 'The Human Preference for Excess Salt', *American Scientist*, 75 (1987), pp. 27–33.

20 G. K. Beauchamp and K. Engleman, 'High Salt Intake – Sensory and Behavioural Factors', *Hypertension*, 17, suppl. 1 (1991), pp. 1176–81.

21 G. K. Beauchamp, M. Bertino and K. Engleman, 'Effects of Sodium Depletion on Salt Taste and Food Preference in Human Volunteers', *Chemical Senses*, 14 (1989), p. 183.

22 K. Ikeda, 'New Seasonings', *Chemical Senses*, 27 (2002), pp. 847–9.

23 F. Bellisle, M. O. Monneuse, M. Chabert, C. Laure-Achagiotis, M. T. Lanteaume and J. Louis-Sylvestre, 'Monosodium Glutamate as a Palatability Enhancer in the European Diet', *Physiology & Behavior*, 44 (1991), pp. 869–74.

24 S. Fuke and T. Shimizu, 'Sensory and Preference Aspects of Umami', *Trends in Food Science & Technology*, 4 (1993), pp. 246–51.

25 M. Naim, I. Ohara, M. R. Kare and M. Levinson, 'Interaction of MSG Taste with Nutrition: Perspectives in Consummatory Behavior and Digestion', *Physiology & Behavior*, 49 (1991), pp. 1019–24.

26 M. Vazquez, P. B. Pearson and G. K. Beauchamp, 'Flavour Preferences in Malnourished Mexican Infants', *Physiology & Behavior*, 28 (1982), pp. 513–19.

27 F. Bellisle, 'Nutritional Effects of Umami in the Human Diet', *Food Reviews International*, 14 (1998), pp. 309–20.

28 P. J. Reeds, D. G. Burrin, B. Stoll and F. Jahoor, 'Intestinal Glutamate Metabolism', *Journal of Nutrition*, 130 (2000), pp. 978s–82s.

29 T. R. Scott and G. P. Mark, 'The Taste System Encodes Stimulus Toxicity', *Brain Research*, 414 (1987), pp. 197–203.

30 G. K. Beauchamp, M. Bertino and K. Engleman, 'Factors Responsible for Changes in Salt Taste Preference following Alterations in Dietary Sodium Intake in Human Adults', *Chemical Senses*, 12 (1987), p. 640.

31 W. Schivelbusch, *Tastes of Paradise: A Social History of Spices, Stimulants, and Intoxicants* (New York, 1993).

3 We Like What We Eat

1 P. Pliner, and M. L. Pelchat, 'Neophobia in Humans and the Special Status of Foods of Animal Origin', *Appetite*, 16 (1991), pp. 205–18.

2   L. Cooke, C.M.A. Haworth and J. Wardle, 'Genetic and Environmental Influences on Children's Food Neophobia', *American Journal of Clinical Nutrition*, 86 (2007), pp. 428–33; A. Knaapila, H. Tuorila, K. Silventoinen, K. Keskitalo, M. Kallela, M. Wessman, L. Peltonen, L. F. Cherkas, T. D. Spector and M. Perola, 'Food Neophobia Shows Heritable Variation in Humans', *Physiology & Behavior*, 91 (2007), pp. 573–8.

3   E. Rozin and P. Rozin, 'Culinary Themes and Variations', *Natural History*, 90 (1981), pp. 6–14.

4   M. L. Pelchat and P. Pliner, '"Try It. You'll Like It." Effects of Information on Willingness to Try Novel Foods', *Appetite*, 24 (1995), pp. 153–66.

5   P. Pliner and K. Hobden, 'Development of a Scale to Measure the Trait of Food Neophobia in Humans', *Appetite*, 19 (1992), pp. 105–20.

6   H. Tuorila, L. Lahteenmaki, L. Pohjalainen and L. Lotti, 'Food Neophobia Among the Finns and Related Responses to Familiar and Unfamiliar Foods', *Food Quality and Preference*, 12 (2001), pp. 29–37.

7   L. Cooke, S. Carnell and J. Wardle, 'Food Neophobia and Mealtime Food Consumption in 4–5-year-old Children', *International Journal of Behavioral Nutrition and Physical Activity*, 3 (2006), pp. 1–6.

8   C. G. Russell and A. Worsley, 'A Population-based Study of Preschoolers' Food Neophobia and Its Associations with Food Preferences', *Journal of Nutrition Education and Behavior*, 40 (2008), pp. 11–19.

9   R. F. Bornstein, 'Exposure and Affect: Overview and Meta-analysis of Research, 1968–1987', *Psychological Bulletin*, 106 (1989), pp. 265–89.

10 W. R. Kunst-Wilson and R. B. Zajonc, 'Affective Discrimination of Stimuli That Cannot Be Recognized', *Science*, 207 (1980), pp. 557–8.

11 S. A. Sullivan and L. L. Birch, 'Pass the Sugar, Pass the Salt: Experience Dictates Preference', *Developmental Psychology*, 26 (1990), pp. 546–51.

12 J. Wardle, M.-L. Herrera, L. Cooke and E. L. Gibson, 'Modifying Children's Food Preferences: The Effects of Exposure and Reward on Acceptance of an Unfamiliar Vegetable', *European Journal of Clinical Nutrition*, 57 (2003), pp. 341–8.

13 J. Prescott and B. Khu, 'Changes in Preference for Saltiness within Soup as a Function of Exposure', *Appetite*, 24 (1995), p. 302.

14 C. A. Forestell and J. A. Mennella, 'Early Determinants of Fruit and Vegetable Acceptance', *Pediatrics*, 120 (2007), pp. 1247–54.

15 J. A. Mennella, C. P. Jagnow and G. K. Beauchamp, 'Prenatal and Postnatal Flavor Learning by Human Infants', *Pediatrics*, 107 (2001), p. E88.

16 Ibid.

17 J. A. Mennella, C. E. Griffin and G. K. Beauchamp, 'Flavor Programming during Infancy', *Pediatrics*, 113 (2004), pp. 840–45.

18 R. Haller, C. Rummel, S. Henneberg, U. Pollmer and E. P. Koster, 'The Influence of Early Experience with Vanillin on Food Preference Later in Life', *Chemical Senses*, 24 (1999), pp. 465–7.

19 C. J. Gerrish and J. A. Mennella, 'Flavour Variety Enhances Food Acceptance in Formula-fed Infants', *American Journal of Clinical Nutrition*, 73 (2001), pp. 1080–85.

20 T. McFarlane and P. Pliner, 'Increasing Willingness to Taste Novel Foods: Effects of Nutrition and Taste Information', *Appetite*, 28 (1997), pp. 227–38.

21 A. T. Galloway, L. M. Fiorito, L. A. Francis and L. L. Birch, '"Finish Your Soup": Counterproductive Effects of Pressuring Children to Eat on Intake and Affect', *Appetite*, 46 (2006), pp. 318–23.

22 L. L. Birch, D. W. Marlin and J. Rotter, 'Eating as the "Means" Activity in a Contingency: Effects on Young Children's Food Preference', *Child Development*, 55 (1984), pp. 431–9.

23 Wardle et al., 'Modifying Children's Food Preferences'.

24 Pelchat and Pliner, '"Try It. You'll Like It"'.

25 S. Mustonen, R. Rantanen and H. Tuorila, 'Effect of Sensory Education on School Children's Food Perception: A 2-year Follow-up Study', *Food Quality and Preference*, 20 (2009), pp. 230–40.

26 P. J. Horne, C. F. Lowe, P.F.J. Fleming and A. J. Dowey, 'An Effective Procedure for Changing Food Preferences in 5–7 Year-old Children', *Proceedings of the Nutrition Society*, 54 (1995), pp. 441–52.

27 K. Hobden and P. Pliner, 'Effects of a Model on Food Neophobia in Humans', *Appetite*, 25 (1995), pp. 101–14.

28 P. Pliner and C. Stallberg-White, '"Pass the Ketchup, Please": Familiar Flavours Increase Children's Willingness to Taste Novel Foods', *Appetite*, 34 (2000), pp. 95–103.

4 Learning to Like

1 J. De Houwer, S. Thomas and F. Baeyens, 'Associative Learning of Likes and Dislikes: A Review of 25 Years of Research on Human Evaluative Conditioning', *Psychological Bulletin*, 127 (2001), pp. 853–69.

2 D. A. Zellner, P. Rozin, M. Aron and C. Kulish, 'Conditioned Enhancement of Human's Liking for Flavour by Pairing with Sweetness', *Learning and Motivation*, 14 (1983), pp. 338–50.

3 F. Baeyens, P. Eelen, O. Van den Bergh and G. Crombez, 'Flavour-flavour and Colour-flavour Conditioning in Humans', *Learning and Motivation*, 21 (1990), pp. 434–55.

4 F. Baeyens, D. Vansteenwegen and J. De Houwer, 'Observational Conditioning of Food Valence in Humans', *Appetite*, 27 (1996), pp. 235–50.

5 L. L. Birch, 'Effects on Peer Models' Food Choices and Eating Behaviours on Preschoolers' Food Preferences', *Child Development*, 51 (1980), pp. 489–96.

6 R. B. Zajonc, 'Mere Exposure: A Gateway to the Subliminal', *Current Directions in Psychological Science*, 10 (2001), pp. 224–8.

7 H. L. Meiselman, J. L. Johnson, W. Reeve and J. E. Crouch, 'Demonstrations of the Influence of the Eating Environment on Food Acceptance', *Appetite*, 35 (2000), pp. 231–7.

8 J. D. Troisi and S. Gabriel, 'Chicken Soup Really Is Good for the Soul: "Comfort Food" Fulfills the Need to Belong', *Psychological Science*, 22 (2011), pp. 747–53.

9   D. A. Zellner, W. F. Stewart, P. Rozin and J. M. Brown, 'Effect of Temperature and
    Expectations on Liking for Beverages', *Physiology & Behavior*, 44 (1988), pp. 61–8.

10 M. R. Yeomans, L. C. Chambers, H. Blumenthal and A. Blake, 'The Role of
    Expectancy in Sensory and Hedonic Evaluation: The Case of Smoked Salmon
    Ice-cream', *Food Quality and Preference*, 19 (2008), pp. 565–73.

11 M. R. Yeomans, M. Leitch, N. J. Gould and S. Mobini, 'Differential Hedonic,
    Sensory and Behavioral Changes Associated with Flavour-nutrient and
    Flavour-flavour Learning', *Physiology & Behavior*, 93 (2008), pp. 798–806.

12 B. J. Baker and D. A. Booth, 'Genuinely Olfactory Preferences Conditioned
    by Protein Repletion', *Appetite*, 13 (1989), pp. 223–7. D. A. Booth, 'Learned
    Ingestive Motivation and the Pleasures of the Palate', in *The Hedonics of Taste*,
    ed. R. C. Bolles (Hillsdale, NJ, 1991), pp. 29–58.

13 L. L. Birch, L. McPhee, L. Steinberg and S. Sullivan, 'Conditioned Flavour
    Preferences in Young Children', *Physiology & Behavior*, 47 (1990), pp. 501–5.

14 S. Mobini, T. D. Elliman and M. R. Yeomans, 'Changes in the Pleasantness of
    Caffeine-associated Flavours Consumed at Home', *Food Quality and Preference*,
    (2005), pp. 659–66.

15 J. Prescott, 'Effects of Added Glutamate on Liking for Novel Food Flavours',
    Appetite, 42 (2004), pp. 143–50.

16 M. R. Yeomans and S. Mobini, 'Hunger Alters the Expression of Acquired
    Hedonic but Not Sensory Qualities of Food-paired Odours in Humans', *Journal
    of Experimental Psychology: Animal Behavior Processes*, 32 (2006), pp. 460–66.

17 Baker and Booth, 'Genuinely Olfactory Preferences Conditioned by Protein
    Repletion'.

18 I. L. Bernstein, 'Taste Aversion Learning: A Contemporary Perspective', *Nutrition*,
    15 (1999), pp. 229–34.

19 J. Garcia, P. S. Lasiter, F. Bermudez-Rattoni and D. A. Deems, 'A General Theory of
    Aversion Learning', *Annals of the New York Academy of Sciences*, 443 (1985), pp. 8–21.

20 J. M. Ratcliffe, M. B. Fenton and B. G. Galef, 'An Exception to the Rule: Common
    Vampire Bats Do Not Learn Taste Aversions', *Animal Behaviour*, 65 (2003), pp. 385–9.

21 E. E. Midkiff and I. L. Bernstein, 'Targets of Learned Food Aversions in Humans',
    Physiology & Behavior, 34 (1985), pp. 839–41.

22 Ibid.

23 Bernstein, 'Taste Aversion Learning: A Contemporary Perspective'.

24 R. C. Havermans, S.-J. Salvy and A. Jansen, 'Single-trial Exercise-induced Taste
    and Odour Aversion Learning in Humans', *Appetite*, 53 (2009), pp. 442–5.

25 W. R. Batsell and A. S. Brown, 'Human Flavour-aversion Learning: A Comparison
    of Traditional Aversions and Cognitive Aversions', *Learning and Motivation*, 29
    (1998), pp. 383–96.

26 M. A. Andrykowski and M. L. Otis, 'Development of Learned Food Aversions in
    Humans: Investigation in a "Natural Laboratory" of Cancer Chemotherapy',
    Appetite, 14 (1990), pp. 145–58.

27 R. D. Mattes, C. Arnold and M. Boraas, 'Management of Learned Food Aversions
    in Cancer Patients Receiving Chemotherapy', *Cancer Treatment Reports*, 71 (1987),
    pp. 1071–8.

5 Too Much of a Good Thing

1 J. E. Blundell, 'The Biology of Appetite', *Clinical and Applied Nutrition*, 1 (1991), pp. 21–31.

2 R. D. Mattes, 'Physiologic Responses to Sensory Stimulation by Food: Nutritional Implications', *Journal of the American Dietetic Association*, 97 (1997), pp. 406–13.

3 R. D. Mattes, 'Oral Fat Exposure Alters Postprandial Lipid Metabolism in Humans', *American Journal of Clinical Nutrition*, 63 (1996), pp. 911–17.

4 M. R. Yeomans, J. E. Blundell and M. Leshem, 'Palatability: Response to Nutritional Need or Need-free Stimulation of Appetite?', *British Journal of Nutrition*, 92, suppl. 1 (2004), pp. s3–14.

5 M. R. Yeomans, R. W. Gray, C. J. Mitchell and S. True, 'Independent Effects of Palatability and Within-meal Pauses on Intake and Appetite Ratings in Human Volunteers', *Appetite*, 29 (1997), pp. 61–76.

6 K. C. Berridge, 'Food Reward: Brain Substrates of Wanting and Liking', *Neuroscience and Biobehavioral Reviews*, 20 (1996), pp. 1–25.

7 M. R. Yeomans, N. J. Gould, S. Mobini and J. Prescott, 'Acquired Flavor Acceptance and Intake Facilitated by Monosodium Glutamate in Humans', *Physiology & Behavior*, 93 (2008), pp. 958–66.

8 P. Winkielman, K. C. Berridge and J. L. Wilbarger, 'Unconscious Affective Reactions to Masked Happy Versus Angry Faces Influence Consumption Behavior and Judgments of Value', *Personality and Social Psychology Bulletin*, 31 (2005), pp. 121–35.

9 R. Mattes, 'Soup and Satiety', *Physiology & Behavior*, 83 (2005), pp. 739–47.

10 P. S. Hogenkamp, A. Stafleu, M. Mars, J. M. Brunstrom and C. deGraaf, 'Texture, Not Flavor, Determines Expected Satiation of Dairy Products', *Appetite*, 57 (2011), pp. 635–41.

11 P. Rozin, S. Dow, M. Moscovitch and S. Rajaram, 'What Causes Humans to Begin and End a Meal? A Role for Memory for What Has Been Eaten, as Evidenced by a Study of Multiple Meal Eating in Amnesic Patients', *Psychological Science*, 9 (1998), pp. 392–6.

12 B. Wansink, J. E. Painter and J. North, 'Bottomless Bowls: Why Visual Cues of Portion Size May Influence Intake', *Obesity Research*, 13 (2005), pp. 93–100.

13 C. de Graff, 'Why Liquid Energy Results in Overconsumption', *Proceedings of the Nutrition Society*, LXX/2 (2011), pp. 162–70.

14 G. B. Haber, K. W. Heaton, D. Murphy and L. F. Burroughs, 'Depletion and Disruption of Dietary Fibre: Effects of Satiety, Plasma-glucose and Serum Insulin', *The Lancet* (1 October 1977), pp. 679–82.

15 J. Li, N. Zhang, L. Hu, Z. Li, R. Li, C. Li and S. Wang, 'Improvement in Chewing Activity Reduces Energy Intake in One Meal and Modulates Plasma Gut Hormone Concentrations in Obese and Lean Young Chinese Men', *American Journal of Clinical Nutrition*, 94 (2011), pp. 709–17

16 M. Bertino, G. K. Beauchamp and K. Engelman, 'Naltrexone, an Opioid Blocker, Alters Taste Perception and Nutrient Intake in Humans', *American Journal of Physiology – Regulatory Integrative and Comparative Physiology*, 261 (1991), pp. R59–R63.

17 M. Cabanac and R. Duclaux, 'Specificity of Internal Signals in Producing Satiety for Taste Stimuli', *Nature*, 227 (1970), pp. 966–7.

18 M. Mori, T. Kawada, T. Ono and K. Torii, 'Taste Preference and Protein Nutrition and L-amino Acid Homeostasis in Male Sprague-Dawley Rats', *Physiology & Behavior*, 49 (1991), pp. 987–96.

19 M. Vazquez, P. B. Pearson and G. K. Beauchamp, 'Flavor Preferences in Malnourished Mexican Infants, *Physiology & Behavior*, 28 (1982), pp. 513–9.

20 E. T. Rolls, B. J. Rolls and E. A. Rowe, 'Sensory-specific and Motivation-specific Satiety for the Sight and Taste of Food and Water in Man', *Physiology & Behavior*, 30 (1983), pp. 185–92.

21 B. J. Rolls, M. Hetherington and V. J. Burley, 'The Specificity of Satiety: The Influence of Foods of Different Macronutrient Content on the Development of Satiety', *Physiology & Behavior*, 43 (1988), pp. 145–53.

22 E. T. Rolls and J. H. Rolls, 'Olfactory Sensory-specific Satiety in Humans', *Physiology & Behavior*, 41 (1997), pp. 461–73.

23 J. Johnson and Z. Vickers, 'Sensory-specific Satiety for Selected Bread Products', *Journal of Sensory Studies*, 6 (1991), pp. 65–79.

24 B. J. Rolls, 'Sensory-specific Satiety', *Nutrition Reviews*, 44 (1986), pp. 93–101.

25 M. Cabanac and E. F. Rabe, 'Influence of a Monotonous Food on Body Weight Regulation in Humans', *Physiology & Behavior*, 17 (1976), pp. 675–8.

26 H. L. Meiselman, C. de Graaf and L. L. Lesher, 'The Effects of Variety and Monotony on Food Acceptance and Intake at a Midday Meal', *Physiology & Behavior*, 70 (2000), pp. 119–25.

27 E. S. Hirsch, F. M. Kramer and H. L. Meiselman, 'Effects of Food Attributes and Feeding Environment on Acceptance, Consumption and Body Weight: Lessons Learned in a Twenty-year Program of Military Ration Research: US Army Research (pt 2), *Appetite*, 44 (2005), pp. 33–45.

28 E. T. Rolls and A.W.L. De Waal, 'Long-term Sensory-specific Satiety: Evidence from an Ethiopian Refugee Camp', *Physiology & Behavior*, 34 (1985), pp. 1017–20.

29 D. E. Berlyne, 'Novelty, Complexity, and Hedonic Value', *Perception & Psychophysics*, 8 (1970), pp. 279–86.

6 Consuming Passions

1 L. Wilkins and C. P. Richter, 'A Great Craving for Salt by a Child with Cortico-adrenal Insufficiency', *Journal of the American Medical Association*, 114 (1940), pp. 866–8.

2 M. J. Morris, E. S. Na and A. K. Johnson, 'Salt Craving: The Psychobiology of Pathogenic Sodium Intake', *Physiology & Behavior*, 94 (2008) pp. 709–21.

3 Ibid.

4 C. Davis, 'Results of the Self-selection of Diets by Young Children', *Canadian Medical Association Journal*, 41 (1939), pp. 257–61, p. 260.

5 S. L. Young, 'Pica in Pregnancy: New Ideas About an Old Condition', *Annual Review of Nutrition*, 30 (2010), pp. 403–22.

6 H. P. Weingarten and D. Elston, 'Food Cravings in a College Population', *Appetite*, 17 (1991), pp. 167–75.

7   L. Christensen and L. Pettijohn, 'Mood and Carbohydrate Cravings', *Appetite*, 36 (2001), pp. 137–45.

8   D. A. Zellner, A. Garriga-Trillo, E. Rohm, S. Centeno and S. Parker, 'Food Liking and Craving: A Cross-cultural Approach', *Appetite*, 33 (1999), pp. 61–70.

9   S. Parker, N. Kamel and D. Zellner, 'Food Craving Patterns in Egypt: Comparisons with North America and Spain', *Appetite*, 40 (2003), pp. 193–5.

10 B. Knox, J. Kremer and J. Pearce, 'Food Preference during Pregnancy: A Review', *Food Quality and Preference*, 2 (1990), pp. 131–54.

11 Ibid.

12 A. J. Hill and C.F.L. Weaver, 'Food Craving, Dietary Restraint and Mood', *Appetite*, 17 (1991), pp. 187–97.

13 A. Drewnowski, D. D. Krahn, M. A. Demitrack, K. Nairn and B. A. Gosnell, 'Taste Responses and Preferences for Sweet High-fat Foods: Evidence for Opioid Involvement', *Physiology & Behavior*, 51 (1992), pp. 371–9.

14 M. Pelchat, A. Johnson, R. Chan, J. Valdez and J. D. Ragland, 'Images of Desire: Food-craving Activation during fMRI', *NeuroImage*, 23 (2004), pp. 1486–93.

15 W. Michener and P. Rozin, 'Pharmacological Versus Sensory Factors in the Satiation of Chocolate Craving', *Physiology & Behavior*, 41 (1994), pp. 419–22.

16 P. J. Rogers and H. J. Smit, 'Food Craving and Food "Addiction": A Critical Review of the Evidence from a Biopsychosocial Perspective', *Pharmacology Biochemistry and Behavior*, 46 (2000), pp. 3–14.

17 W. Timberlake and V. A. Farmerdougan, 'Reinforcement in Applied Settings – Figuring Out ahead of Time What Will Work', *Psychological Bulletin*, 110 (1991), pp. 379–91.

18 Hill and Weaver, 'Food Craving, Dietary Restraint and Mood'.

19 M. R. Lowe and M. L. Butryn, 'Hedonic Hunger: A New Dimension of Appetite?', *Physiology & Behavior*, 91 (2007), pp. 432–9.

20 C. Cornell, J. Rodin and H. Weingarten, 'Stimulus-induced Eating When Satiated', *Physiology & Behavior*, 45 (1989), pp. 695–704.

21 Christensen and Pettijohn, 'Mood and Carbohydrate Cravings'.

22 E. Kemps and M. Tiggeman, 'A Cognitive Experimental Approach to Understanding and Reducing Food Cravings', *Current Directions in Psychological Science*, 19 (2010), pp. 86–90.

7 Just Disgusting

1   C. Darwin, *The Expression of Emotions in Man and Animals* (London, 1872), p. 257.

2   P. Ekman and W. V. Friesen, 'Constants across Cultures in the Face and Emotion', *Journal of Personality and Social Psychology*, 17 (1971), pp. 124–9.

3   P. Ekman, W. V. Friesen, M. O'Sullivan, A. Chan, I. Diacoyanni-Tarlatzis, K. Heider, R. Krause, W. A. LeCompte, T. Pitcairn, P. E. Ricci-Bitti, K. Scherer, M. Tomita and A. Tzavaras, 'Universals and Cultural Differences in the Judgments of Facial Expressions of Emotion', *Personality Processes and Individual Differences*, 4 (1987), pp. 712–17.

4 J. Simpson, S. H. Anthony, S. Schmeer and P. G. Overton, 'Food-related Contextual Factors Substantially Modify the Disgust Response', *Food Quality and Preference*, 18 (2007), pp. 183–9.

5 Y. Martins and P. Pliner, '"Ugh! That's Disgusting!": Identification of the Characteristics of Foods Underlying Rejections Based on Disgust', *Appetite*, 46 (2006), pp. 75–85.

6 P. Rozin and A. E. Fallon, 'A Perspective on Disgust', *Psychological Review*, 94 (1987), pp. 23–41.

7 P. Rozin, L. Lowery and R. Ebert, 'Varieties of Disgust Faces and the Structure of Disgust', *Journal of Personality and Social Psychology*, 46 (1994), pp. 870–81.

8 S. L. Marzillier and G.C.L. Davey, 'The Emotional Profiling of Disgust-eliciting Stimuli: Evidence for Primary and Complex Disgusts', *Cognition and Emotion*, 18 (2004), pp. 313–36.

9 J. Simpson, S. Carter, S. H. Anthony and P. G. Overton, 'Is Disgust a Homogeneous Emotion?', *Motivation and Emotion*, 30 (2006), pp. 31–41.

10 M. J. Oaten, R. J. Stevenson and T. I. Case, 'Disgust as a Disease-avoidance Mechanism', *Psychological Bulletin*, 135 (2009), pp. 303–21.

11 V. Curtis, R. Aunger and T. Rabie, 'Evidence that Disgust Evolved to Protect from Risk of Disease', *Proceedings of the Royal Society: Biological Sciences*, 271, suppl. 4 (2004), pp. S131–3.

12 P. Rozin, A. Fallon and M. Augustoni-Ziskind, 'The Child's Conception of Food: The Development of Contamination Sensitivity to "Disgusting" Substances', *Developmental Psychology*, 21 (1985), pp. 1075–9.

13 M. Siegal, 'Becoming Mindful of Food and Conversation', *Current Directions in Psychological Science*, 4 (1995), pp. 177–81.

14 Rozin et al., 'The Child's Conception of Food'.

15 R. J. Stevenson, M. J. Oaten, T. I. Case, B. M. Repacholi and P. Wagland, 'Children's Response to Adult Disgust Elicitors: Development and Acquisition', *Developmental Psychology*, 46 (2010), pp. 165–77.

8 You Eat What You Are

1 J. Prescott, 'Genetic Influences on Taste', in *Flavour in Food*, ed. A. Voilley and P. Etievant (Cambridge, 2006), pp. 308–26.

2 L. M. Bartoshuk, 'The Biological Basis of Food Perception and Acceptance', *Food Quality and Preference*, 4 (1993), pp. 21–32.

3 Those who have been paying attention will be asking whether there are cross-cultural differences in the proportions of sweet likers and dislikers (see chap. 8). Unfortunately, this is not known. A. L. Fox, 'Six in Ten "Tasteblind" to Bitter Chemical', *Science Newletter*, 9 (1931), p. 249.

4 J.-A. Brillat-Savarin, *The Physiology of Taste* [1825] (London, 1994), p. 39.

5 I. J. Miller and F. E. Reedy, 'Variations in Human Taste Bud Density and Taste Intensity Perception', *Physiology & Behavior*, 47 (1990), pp. 1213–19.

6 J. Prescott, J. Soo, J. Campbell and C. Roberts, 'Responses of PROP Taster Groups to Variations in Sensory Qualities within Foods and Beverages', *Physiology &*

Behavior, 82 (2004), pp. 459–69.

7   B. Turnbull and E. Matisoo-Smith, 'Taste Sensitivity to 6-n-Propylthiouracil Predicts Acceptance of Bitter-tasting Spinach in 3-6-y-old Children', *American Journal of Clinical Nutrition*, 76 (2002), pp. 1101–5.

8   J. E. Hayes and G. J. Pickering, 'Wine Expertise Predicts Taste Phenotype', *American Journal of Enology and Viticulture* (2011).

9   R. S. Herz, 'Taste Sensitivity is Related to Visceral But Not Moral Disgust', *Chemosensory Perception*, 4 (2011), pp. 72–9.

10   A. S. Teller, H. J. Wiener, L. M. Bartoshuk and S. E. Marino, 'Variation in Bitter Taste Perception between Moral Vegetarians and Non-vegetarians', presentation given at the conference *Association for Chemoreception Sciences* (St Petersburg, FL, 2011).

11   J. E. Hayes, B. S. Sullivan and V. B. Duffy, 'Explaining Variability in Sodium Intake through Oral Sensory Phenotype, Salt Sensation and Liking', *Physiology & Behavior*, 100 (2010), pp. 369–80.

12   J. E. Hayes and V. B. Duffy, 'Oral Sensory Phenotype Identifies Level of Sugar and Fat Required for Maximal Liking', *Physiology & Behavior*, 95 (2008), pp. 77–87.

13   B. J. Tepper, E. A. White, Y. Koelliker, C. Lanzara, P. d'Adamo and P. Gasparini, 'Genetic Variation in Taste Sensitivity to 6-n-Propylthiouracil and Its Relationship to Taste Perception and Food Selection', *Annals of the New York Academy of Science*, 1170 (2009), pp. 126–39.

14   R. M. Pangborn, 'Individual Variation in Affective Responses to Taste Stimuli', *Psychonomic Science*, 21 (1970), pp. 125–6.

15   K. Keskitalo, A. Knaapila, M. Kallela, A. Palotie, M. Wessman, S. Sammalisto, L. Peltonen, H. Tuorila and M. Perola, 'Sweet Taste Preferences Are Partly Genetically Determined: Identification of a Trait Locus on Chromosome 16(1–3)', *American Journal of Clinical Nutrition*, 86 (2007), pp. 55–63.

16   M. R. Yeomans, J. Prescott and N. J. Gould, 'Acquired Hedonic and Sensory Characteristics of Odours: Influence of Sweet Liker and Propylthiouracil Taster Status', *Quarterly Journal of Experimental Psychology*, 42 (2009), pp. 1648–64.

17   F. M. Breen, R. Plomin and J. Wardle, 'Heritability of Food Preferences in Young Children', *Physiology & Behavior*, 88 (2006), pp. 443–7.

18   B. Teucher, J. Skinner, P.M.L. Skidmore, A. Cassidy, S. J. Fairweather-Tait, L. Hooper, M. A. Roe, R. Foxall, S. L. Oyston, L. F. Cherkas, U. C. Perks, T. D. Spector and A. J. MacGregor, 'Dietary Patterns and Heritability of Food Choice in a UK Female Twin Cohort', *Twin Research and Human Genetics*, 10 (2007), pp. 734–48.

19   N. L. Caine-Bish and B. Scheule, 'Gender Differences in Food Preferences of School-aged Children and Adolescents', *Journal of School Health*, 79 (2009), pp. 532–40.

20   A. N. Gilbert and C. J. Wysocki, 'The Smell Survey Results', *National Geographic* (October 1987), pp. 514–25.

21   D. A. Deems, R. L. Doty, R. G. Settle, V. Moore-Gillon, P. Shaman, A. F. Mester, C. P. Kimmelman, V. J. Brightman and J. B. Snow, 'Smell and Taste Disorders: A Study of 750 Patients from the University of Pennsylvania Smell and Taste Center', *Archives of Otolaryngology – Head and Neck Surgery*, 117 (1991), pp. 519–28.

22 J. Corwin, M. Loury and A. N. Gilbert, 'Workplace, Age, and Sex as Mediators of Olfactory Function: Data from the National Geographic Smell Survey', *Journal of Gerontology: Psychological Sciences*, 50 (1995), pp. 179–86.

23 R. E. Frye, B. S. Schwartz and R. L. Doty, 'Dose-related Effects of Cigarette Smoking on Olfactory Function', *Journal of the American Medical Association*, 263 (1990), pp. 1233–6.

24 R. L. Doty, P. Shaman, S. L. Applebaum, R. Giberson, L. Siksorski and L. Rosenberg, 'Smell Indentification Ability: Changes with Age', *Science*, 226 (1984), pp. 1441–3.

25 C. Murphy, 'Flavor Preference for Monosodium Glutamate and Casein Hydrolysate in Young and Elderly Persons', in *Umami: A Basic Taste*, ed. Y. Kawamura and M. R. Kare (New York, 1987), pp. 139–51.

26 S. S. Schiffman, 'Sensory Enhancement of Foods for the Elderly with Monosodium Glutamate', *Food Reviews International*, 14 (1998), pp. 321–34.

27 R. Doty and E. L. Camerson, 'Sex Differences and Reproductive Hormone Influences on Human Odor Perception', *Physiology & Behavior*, 97 (2009), pp. 213–28.

28 P. Dalton, N. Doolittle and P.A.S. Breslin, 'Gender-specific Induction of Enhanced Sensitivity to Odors', *Nature Neuroscience*, 5 (2002), pp. 199–200.

29 A. N. Gilbert and S. E. Kemp, 'Odor Perception Phenotypes: Multiple, Specific Hyperosmias to Musks', *Chemical Senses*, 21 (1996), pp. 411–16.

30 C. J. Wysocki and G. K. Beauchamp, 'Ability to Smell Androstenone Is Genetically Determined', *Proceedings of the National Academy of Sciences of the USA*, 81 (1984), pp. 4899–902.

31 C. J. Wysocki, K. M. Dorries and G. K. Beauchamp, 'Ability to Perceive Androstenone Can Be Acquired by Ostensibly Anosmic People', *Proceedings of the National Academy of Sciences of the USA*, 86 (1989), pp. 7976–8.

32 J. Prescott, S. M. Lee and K. O. Kim, 'Analytic Approaches to Evaluation Modify Hedonic Responses', *Food Quality and Preference*, 22 (2011), pp. 391–3.

9 Diner in a Strange Land

1 P. Rozin and T. A. Vollmecke, 'Food Likes and Dislikes', *Annual Review of Nutrition*, 6 (1986), pp. 433–56.

2 B. J. Tepper, 'Nutritional Implications of Genetic Taste Variation: The Role of PROP Sensitivity and Other Taste Phenotypes', *Annual Review of Nutrition*, 28 (2008), pp. 367–88.

3 J. Prescott, 'Comparisons of Taste Perceptions and Preferences of Japanese and Australian Consumers: Overview and Implications for Cross-cultural Sensory Research', *Food Quality and Preference*, 9 (1998), pp. 393–402.

4 H. R. Moskowitz, V. Kumaraiah, K. N. Sharma, H. L. Jacobs and S. D. Sharma, 'Cross-cultural Differences in Simple Taste Preferences', *Science*, 190 (1975), pp. 1217–18.

5 J. Prescott, O. Young and L. O'Neill, 'The Impact of Variations in Flavour Compounds on Meat Acceptability: a Comparison of Japanese and New Zealand Consumers', *Food Quality and Preference*, 12 (2001), pp. 257–64.

6   M. Kawai, 'On the Newly-acquired Behaviors of the Natural Troop of Japanese
    Monkeys on Koshima Island', in *Seventh Annual Meeting of the Society for Primate
    Researches* (Inuyama, Japan, 1962).

7   J. Prescott and R. J. Stevenson, 'Pungency in Food Perception and Preference',
    Food Reviews International, 11 (1995), pp. 665–98.

8   F. Wey, *Les Anglais chez eux* (Paris, 1859), p. 63.

9   P. Rozin, 'Getting to Like the Burn of Chili Pepper. Biological, Psychological, and
    Cultural Perspectives', in *Irritation*, ed. B. G. Green, J. R. Mason and M. R. Kare
    (New York, 1990), pp. 231–69.

10 E. Rozin and P. Rozin, 'Culinary Themes and Variations', *Natural History*, 90
    (1981), pp. 6–14.

11 C. Stallberg-White and P. Pliner, 'The Effects of Flavor Principles on Willingness
    to Taste Novel Foods', *Appetite*, 33 (1999), pp. 209–21.

12 J. Prescott, O. Young, L. O'Neill, N.J.N. Yau and R. Stevens, 'Motives for Food
    Choice: A Comparison of Consumers from Japan, Taiwan, Malaysia and New
    Zealand', *Food Quality and Preference*, 13 (2002), pp. 489–95.

10 Future Taste: Art and Science

1   S. S. Schiffman and C. A. Gatlin, 'Sweeteners: State of Knowledge Review',
    Neuroscience and Biobehavioral Reviews, 17 (1993), pp. 313–45.

2   A. T. Woods, D. M. Lloyd, J. Kuenzel, E. Poliakoff, G. B. Dijksterhuis and A.
    Thomas, 'Expected Taste Intensity Affects Response to Sweet Drinks in Primary
    Taste Cortex', *Neuroreport*, 22 (2011), pp. 365–9.

3   C. Spence, 'Multisensory Integration, Attention and Perception', in *Signals and
    Perception: The Fundamentals of Human Sensation*, ed. D. Roberts (London, 2004),
    pp. 345–54.

4   R. J. Stevenson, J. Prescott and R. A. Boakes, 'Confusing Tastes and Smells: How
    Odours Can Influence the Perception of Sweet and Sour Tastes', *Chemical Senses*, 24
    (1999), pp. 627–35.

5   R. A. Frank and J. Byram, 'Taste-smell Interactions Are Tastant and Odorant
    Dependent', *Chemical Senses*, 23 (1988), pp. 445–55.

6   G. Lawrence, C. Salles, C. Septier, J. Busch and T. Thomas-Danguin,
    'Odour–taste Interactions: A Way to Enhance Saltiness in Low-salt Content
    Solutions', *Food Quality and Preference*, 20 (2009), pp. 241–8.

7   K. C. Berridge, 'Food Reward: Brain Substrates of Wanting and Liking',
    Neuroscience and Biobehavioral Reviews, 20 (1996), pp. 1–25; I. E. de Araujo, E. T.
    Rolls, M. L. Kringelbach, F. McGlone and N. Phillips, 'Taste-olfactory
    Convergence, and the Representation of the Pleasantness of Flavour, in the
    Human Brain', *European Journal of Neuroscience*, 18 (2003), pp. 2059–68; D. M.
    Small, R. J. Zatorre, A. Dagher, A. C. Evans and M. Jones-Gotman, 'Changes in
    Brain Activity Related to Eating Chocolate. From Pleasure to Aversion', *Brain*, 124
    (2001), pp. 1720–33.

8   H. This, 'Food for Tomorrow?', EMBO *Reports*, 7 (2006), pp. 1062–6.

9   H. Blumenthal, *The Big Fat Duck Cookbook* (London, 2008), p. 135.

10 My thanks to Rick Mattes, Professor of Nutrition Science at Purdue University, USA, for this evocative phrase.

11 N. Myhrvold, 'The Art in Gastronomy: A Modernist Perspective', *Gastronomica: The Journal of Food and Culture*, 11 (2011), p. 13.

12 A.-C. Roudot, 'Food Science and Consumer Taste', *Gastronomica: The Journal of Food and Culture*, 9 (2004), pp. 41–6.

13 E. David, *Italian Food*, 3rd edn (London, 1987), p. 61.

11 Beyond Survival: Uncoupling Taste and Nutrition

1 *Sydney Morning Herald*, 1 March 2011.

2 P. Rozin, M. Ashmore and M. Markwith, 'Lay American Conceptions of Nutrition: Dose Insensitivity, Categorical Thinking, Contagion, and the Monotonic Mind', *Health Psychology*, 15 (1996), pp. 438–47.

3 P. Rozin, 'Food is Fundamental, Fun, Frightening, and Far-reaching', *Social Research*, 66 (1999), pp. 9–30.

4 V. Provencher, J. Polivy and C. P. Herman, 'Perceived Healthiness of Food. If It's Healthy, You Can Eat More!', *Appetite*, 52 (2009), pp. 340–44.

12 Palatability and the Energy Crisis

1 C. P. Herman and J. Polivy, 'External Cues in the Control of Food Intake in Humans: The Sensory-normative Distinction', *Physiology & Behavior*, 94 (2008), pp. 722–8.

2 B. Wansink and J. Kim, 'Bad Popcorn in Big Buckets: Portion Size Can Influence Intake as Much as Taste', *Journal of Nutrition Education and Behavior*, 37 (2005), pp. 242–5.

3 L. R. Vartanian, C. P. Herman and B. Wansink, 'Are We Aware of the External Factors That Influence Our Food Intake?', *Health Psychology*, 27 (2008), pp. 533–8.

4 S. Schachter and L. P. Gross, 'Manipulated Time and Eating Behavior', *Journal of Personality and Social Psychology*, 10 (1968), pp. 98–106.

5 R. E. Nisbett, 'Taste, Deprivation, and Weight Determinants of Eating Behavior', *Journal of Personality and Social Psychology*, 10 (1968), pp. 107–16.

6 W. Hofmann, G. M. van Koningsbruggen, W. Stroebe, S. Ramanathan and H. Aarts, 'As Pleasure Unfolds: Hedonic Responses to Tempting Food', *Psychological Science*, 21 (2010), pp. 1863–70.

7 B. Wansink, C. R. Payne and P. Chandon, 'Internal and External Cues of Meal Cessation: The French Paradox Redux?', *Obesity*, 15 (2007), pp. 2920–24.

8 E. Schur, C. Noonan, J. Polivy, J. Goldberg and D. Buchwald, 'Genetic and Environmental Influences on Restrained Eating Behavior', *International Journal of Eating Disorders*, 42 (2009), pp. 765–72.

9 I. Fedoroff, J. Polivy and C. P. Herman, 'The Effect of Pre-exposure to Food Cues on the Eating Behavior of Restrained and Unrestrained Eaters', *Appetite*, 28 (1997), pp. 33–47.

10 A. W. Logue and G. R. King, 'Self-control and Impulsiveness in Adult Humans When Food Is the Reinforcer', *Appetite*, 17 (1991), pp. 105–20.

11 J. M. Brunstrom and G. L. Mitchell, 'Flavour-nutrient Learning in Restrained and Unrestrained Eaters', *Physiology & Behavior*, 90 (2007), pp. 133–41.

12 E. J. Bryant, N. A. King and J. E. Blundell, 'Disinhibition: Its Effects on Appetite and Weight Regulation', *Obesity Reviews*, 9 (2007), pp. 409–19.

13 A. J. Stunkard and S. Messick, 'The Three-factor Eating Questionnaire to Measure Dietary Restraint, Disinhibition and Hunger', *Journal of Psychosomatic Research*, 29 (1985), pp. 71–83.

14 K. Keskitalo, A. Knaapila, M. Kallela, A. Palotie, M. Wessman, S. Sammalisto, L. Peltonen, H. Tuorila and M. Perola, 'Sweet Taste Preferences Are Partly Genetically Determined: Identification of a Trait Locus on Chromosome 16(1–3)', *American Journal of Clinical Nutrition*, 86 (2007), pp. 55–63.

15 M. R. Yeomans, S. Mobini, E. J. Bertenshaw and N. J. Gould, 'Acquired Liking for Sweet-Paired Odours is Related to the Disinhibition but Not Restraint Factor from the Three Factor Eating Questionnaire', *Physiology & Behavior*, 96 (2009), pp. 244–52.

16 M. R. Yeomans and E. Coughlan, 'Mood-induced Eating. Interactive Effects of Restraint and Tendency to Overeat', *Appetite*, 52 (2009), pp. 290–98.

17 B. Soetens, C. Braet, L. Van Vlierberghe and A. Roets, 'Resisting Temptation: Effects of Exposure to a Forbidden Food on Eating Behaviour', *Appetite*, 51 (2008), pp. 202–5.

18 L. Chambers and M. R. Yeomans, 'Individual Differences in Satiety Response to Carbohydrate and Fat. Predictions from the Three Factor Eating Questionnaire (TFEQ)', *Appetite*, 41 (2011), pp. 316–23.

19 E. Papies, W. Stroebe and H. Aarts, 'Pleasure in the Mind: Restrained Eating and Spontaneous Hedonic Thoughts about Food', *Journal of Experimental Social Psychology*, 43 (2007), pp. 810–17.

20 J. Polivy, J. Coleman and C. P. Herman, 'The Effect of Deprivation on Food Cravings and Eating Behavior in Restrained and Unrestrained Eaters', *International Journal of Eating Disorders*, 38 (2005), pp. 301–9.

21 J. M. Brunstrom, 'The Control of Meal Size in Human Subjects: A Role for Expected Satiety, Expected Satiation and Premeal Planning', *Proceedings of the Nutrition Society*, 70 (2011), pp. 155–61.

22 J. Polivy, 'Psychological Consequences of Food Restriction', *Journal of the American Dietetic Association*, 96 (1996), pp. 589–92.

23 J. Polivy, 'Restricting Food Intake in an Environment Where Food is Abundant. The Effects of Food Cues on Food Intake and Weight' [Se restreindre dans un environnement d'abondance alimentaire. Les effets des stimuli alimentaires sur la consommation et le poids], *Obésité*, 4 (2009), pp. 105–11.

Acknowledgements

It is hard to know what to expect when writing a first book. It is certainly a different task to writing scientific papers. For one thing, a book has to maintain a reader's interest over quite some distance. It also hopefully ends with something more interesting than 'more research is needed'. A bit of a rethink about how one uses language is crucial – the jargon, the passive tense, the well-developed detachment that are typical of journal articles must go. Quite a few people helped me with these and other 'writing issues' by reading drafts and making encouraging noises such as 'isn't that book finished yet?' Foremost among these was my wife, Anne-Marie Feyer, who has with good humour put up with the 'idea' of such a book for . . . well, years. Thanks are due to other readers including Natalia Bradshaw and Theresa White for valuable feedback on writing and technical content. Several of the people mentioned in the book generously provided material either in the form of interesting anecdote or observation. Some even gave their permission to use the material. I'd like also to mention Sandra Ferman because she wanted to be in the book . . . and didn't care where. Heston Blumenthal kindly agreed to write the foreword, despite recently being officially declared the busiest man on the planet. Thank you. I am grateful too to my colleagues (and many friends) who are responsible for the often brilliant research on which the book is based. Any misinterpretations of your data must have occurred in the editing stage. Finally, thanks are due to my editor at Reaktion Books, Vivian Constantinopoulos, for her support and guidance. Once again, I wasn't sure what to expect in this process but her approach made it as pain-free as I could imagine.

Photo Acknowledgements

Photographs courtesy of Prof. Linda Bartoshuk: p. 126; used with permission of Paul Ekman, PhD/ Paul Ekman Group, LLC: p. 113; reproduced with permission from C. Forestell and J. Mennella, 'Early Determinants of Fruit and Vegetable Acceptance', *Pediatrics*, vol. 120, pp. 1247–54, © 2007 by the American Academy of Pediatrics: p. 52; photos courtesy of Prof. Jacob Steiner: p. 32.

Index